French, Albert.

Patches of fire.

$22.95

D0561061

PATCHES OF FIRE

ALSO BY ALBERT FRENCH

Billy

Holly

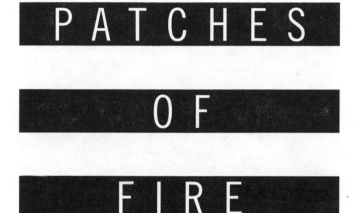

PATCHES OF FIRE

A Story of War and Redemption

ALBERT FRENCH

Anchor Books
Doubleday
New York   London   Toronto   Sydney   Auckland

AN ANCHOR BOOK

PUBLISHED BY DOUBLEDAY

a division of Bantam Doubleday Dell Publishing Group, Inc.

1540 Broadway, New York, New York 10036

ANCHOR BOOKS, DOUBLEDAY, and the portrayal of an anchor
are trademarks of Doubleday, a division of
Bantam Doubleday Dell Publishing Group, Inc.

Book design by Chris Welch

Library of Congress Cataloging-in-Publication Data
French, Albert.
Patches of fire : a story of war and redemption / Albert French. —
1st Anchor Books ed.
p.   cm.
1. Vietnamese Conflict, 1961–1975—Afro-Americans—Fiction.
2. Vietnamese Conflict, 1961–1975—Veterans—Fiction.   3. Afro-
American men—Fiction.   I. Title.
PS3556.R3948P38   1997
813'.54—dc21   96-45682
CIP

ISBN 0-385-48363-5
Copyright © 1997 by Albert French
All Rights Reserved
Printed in the United States of America
First Anchor Books Edition: January 1997
1   3   5   7   9   10   8   6   4   2

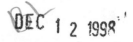

To the echoes of E-2/7

Thanks to Geoffrey Mulligan,
a quiet voice in the storms.

How sweet the sound
that saved a wretch like me.
—John Newton,
"Amazing Grace" (1750)

PART I

The story of a young man's encounter
with a war and deaths beyond his understanding; of his return to a country
torn by racial unrest; and of his pain-
staking efforts to defeat his inner
demons and make a place for himself as
a black man in white America.

1

THE FEELING

The train had come a long time ago; now it was winding through the Pennsylvania mountains and further into the night. In the morning, green grass with patches of snow sped by my window. The rocking of the train teased my excitement. Washington, D.C., was the next stop, President Kennedy and only things on TV.

My world was changing; the stop in D.C. was brief, switching trains only and off again, further than I'd ever been. I sat looking out the window. It was pretty at first. The January morning was bright and fresh as the train rolled through the green hills of Virginia. Then it must have been the fast track, the back track, the way I'd have to go. North Carolina now, and brown shacks and sheds barely standing, yet I felt they had been there forever. Old bony mules grazed on bare brown ground. The mules seemed to be the same tobacco color as the brown shacks and sheds. Dark-brown-skinned children with pale-colored coats and jackets sometimes stood staring at the train.

The hills had flattened, the day had faded into night. South Carolina now; the hour was late, way past midnight. The train slowed, then stopped and seemed to quiver on the tracks.

Shouts came into the train.

"Get up on your feet, goddamnit. Move it, move it. Why are you asshole little girls starin' at me? When I say move it, goddamnit, move. Move, move, move."

3

The shouting voice roared through the car and into my sleep. Time spun wild, twisting and turning my feeling of everything, any yesterday and any fucking tomorrow.

Shouts called the cadence of our time.

"Hut ta three, hey da la, hey da la, hey da la. Hut ta three, hay da la, hey low, hey la, hey low, hey da la."

"Column left, hut.

"Right shoulder, arms."

"Platoon, hut.

"Goddamnit, move it."

"If Jesus Christ comes here, he'll shave, shoot straight too. Or I'll kick his ass out of my Marine Corps."

"This is your rifle. It kills. The only reason you are here is to use this weapon."

Oceans, gray ships, green shirts, and blackjack came to play. Fast cars, lonely highways, brown girls in W-town with bright skirts put color in the night. Sweat and wine and sound of song came alive in the night, lived quick but longer than Presidents.

Bright skirts and "Dancin' past the midnight hour . . . Yeah baby, let the night catch on fire . . ." and I could shoot straight too.

Arthur was there one day; he came from before, back then, up the way, schoolbells and blue band jackets. When streets had stop signs and I knew the faces on the porch. He was older than me, hung with the big boys, running touchdowns and big-timing at parties. Got him a nice scholarship too, went to a big school. But he was here now; he was in my world, my oceans and my brown-girl towns.

Arthur was waving and talking now. "Hey man, that you? Hey, home, when you come in?"

I spoke. "Hey man, what ya doin' way down here? I been in for about two years. Just got back from fucking around in Panama. How long you been in?"

"Shit, man," Arthur was saying, "I been in for about seven months. I'm in motor T, over behind Tenth Marines."

"Yeah," I said, "I'm with three-eight L Company. I saw Ramsey, he's up in air wing. He got it made, he got a nice woman up in K-town."

"Damn," Arthur said, looking at me, "you make corporal?"

"Yeah," I said, "I made it a couple months ago."

I hadn't liked Arthur too much before—his "Hey man's" were too quick, he only saw you if he bumped into you—but he had fallen from his world and I had emerged in mine.

Time was screaming, "Move, move, move."

Arthur looked away but was saying, "I got my papers, I'm bein' shipped over the way. Man, this is some shit comin'—fuckin' Nam, man."

I spoke quickly. "Yeah, I got my shit too. I got some leave time coming, then I got to be on the West Coast at the end of the month."

"Same shit here." Arthur was looking back and saying, "Let's get together up the way. Paul's havin' a party. Here, let me get your number up the way, shit, maybe we can get together, get some partying in?"

"That's cool," I said quickly as I scratched my number down on something. "I'll check you out up the way."

Trains were slow, too slow, stopped too many times. The tobacco-colored shacks and sheds were still there; the green hills were there too, if I looked. The Chevy moved through the night and into the day and back to before.

"Good to see ya, man, when ya get back in town? Saw Pee Wee last week sometime. Yeah, man, he's still crazy, still bangin' Debbie. Kenny got busted behind some shit, him and Melvin stickin' guns up in people's face. Hank's doin' fine, man, got him a nice thing goin', drivin' one of 'em gas trucks. Yeah, man, I heard ya were home, how long ya got? Yeah, I'll be checkin' ya out before ya be leavin'."

Streetcars and stop signs, stop sometimes but keep on trucking. Party lights sparkled, home faces smiled, laughed too. I ran into Arthur down at the club, dressed in his uniform, tie loose and just dangling from his neck. The band music blasted, bright skirts wiggled, and Arthur was there swaying with the sounds.

"Hey man," he would say, "I think I'm stayin' here, fuck some over the ocean."

The gin danced in his eyes. My wine was talking. "Yeah, fuck that shit."

The drums were pounding; we could hardly hear, our hands grasped in a home shake. "Stop up Paul's," he shouted. "I'll be up Paul's, stop up if you can."

The time came, the time to move, hurry, not enough time for slow words, too fast a time for Mom.

"You got everything you need?" she said, milling around.

"Yeah," I answered quickly.

"Don't forget to call your grandmother, she's waiting."

"I'll call." My words were quick.

I looked around my room, looked at the things on the wall, looked at the pictures on the dresser, thought some things before I went downstairs. I knew it would have to be quick; it had to, I had to go.

"Listen, Mom," I was saying, "I don't want you to worry. A year's not that long."

"We'll be okay," she was saying, fumbling with something in her hands.

"Where's Sherry and Stacy?" I remember asking for my little sisters.

"They're out on the porch with your father," Mom answered, as I saw the tears coming to her eyes.

My father sat quietly on the porch. There was a quick handshake, fast words, and a good look into the eyes. I turned quickly; he knew I had to go. My sisters, just children, I called to.

"Come here, give me a kiss and hug. You be good," I would say, but the hug would be more. The hug would be the smell of their hair, the wetness of their tears on their cheeks, a quick turn with their faces deep in my mind. I had to go.

The car was packed; my friends John and Walt stood waiting to take me to the airport. My eyes would glance at the house, the porch, the home, now, quickly. It had to be done.

"Mom, I got to go. I love you." Her arms held me tightly. Then I was gone.

Down the corner, one look back. The waves were still there, as the silence was still in the car. "Fuck it, let's go." I sighed and turned away.

Met Arthur at the airport. The plane and gin flew into the night. Chicago was there, but not too long; a couple of looks and we were back in the sky. Talk was easy and slow.

Arthur was saying, "You lucky man, you be out as soon as you get back."

"Yeah," I was saying.

The miles and the moments kept flying by.

Arthur settled deeper in his gin, then was saying slowly, "I hate this shit, man."

I sighed some, saying, "It's not all that bad. W-town was somethin'. The shit ain't that bad all the time. You get used to it—it's better than the streets. Half the dudes in jail already, ain't a job nowhere, mills ain't doin' shit."

Arthur got quiet. I did too. The plane flew on into the night. I didn't say it—maybe I should have—but it was good not to be alone. Arthur was here in my world, he was in it like me, and it was moving too fast for us to let go.

Los Angeles was the bus station, a wee hour in the night, and some dude with a clean Chevy convertible parked outside with the radio blasting song. Then we were gone further into the night.

"Corporal, the barracks are up on the right. You'll be in Unit 106. Reveille goes 0600, chow goes 0700. Here, keep these orders with you."

"What's your papers say?" Arthur asked as he fumbled through his.

"Looks like I'm going by ship next week," I answered, then asked, "What's yours say?"

"Damn," Arthur said, "looks like I'm flyin' out the end of the week. Shit, look at this—looks like they got about ten damn planeloads flyin' out. Shit, that ain't too long. Fuck."

I spoke quickly. "Fuck it, man, at least we got a few days to check out L.A."

Back to L.A., searching streets for song, bright skirts, with fast thoughts and slow hellos. Strangers among strangers, dark smiles smiling at the nights. Everything was spinning; time was dancing, swinging and swaying. Yeah, we were here.

The hot days spun by and the nights and wine remained hot, but there was a chill somewhere deep in the night. I wasn't certain what it was, but it wasn't in the bright skirts or the faceless faces flashing by. But I could feel a chill.

I remember the walk. Arthur's plane was flying out that night, and I walked him down to the pay phones. I stood off to the side as Arthur called home and spoke to his mother. I could hear him ending with "I love you, Mom. I'll write soon."

He turned, and his face was just there, his look silent. I joked, "Damn, man, you won't have any money till Christmas the way you fucked your pay up on parting."

He was quiet for a while as we walked through the night. Then his voice was low, but his words were clear. "I'm not worried about it. I got a feeling I'm going to die."

I said, "Damn, man, knock that shit off."

He spoke again. His words were faint; he seemed to be letting go of everything, ready to get off. "I just feel it. I just know it."

"Look, man." I spoke slowly. "You'll be okay. I talked to a guy yesterday that just got back. He said that just one guy in the whole company got killed. You're going to be in motor T, that should be okay. They're not going to stick you in some foxhole."

I kept talking.

Arthur's steps were steady; his head was up, and he stared out into the night as we walked. I could hear him saying, "I just got this weird feeling, I know I'm going to die. I can't explain it. I just feel it."

I didn't know him then—I wanted to, but I didn't. The night huddled around us. He was older, a year or two ahead of me in school, distant from me, only a face in the hall, a quick "Hey man" here and there. But now he was closer than the dark in the night.

I spoke slowly again. "I'll be there soon. Heard most of us are going to Da Nang. The shit is not going to last long—we'll probably be back stateside come Christmas."

I listened for him to speak. I wanted him to laugh, say, "Oh, fuck it," say something. I wanted him to get back on, but he was quiet. Our hands grasped in the night. "Look, man," I said as we shook, "you'll be fine."

"Okay." He sighed and walked away.

"I'll check you out when I get there," I shouted as he got farther away.

The night spun into morning and chow time came—orange juice, eggs and bacon, and a thousand faces. I could hear some of their words.

"Hey man, when you get here? Walker's here too. Did you see that one girl last night? She was something. We're going back down tonight. Did you hear what happened last night? One of them planes went down, flew into the side of a mountain."

I stopped eating and looked up from the table. I sighed and then spoke, asking, "Anybody make it?"

The stranger looked over, then said, "I don't think so. The word is, everybody got fucked. They got the list over HQ."

I ate quickly but didn't taste the food.

Eleven planes flew out. I knew it just could not be. I walked up the steps to the HQ. I felt uneasy, off-balance, but I spoke quickly to the guy behind the counter.

"I got a buddy that flew out last night."

"What was his name?" the guy asked as he got up from his desk and came to the counter.

"Arthur Slaughter, PFC."

"Slaughter, Slaughter," the guy mumbled as he opened a thick file on the counter and started sliding his finger up and down the page. I watched his finger slide, then stop. He closed the file and looked up and shook his head.

Arthur was dead.

I turned and left. Outside I felt distant, didn't seem to hear or see things around me, but I had to move on. Everything seemed so long ago, even last night, but I could still feel its chill.

How did Arthur know? Was I going to know? Or did I already know?

Eighty-five guys died when the plane crashed into the mountain, but I watched Arthur die before the plane flew into the night.

2

THE SEA

I don't remember the night, just the morning when the long line
of buses was waiting. It was early morning, when it's still gray
and foggy. I remember looking out of the barracks window and
seeing the yellow fog lights on the buses burning dimly through the
fog.

The shouts, yells, and moans were about. *"Let's go, people, let's go,
move it out, get your gear on the buses."*

"It's too fuckin' early for this shit."

"Let's go, people."

"Shit."

"Let's move it out."

The shouts and moans were about, yet the morning was quiet in its
own way, and our way; there was a silence about.

The big green seabags we carried were heavy. All we were was
stuffed inside of them—extra boots, uniforms, writing paper, little pictures of home, anything that we might need and little pieces of things
that were just yours and nobody else's. We shouldered the bags and
moved toward the buses.

It was early summer 1965, Camp Pendleton, California. San Diego
Naval Base would be next, in about an hour or two—not a long time in
our time, not far on our roads.

The buses slowed from the highway and turned into the neat little streets that wound through the naval base and down to the pier where the ship was docked.

"Let's go, people, outside, fall in formation, answer up when your name is called." The commands were subtle now as we unloaded from the buses and moved toward the big gray ship.

The steps to the ship were slow and awkward as we carried our heavy bags. I remember one step, one moment, that I seemed to hold in reverence, one step that I watched for and felt. I know I looked down as I stepped from the pier onto the ship's steep ladder. I know I did not look back, didn't turn around and look around. I just thought a thought and kept going.

We climbed the steep ladder until we reached the deck of the ship, then followed the Navy guy down through the narrow, steeper steps and ladderways until we were in the bottom of the ship and its rooms and racks. Racks piled five or so high, maybe fifty to a room. The rack would be your space, your sleeping space and thinking space, your little space of everything.

I had sailed before, seen the sea, felt its waves, its ways. I knew soon the ship would jolt, shake. Then, without looking, I'd know we were moving, gliding through the soft port waters to the sea. We were going to Okinawa. From there most of us would be flown into Vietnam. I knew I would be on one of the planes that would fly from Okinawa.

I was twenty-one, a corporal. I had joined the Marines in January of 1963, when I was nineteen. I was an O331, little numbers that told you what you were and what you did. I was a machine gunner in the infantry.

Vietnam to me was silent moments, moments when I would try to see it in my mind, moments of trying to feel what it was going to be like. Long moments sometimes, trying to see beyond this time, see to back home and that me I could not see. Somehow, now had to be the only time.

I knew I was going beyond what I was, going into an unknown that was already pulling and jerking on letters to home, dances in the night, Christmas lights, my red-and-white Chevy. Only my songs seemed to linger with me, and they too seemed to drift and leave me alone with me.

I could feel the ship moving.

It began with me, with a Christmas and black-and-white stuffed puppy dogs. When I look back, it was that foggy and misty time, that time when you can only see some things, big things. That kind of time when you can almost hear feelings, hear the chord of what you are and what you are to be.

There was a little white rocking horse, a piano in one room, table and chairs in the kitchen and a stove and a white icebox. Upstairs was night and dark, but morning too. It's hard to remember summer or winter; can't remember snow and cold at all. Summer was outside, but warmth was inside, warmth was my mother, warmth cuddled me, kept me close where I could be warm and not feel the chills of my fears.

I can see the end house on the yellow brick row. I can see the lot next to it with its tall weeds, and if you went through the weeds, you could see the big gray fence and you might see Mr. Toto. He might have been standing there, leaning over the fence, but if he was, his big brown face would look at you, and when he smiled or laughed, you could see his bright shiny gold teeth. That was as far as my world went, across that lot or maybe out front to see Aunt Lanny or the junkman's horse.

I can see and even hear the time, see my mother, see my grand-mother, Ma-Ma, standing in the kitchen with the flowers on her dress. See my aunt Neenee, my uncle Ote, but if that time had a cadence, a drumbeat, loud and clear and sudden, it was my grandfather. He would fill the house with his presence. I'd look up, way up, and he was there. He'd pick me up and the room would spin and the chairs and table would be way down below, 'cause I'd be up there. I can still smell his tobacco, feel the whiskers on his face, but mostly I can hear:

> *A froggy went a-courtin' and he did ride, ah huh, ah huh.*
> *The froggy went a-courtin' and he did ride,*
> *Sword and pistol at his side, ah huh, ah huh.*

He would sing and sway until I could hear the froggy singing and see him dancing too.

I did not know it then, but we were colored. The little row house was Casino Way, the big street out front where Aunt Lanny lived was Ti-oga, and it was Homewood and Pittsburgh and America. It must have been the war years, 1945 or so, brown army suits, people coming and going. I'd see the people sometimes; if I didn't know them, I'd just peek at them, wouldn't let them hold me. I'd go away, run to the kitchen. Ma-Ma would be there, and I might hear the radio.

I didn't hear the radio, it sat on a table all the time, but I didn't understand the world it spoke of. Sometimes I'd sneak behind it and look in at the little lights, but I'd be trying to see the little people talking, maybe see Cowboy Phil shooting and singing. I couldn't see them, but I'd look again anyway—and sometimes they were there, I could see them.

One day in the kitchen, Cowboy Phil wasn't there, wasn't singing and shooting in the radio. Slow music played, drums beat slowly, but I rode the little white rocking horse. I would know much later that they buried President Roosevelt that day. And there was another time, another time when the radio said something that stuck in my mind and stayed there until it was understood, then just stayed. I can hear the radio now, its scratchy voice saying words, words that were big and different, words that didn't make me stop riding and rocking on my rocking horse, but words that made me ask, "Ma-Ma, what's a Japan? Ma-Ma, what's a tomic bomb?" I can't remember what my grandmother said, but I remember the words, their sounds, and me asking what they said.

I didn't know who we were, or what we were. It was just warm and I was there. But there was always something outside, something beyond Mr. Toto's fence, something far away, something that was not allowed in the house, something my grandfather knew but wouldn't tell. Something he carried but wouldn't let me see, wouldn't show me. I didn't know what it was, so I could not ask to see it, but it gave me the same feeling as peeking behind the radio, looking for the little people and Cowboy Phil but only seeing the little lights or maybe just the darkness.

We moved from the little row house and way away from Mr. Toto and Aunt Lanny. I was told later that Aunt Lanny was almost one hundred years old. I remember Aunt Lanny, who was not my aunt; I was told that everyone called her Aunt Lanny. My mother would take me to see her, take me up those steps. She would be sitting up there in that old chair, and when she saw me, she would start smiling and make me come close to her. I'd go. She would always give me a shiny penny. I'd take the penny and hold it in my hand real tight. My mother would always make me say thank you, and make me give Aunt Lanny a kiss. Then Aunt Lanny would try to kiss me until I squirmed away. I guess

Aunt Lanny would have been born in the 1840s, a young girl of twenty or so when Billy the Kid and Comanche Indians woke with the sun, when the North rode against the South, when Lincoln stood at Gettysburg. Aunt Lanny knew the penny before Lincoln was on it.

We moved a couple of streets over, next to the railroad tracks and trains. I saw the trains go by, and 1951 came.

It was a Sunday, late in the year, the Sunday after Christmas. It was morning. I was downstairs in the living room with my grandfather. We were watching a preacher show on TV, and he stood and swayed a little and seemed to rock as he tried to walk. I could hear him climb the hallway steps, hear the steps squeak until he reached the top. Then the house shook and kept trembling with the sound of his fall. I heard my grandmother scream. I was alone downstairs, but I knew. I ran out into the kitchen, even went out on the back porch. My heart was pounding. Soon people came, took the Christmas tree down, and my mother took me and told me in words what I already knew: "Daddy died."

More people came, and soon the door, that one that went to the hallway and the steps, was closed, but I could still hear the slow thumps and squeaks as they carried him down the steps.

I didn't know it then, no one did, but later, in a different time, in the 1970s and 1980s, people would read about my grandfather, my grandmother, their times and their ways. My cousin John would become an author and storyteller of Homewood and those times.

I did not know then, and did not know even when I passed them, that those brown slanted shacks in Virginia had been my grandfather's home. I did not know, would never have been able to put it together, make a meaning, if it meant anything at all, of his bright yellow-white skin. Of his halfness, half of chains and its total lingering decay, half of freeness and its everlasting fear of conquest. My grandmother, with her light skin and long black hair, was a daughter of Beethoven and the blues. Half what she knew and was, half what she didn't know but could only feel. I didn't know that the sum of a half of a half and a half of a half could make the total whole of something else, and it would be my home of homes. My mother's blue eyes.

Nineteen fifty-two came, and I ran through it, playing in the lots and alleyways. Macky, Georgie, and Nooty came, moved in a few houses down, played together all the time. Macky, Georgie, and Nooty's daddy came to see them. They said he was from Texas, used to live down there. Sometimes I would see him, would stand off to the side as he came and they ran to him. Sometimes he'd ask me how I was. I didn't know him, I didn't know why he asked, only that I had to remember that he did.

Harry came one day, and I had a father, but I didn't know what that was. We moved from Homewood to the edge of the other side of the city. I became a lot of things around me; I loved the woods down over the hill from the new projects we moved into, would spend all day down in the woods just looking at rabbits, trying to catch a snake, swinging on the vines. Looking back, I guess it was the different things, the wild, that were tickling me, and I was teasing them back, and would always go further than I was allowed.

My first little sister came and I was a brother. Soon music came, Frankie Lymon and the Teenagers; then girls became an exciting mystery and I was curious. Dance came, but before dance came nigger, came colored and white. Before Little Rock and TV showing colored people being beaten and kicked by white people came nigger. Nigger came from porches sometimes—"Hey nigger, nigger, nigger." Nigger came from Stan Helinsky; as I sat on his porch waiting for him to come out to play baseball, I would hear his father saying, "I told you to stay away from them goddamn niggers." Nigger came as a feeling, and from feelings. "Watch out where you go, don't go that way, we can't go there, they only let white kids swim there." Somehow the line had been drawn. I didn't know that it was always there and I was on one side of it.

Nineteen fifty-eight and we moved back to my grandfather's land, Homewood. Homewood became my world—the streets and their ways, the song and its dance. Homewood wasn't on TV, it was our way, just our way. Looking back, Homewood was its own nation and had its own laws and borders. School became Westinghouse, all colored faces. The other world was only on TV. We were bad, could kick anybody's ass. I was bad, had my walk and my way, had my dance and my song. Went to school, never brought home books, knew enough. Battled for the street corners, sometimes went across the tracks, crossed our borders and went up into rich people's land, fucked up a few white boys up there—"They better not call us niggers."

Homewood was home, any day was home. Mondays and Tuesdays could be good days. Friday and Saturday nights, a bottle of wine and dance time. Homewood had Sundays, too. Jesus came on Sunday; dark faces with eyes dimly lit with hope waited, then smiled. In a way, as in a circle of days, the further you got from Sunday, the closer it was. I remember Sundays.

Nineteen sixty, we moved again. Now roads and trees and yellow school buses, white kids and me on the bus, brand-new school with bright halls and seventy-five dark faces speckled in three thousand white. Birmingham was burning, King was on the march, and Kennedy was on TV telling people to put the fires out, that's not nice, don't do colored people that way.

I lived in three worlds, same time—yellow school buses with white faces and me, back in Homewood come weekends, and a different world, a changing me. I could feel the change, sometimes see it. Could say, "How are you doing today? Is that your dad's car? That's a nice car." Yeah, I could say that and still be thinking, "Hey man, glad I checked ya out, what's going down? Is that your raise's ride? That's bad, man." I could talk one way and think another. Even took books home—wasn't nothing else to do.

Had a girlfriend lived in Homewood, got to talking about what-all everything was about. I started asking questions and there was no one to answer, but I didn't ask anyone either, just asked.

Nineteen sixty-two and my second little sister came; another care. June 1962, graduation time and what? The mills, the service, the streets—fuck school, I was too dumb and poor anyway.

January 1963, the train came and Parris Island, South Carolina, United States Marine Corps. These motherfuckers were crazy, stood in your face and told you all about your ass. Told you what you were didn't have a goddamn thing to do with what you were going to be. Made you stand in the dark and see yourself, run an hour past the minute you thought you'd drop. Made it very clear: you'd be the first, you better be the best, think fast and kill quick. In a way it all made sense, but in another way it said look over the edge. Then the sense became crazy, because it was real and I was on the edge.

April 1963, Rocky Mountain train station. The signs were very clear, WHITE ONLY, COLORED ONLY, and I had my green suit on. Sometime late in '63, on the outskirts of Wilmington, North Carolina, the cross burned in the field and the Halloween sheet motherfuckers stood watching the fire.

The sea came too—Cuba, Puerto Rico, Panama, and the first faces look like Mr. Toto. I wonder where Ricky Ricardo is. I don't know what the fuck is going on, care and then don't care, ride the ships, run the highways, and party the towns. Fuck the Klan and the speed limits; I go as fast as the Chevy can go, as far as the ships sail, drink wine in the night and stand straight in the morning.

Nineteen sixty-four, gray ocean waves, the wind, Spain, and a breeze of death. Choppers crash in the air, twenty guys die; I saw the fires. Smiling white faces in England and France. I could go anywhere. Harlem sparks, Mississippi and Alabama burn, Kennedy's dead, King's telling Mother America she's fucking up her black babies. I could tell you all about the machine gun.

Life was whatever day it was and wherever we were. It was my way, our way; *our* was us. We were from all over the place—colored guys from New York, Chicago, Florida, and Alabama too, white guys from Maine, Jersey, Ohio, Mississippi, and everyplace else. In our own way we weren't very different. Fought some but not too much, told secrets to one another too. Came close in our own way.

Spring 1965, Panama, and the ships sailed back to North Carolina and the papers were flying, orders to Third Marine Division, Fleet Marine Force, Western Pacific. The word was spreading, the shit and the fan had had a collision. The Ninth Marines had been sent to Da Nang, the Fourth Marines were at Chu Lai. Guys were getting fucked over there, and our asses were on the way.

The ship was moving now, I could feel it surging through the water. I was climbing through its little passageways and up its little steep ladders, up to its deck. I could see the faraway gray buildings and even the little people moving about on the distant docks, and then I couldn't see them, only the wiggly gray lines beneath a pale blue sky. Looking down, I saw the waves breaking at their peaks, blue-gray water splashed into white sparkling drops of sea. Looking ahead, looking out to sea, just water and sky.

I was not leaving a lot behind, real things like a house, kids, wife, or even a girlfriend. If I thought of home and took a deep breath, I'd be thinking of faces, faces in me, faces so close to me they were me—my mother, little sisters, Harry, my grandmother, just those faces. That was about all I'd hurt for. If I'd known where I was going, could have seen over the distant horizon, flipped the pages, peeked beyond, I don't know if it would have made a difference. The ship was sailing away.

Ship days can be long days, long days of just being. It would not take too long to find yourself in strangers, find a "Hey home, where you from?"

"Pittsburgh, man, where you from?"

"Shit, man, seem like everybody from up north. I'm from South Carolina."

And then the games.

"You in, man? We playin' a buck a hand, blackjack. Five-card charlie pays double."

There would always be a corner somewhere close to where you were, small enough to hide to the side but big enough to get into a different world.

"Hey man, I'm good, see the next man."

"Hit me, man, easy. Shit."

"Give me one more, down and dirty."

"Man, cut those fuckin' cards."

"Blackjack, motherfucker."

The game would become real. The cards might die in your hands, but the chance was still there, winking at you, flirting with your hard-on for it.

We were all strangers to one another, different faces, different looks, but in a way, our way, saying the same words, thinking the same thoughts. Actually, no one talked about Vietnam much. We didn't say the word "Vietnam." If we talked about it, we would just call it "there" or some other little word that could mean a lot of things. We played our cards, wrote our letters, stayed on our racks, and talked and marked time by when it was time to eat, but we sailed in a silence.

I didn't understand too much about Vietnam. I knew where it was, I had looked on a map. I didn't watch TV and really didn't know what was going on, other than that troops had been sent in and we were going to join them. I knew all about the kind of warfare, the booby traps and ambushes. I knew we had been training a lot for jungle and guerrilla warfare, but no one said what the training was for.

Some days I didn't give a fuck, could care less about where I was going, didn't worry too much about getting fucked up, didn't think it could happen to me anyway. Then some days I got this feeling; some-times I'd think about Arthur and his knowing he was going to die. Then it would be hard to know if my feelings about getting killed were just thoughts or some will, some strange thing in the sky or night that was drawing me to it, and I knew it yet couldn't do anything about it. Like Arthur. If Arthur knew, I could know too. Arthur was there, just like me, talking and laughing and all that stuff, he wasn't weird or anything like that, and then he knew he was going to die. All that was in him— that talk and being up on things, wanting to get some leg, hear some song, come back home and be some more of what he was—all that inside stuff just seemed to go away, and I was talking to a shell, a skeleton already. Sometimes I thought each inch the ship moved was taking me closer to dying. Then I'd started killing myself in my mind, thinking and sometimes saying, "Fuck it, let it come."

The sea's nights are different, different from highway nights, party nights, home nights, any night. As far as you can see, the night is dark and silent; even the waves swell, splash, and ripple in silence. Thoughts and time can stand still, stop. No matter who you were, what you were, you could become just a particle of ever, of everything, of never and nothing.

3

THE HOLE

Okinawa, last pussy stop, last days waiting; then the plane flew through the air and a space. Not a space of time or emptiness but a space of change. The thought of Vietnam—over the way, there, Nam—became a feeling fleeing, a dead thought and then a ghost. A ghost of a past, a ghost of you.

Now Da Nang, heat hotter than Panama, heat that wouldn't let your mind think of anything else. The airstrip was a wait in the sun, fighter jets poised, muddy brown sandbag bunkers with black guns sticking out. The truck was a ride down some baked dusty road and then the sea again, a small boat waiting and a young beautiful girl up in the rocks and bushes near the beach. We watched the girl. She veered from the path she was on, pulled her black pajamas down, and pissed and shit.

I was going to Chu Lai, but the openness had already come. Green distant treelines, shaded shadows, began to lurk and poke out at me. The sea was half safe, half open waters where your mind could wander, run, half the near shoreline with its silent shadows, where your mind could not wander or run.

Chu Lai was a fading sun, another baked road. The jeep driver stopped and barely muttered, "That's Alpha Company up there on the hill."

I stood looking up the hill. I could see about four or five dark green sagging tents; there were beaten mud paths weaving between them and patches of weeds all around. The top of the hill seemed bare and blended in with the evening sky. I could hear muddled voices coming from some of the tents. There were some guys on top of the hill and this guy coming down the path.

"Hi, I'm Kearns, acting supply sergeant. XO says get you guys some gear. Most of you guys be goin' to first platoon—they're up there." He was pointing now, throwing his arm over his shoulder and extending his thumb to the tents above.

He was a short guy, sort of thin, dark hair and a sand-colored face. His green faded shirt was open and hung loosely over his waist; his green mud-stained pants sagged from his hips. "Come on over to the supply tent," he was saying. "We can get your gear over there. Gear's a little fucked, but it's all we have. We're supposed to get some new shit in."

He turned and we followed.

Inside the supply tent, brown and green gear—packs, canteens, ponchos, helmets, belts, rifles, and ammo—lay about. After lighting a cigarette, Kearns was rifling through the piles of gear.

"These rifles are beat, need to be cleaned real good. This one's a automatic, you want it?" he said, holding the rifle out to me. I took it and slung it over my shoulder, then picked the rest of the gear up in my arms and started to turn.

"How many grenades ya want?" Kearns was saying as he held his cigarette in his mouth and fumbled with two handfuls of grenades. "Here, take a few. Ya get time, tape those pins down on them. Guy up in Bravo Company got a pin stuck on something getting on a truck, the pin popped out. Couple guys got sapped and about six or so got wounded."

I followed Kearns up the hill to one of the tents. In a while I met the platoon sergeant—a few quick words and a "Sit tight, we'll have time to go over things later" as he left.

The night came quickly. I lit a candle and was sitting on a rack in the empty tent. In the distance the booming sound of artillery could be heard, and from time to time a burst of machine-gun fire.

I was sitting on the rack cleaning the rifle and loading the bullets into the ammo clips when they came in from the night. I had heard their footsteps and watched them come into the tent. They were strangers, new faces, with sweaty skin and muddy, stained clothes and boots.

"You the new corporal? Hi, I'm Bright," the taller one said as he flung his helmet off, sat on his rack, and started looking for a cigarette. He had sweaty blond hair that hung down over his forehead and a schoolkid's face.

"Hey, I'm Lee. Welcome to the squad, what there is left of it," the other one said as he let his helmet fall to the ground and unbuckled his ammo belt. He was a dark-skinned kid. The light from the candle seemed to make the sweat on his face glisten.

"You takin' over the squad?" Lee asked.

"Yeah," I said.

"That's good news," the blond kid blurted out.

I looked at him but didn't say anything. I waited for a while before asking, "How things going?"

Bright answered quickly, "Not bad. We been on watch. Sergeant Wiggins has sort of been the squad leader. Did you meet him yet?"

"Yeah," I said.

Lee said, "Sergeant Wiggins is the platoon sergeant. He's been runnin' the squad until we get a corporal. I guess that's you."

I lit a cigarette and took a deep drag before asking, "What happened to the squad leader?"

Lee smiled and almost laughed as Bright blurted out, "Ain't no corporals except for Gates. He was the squad leader, but—"

Lee spoke quickly and over Bright's words, saying, "Let's just say it didn't work out."

It was quiet for a while. The artillery boomed in the distance. I heard Lee asking, "Where you from?"

"Pittsburgh."

"You know Willis? He's from Pittsburgh."

"No, I don't think so," I answered. "How many guys left in the squad now?"

"Well," Lee said, then paused. "There's me, Bright, Grunwald— Grunwald will be back, he got shot in the leg. Rayburn and McCabe's on mess duty, and if you want to count Gates, I guess that's it. Let's see." Lee was counting with his fingers and saying, ". . . two, three, five, six if ya want to count Gates."

"That's all?" I asked.

"Well," Lee said, "Shreck got it, he got killed. Griffin got transferred. Pugh got fucked up too that day Shreck and them got it, but Sergeant Wiggins said Pugh might be back."

Both Lee and the blond kid became quiet and then started talking between themselves as a slender, nervous-looking guy came into the tent. He looked around, then looked to where I sat and said quickly, "You the new guy? Sergeant Wiggins says you got last watch, says meet him up the radio shack at 2430."

"Yeah, okay," I answered slowly, then said, "You must be Gates."

"Yeah," he said, then turned quickly. "I got watch now, I got to go."

Gates hurried out of the tent. Lee and Bright both waited for a while before Lee blurted out, "He's fucked up. He almost got us all fucked up over on Pork Chop."

Bright laughed and said, "Gates is a nice guy, man, but he's really screwed."

I blew out the candle. Lee and Bright fell asleep quickly. I lay on the rack, just thinking and listening to the sounds out in the night. The sides of the tent were rolled up, and as far as I could see, everything was dark. The distant sound of guns began to settle in my mind, but the darkness was restless.

I was closing my eyes, resting, then quickly opening them and glancing at my watch. The little green hands seemed frozen. Then I would look again and they might have leaped forward, sometimes too far. I wanted more time, more time to think, more time not to think. I didn't know what was out there, and I didn't know, wasn't sure, what was in me.

If I slept, I didn't dream; I didn't close my mind to the night. But I was up now. I buckled on my ammo belt, stuck those grenades in my pockets, and slung my rifle over my shoulder.

Outside the tent, I could hardly see the path, any path, as I started up the hill. I could hear my own footsteps in the dark, then I heard the garbled sounds of radio voices.

"Alpha, Alpha one, over."

"Alpha one, copy, over."

"Alpha six, come in, six."

I leaned to the sounds of the voice and soon I could see the radio tent. I waited for the garbled voices to quiet, then I spoke into the tent. "Looking for Sergeant Wiggins. I'm to meet him here at 2430."

"Ya must be the new guy. Set tight, he's up with second squad. He'll be down soon."

I remember sitting on an ammo box, waiting but mostly looking further up the hill to its top and wondering what lay on the other side. I could see the outline of the top of the hill and then just black sky. I could hear the static radio voices itching at the silence. I didn't know I was still hearing the guns.

A sudden sound of footsteps came into my thoughts. Quickly I peered up the dark path. I knew it was Wiggins, even though the darkness hid his face. We had talked earlier. "Welcome aboard, corporal," he had said. "I'm Sergeant Wiggins, first platoon sergeant. Glad you're here. You have third squad. The lieutenant is Lieutenant Fargo. He's out with first squad, he'll be back tomorrow, we can get things squared away." We shook hands, but we had only talked a bit.

He was older, clean-shaven, with a high-cheekboned face and a little puggy nose. His shirt was buttoned and his pistol belt was buckled snugly around his waist. He walked with his shoulders erect and his back straight, almost stiffly. I could tell it was him coming down the path.

When he arrived, he took a seat on another ammo box. "You get any sleep?" he asked, then said, "You got the lp. We'll go up in a couple minutes."

He had taken a cigarette out; now the flame from his lighter was dimly lighting his face. He spoke again. "You smoke, better get one now—no smokin' on watch. The password's 'blue horse.' All the patrols are in. We just man the lp at night—it's down over the hill, 'bout seventy yards or so. Should be quiet, but if anything breaks loose, get back up the hill. We got a machine gun on top. Hold your position until morning. Chow goes at 0600. You ready?"

I had lit a cigarette and puffed away quickly as he spoke. Now I followed him up the dark path to the top of the hill. It was flat; steps were easier to take, free from the strain of coming up the hill. I could see some now. In the distance, dark mountains or big hills stood far and high into the sky; closer, down over the hill, it looked like a deep dark valley. I hadn't thought about the stars, and I glanced at the sky. I could see some, but they seemed to hide or shy away from the night.

Wiggins was whispering now and pointing into the darkness. "We got this sector—five positions, machine gun is up there. The lp is down in front of the guns. Just follow me."

I could barely see anything that Wiggins was pointing to. Then, out of the night, I could see a stack of sandbags. "Halt," came a whisper through the dark. Wiggins whispered back, "Sergeant Wiggins."

As we passed the stack of sandbags I could see the outline of a helmet peering over and then the long black barrel of the machine gun pointing out into the night.

We started down the hill.

I could not see anything except for the back of Wiggins. My steps were awkward; the ground was uneven and rocky. The dark forms ahead slowly became bushes and small trees. The sandbags and the barrel of the machine gun were my last discernible vision; even Wiggins had just about become lost in the night, there and not there. When I could not see him, I listened for the sound of his footsteps, and I was following the sound as we curved down through the darkness.

I shuddered.

A frantic whisper jumped out of the darkness. "Halt. Halt, who's that?"

I heard shifting sounds, then Wiggins whispering, "Sergeant Wiggins, Sergeant Wiggins."

Wiggins was kneeling, almost crawling, as we moved toward the sounds ahead. I could see a little now—I could see the shape of a helmet and a dark shaded face that looked as if it were just sticking out of the ground.

We crawled on through the bushes. The shifting sounds of movements hastened and whispers broke the silence.

"Is everything quiet?" I knew it was Wiggins's whisper.

"Yeah," another muffled voice whispered.

I could hear the sounds of ammo belts shaking and the sudden sound of someone rolling or climbing. Then I could see ahead, I could see the hole in the ground. It looked like a small circle of darker blackness. I could see Wiggins and someone with him as I neared the hole.

"Okay, it's your watch," Wiggins was whispering back to me.

"Okay," I whispered.

I was there now, still on my knees, peering down into the hole. I could not see the bottom of it. I eased myself into it and found I could stand; it was chest deep.

"See ya at chow," Wiggins whispered as they began crawling away.

I watched them crawl until I couldn't see them. Then I listened to their sounds until I could no longer hear them.

I looked around.

I stood, staring and looking around, trying to see into the black shapes, trying to take them apart and put them back together in my mind so I could tell what they were. Without knowing, remembering when, at what moment, I had pointed the rifle into the dark and gripped it tightly. Now, very slowly and without taking my eyes from the dark, I eased my hand from the foregrip of the rifle and very slowly reached in my pockets and gently pulled the grenades out, one by one, remembering that I had not taped them. I placed them on the edge of the hole and quietly put my hand back on the rifle.

Something moved and was moving toward me, in me. It moved slowly, but I could feel it. I steadied myself and kept my eyes on the night.

I could feel it moving again, all around me, all in me, all in everything I was. It was there in the silence; it was moving like shadows, yet it was still. But I knew it was closer to me.

It touched me.

I jerked from its touch, but I could still feel it reaching and grabbing for me. My mind turned quickly, slipping, spinning, climbing out of the hole, up the hill, out of the night, but I was still in the hole.

I tried to breathe quietly. I shifted my weight from foot to foot, all along looking and staring into a black world from a black hole. Now sound, any sound—the distant artillery booming, nightbugs buzzing, the wisps of any breeze, my own breathing—picked and poked at me.

I was hiding now, crouching lower into the hole. I could smell the dirt when I breathed, smell its cool dampness. I did not want to die, not now, not here.

I could only see in my mind, see beyond the swells of darkness, see reds and yellows, see memories and briefly feel them, see front porches, see lipstick and feel gentle hugs. Red lipstick and green trees, cars with horns, yellow flowers in the grass, gray sidewalks.

My mouth was dry, but I was trying to whisper, whisper to me, whisper out of me. I was trying to remember how to say it, how it sounded. I could hear it in my mind.

"Yea, yea, though I walk through the valley . . ."

The black barrel of my rifle pointed out into the night.

". . . of death, I will fear no evil . . ."

My finger was pressing on the trigger.

". . . for Thou . . ."

I did not want to die.

I could see the grenades sitting there in the dirt beneath my face, their pins dangling from their sides.

The silence was a time that wouldn't move, the dark that hovered, that wiggly-looking black ugly shape standing in the dark pretending it was a bush, a tree, trying to fool me.

The silence cracked, shook.

I jumped, jerked the rifle, and swung it to the sudden sound, then listened, waited, watched for it to move, crawl. I knew something moved, I heard it. Something was there, I heard it. My finger eased over the point of the trigger. I sank deeper into the hole, didn't breathe, then breathed slowly but quietly as the silence crept back.

My mouth was dry, and when I breathed, I tasted the dry spit on my tongue. My hands were sweating, my finger was sliding on the slippery trigger, but I kept moving the rifle from side to side, watching and waiting.

I saw it.

I saw it this time—it moved, I know it did. It was over there; I could see it, I could see it now. It was still, just waiting for me to turn away from it and stop looking at it, but I wouldn't move, wouldn't breathe, I would wait.

"Come on, motherfucker, come on, move," I wanted to scream, but I was quiet and waited. I knew it saw me; I could feel its eyes watching me.

It moved, it was over *there* now. I heard it. I swung my rifle to it. I heard it, I knew I did. I listened; I could still hear the echoes of its sound darting in my mind. I could hear the night, hear its darkness swaying.

Silence came again, then stillness.

I put my head down and breathed, took a deep breath, then raised my head and looked back into the night. It was so silent, so still.

There was a peace in my mind, a cold chilling peace that gave some comfort to the heat, the hot air, the flames of my fears.

I would kill, I knew it.

I knew that when it came, I would kill it, try to kill it. Pull that trigger in its face.

I knew I would, but I didn't want to know that. I did not want to become a part of what I was in. There was another feeling, not part of the peace; it was deeper and smiled. I didn't want words for it, I wanted to keep it secret from me.

I felt the itch on my neck. The bug had probably been crawling there for a while; now I could feel it nipping and chewing at my skin. Slowly and quietly, and without looking away from the night, I moved my left hand from beneath my rifle and eased it to my neck, then waited. I slowly looked around while the bug chewed or scraped at my skin. Then I opened my hand and quietly pressed it against my neck. I began to rub my hand hard against my neck. I could feel the little legs breaking, the bug crumbling and rolling into little pieces between my hand and my sweaty neck. I kept on rubbing; the sweat made the rubbing easy and soothing. Then, just as slow as the night, I moved my hand back beneath the rifle, where it would wait.

Time would not move.

It seemed like it had always been dark. I knew it was real now and I couldn't even see it. I couldn't get out of this hole, out of this dark. I didn't want to die down here. I wondered if Arthur was laughing at me, if I was seeing the same thing he saw, feeling what he felt, knowing what he knew.

I was reaching now, easing my hand down to my belt, letting my fingers rub over the coarse ammo belt until I could feel the hard handle on the bayonet. I let my fingers grip the handle and quietly pull the bayonet from its case. I looked around and listened, then slowly pulled the rifle in closer to me until I could reach the muzzle and put the bayonet on the end of the barrel. Then I pushed the rifle back down the hill and breathed slowly as I looked at the stark silhouette of the knife sticking into the night.

A sharp light flashed behind me and the ground shook; the whole hill felt like it was breaking apart. Everything was spinning. I spun around, pointing my rifle up the hill, and slung myself against the back side of the hole. My chest was heaving; the echo of the roar was still clawing into the night. Then it was quiet, but I was still shaking, quivering, and looking back up the hill.

The flash of light came again, the roar broke loose, the ground shook, but while the flashing light hovered I could see the huge silhouette of a tank and its long barrel still flaming from its fire. Quickly I turned around and pointed my rifle back down the hill. Everything was black now; the flashes from the tank had burned my vision of the night into crisp darkness.

I hadn't heard them when the tank was firing, but I could hear them now—I could hear dogs barking and howling. Somewhere out there, and not too far, there were dogs, and I couldn't hear anything around me for their howling. Slowly I began to see again. The wiggly forms were still there. The dogs kept barking.

My breathing was slower. I wanted a cigarette. I stood shifting my weight from foot to foot, sometimes almost swaying. My mouth was scorching dry and I wanted a drink of water, but I didn't want to take my hands from my rifle to reach for my canteen.

The night was still and its darkness was at ease.

I could see home, see what I was, see people I knew, see colors again. Then I'd see my mother, my sisters, Harry. I'd look at them for only a moment, maybe just a quick glance, then I'd hurt and turn back to the dark.

The dogs were still barking.

I shuddered. A machine gun was going off somewhere in the distance. It fired one long burst, then a few quick bursts, but it was far away. I kept shifting my weight from foot to foot, watching and waiting.

I could feel the pressure in my gut, the heat in my groin. It had been there for a while. I kept shifting my weight back and forth, but I could not ease the pressure, and now the heat in my groin was burning.

I kept waiting and watching.

Slowly I reached one hand down to the buttons on my pants, while keeping the other hand on the rifle and its finger on the trigger. I unbuttoned each button and pulled my penis out into the night air, then slowly put my hand back beneath the rifle.

I would wait and keep watching the zigzaggy creatures lingering in the dark. The moments dripped by slowly, but I waited and listened to the creeping sounds and the howling of the dogs.

The pressure in my gut kept pounding and surging. I slid to the corner of the hole and waited again. The heat of the night air curled around my penis, teasing it, and it began to throb from the pressure in my gut.

I had to go, I had to piss, but I was not going to piss in this hole. I didn't want to crawl out into the night. I wanted to stay in the hole, hide in the dark, but I had to go. I wasn't pissing in this hole and dying in it too.

Slowly I was climbing up the dirt walls of the hole, then nudging myself out of it. My eyes were frantically spinning around and searching the dark, waiting for it to run at me. My rifle was sticking to my hands, my own sounds were shattering the silence around me. I hurried, then stilled and lay on the ground. Everything was moving. The night was shifting and twisting; wiggly creatures seemed too near.

Quietly I eased myself to my knees, still holding my rifle in both hands and sticking it into the dark. Then I spread my knees apart and waited. It was quiet. I breathed and let the pressure out of my gut. My penis throbbed and the piss splashed on the ground beneath me, but I quickly stopped it from hitting the ground. It made too much noise. I waited, listened. It was silent again, but I kept waiting. Then I breathed again. The piss squirted from my penis and splashed onto the ground. It splattered against the silence, but I couldn't stop it again. I let it splash into the dirt, but I kept looking around, holding the rifle and swinging it back and forth.

Now I was easing back into the hole, quietly sliding down the dirt walls. I stood, searching the night again, but I could smell the sour stench of piss floating through the air. The fucking dogs were still barking.

There was a silence now, not in the night but in me. I didn't want to die, couldn't even see death. I could see funerals with flowers, but not this death out here. Not the kind of death that killed that guy named Shreck. But I had to see it, look it in the face. I was in its hole now.

Fuck the goddamn dogs.

4

FIRST FIRE

I remember it was in the afternoon when I first met Vernon. I don't remember what day, maybe the second or third day, maybe the first, I don't know, but I was coming back from the chow tent. Vernon was sitting outside his tent cleaning a machine gun. I spoke. "Hey man."

"Hey," he said.

"You in guns?" I asked as I slowed.

"Yeah."

"I was in guns in the States." I stopped and looked at the familiar pieces of M-60 spread out on the poncho.

"You in first platoon now?"

"Yeah, I got third squad."

"Yeah, I heard. You took Gates's place," Vernon said with a slight smile. Then he was silent for a moment before asking, "How you like it?"

I laughed a little, then said, "Shit, ain't much of a squad, just Bright, Lee, Grunwald just got back, and some guy named McCabe and some other guy, Rayburn, are still on fuckin' mess duty. Sergeant Wiggins says they ought to be back tomorrow, or sometime soon. Shit, that's still just five guys."

"McCabe in your squad?"

"Yeah, why?"

"Oh, nothin'."

31

"Ya know him?"

"Yeah, everybody knows McCabe."

I didn't ask what Vernon was trying to tell me. I already knew. Mc-Cabe was a fuckup. Rayburn could fuck up too.

Vernon was a stocky guy with brown buckeye skin, and even when he wasn't smiling or laughing, he left half of his last smile still on his face. The guys had nicknamed him VC, because his last name was Carter. I would always call him Vernon, or Vern.

"Did you come over from Pendleton?" Vernon was asking.

"No, we stopped there, were there for a week. I was at LeJeune, Eighth Marines for two years."

"How did you get here?"

"That's what I want to know. We got back from Panama, fuckin' orders were waiting. I got a chance to go home for two weeks, and that was it."

"Where you from?"

"Pittsburgh. Where you from?"

"Florida."

We talked for a while, got to laughing, even laughed when I asked what that tent up on the other side of the road was. He answered, "Graves." I said, "What?" He said, "Graves registration." I remember laughing on the outside and saying, "That's the last fuckin' place I want to register at." Later I sat and stared at it for a while, then turned away.

It was good talking to Vernon. We didn't say anything important; I guess it was the feeling I liked—it was like talking to someone from home.

It didn't take long for the days to melt into just time; they lost their names, as if Tuesday or Thursday, even fuckin' Friday and Saturday nights, didn't mean shit. But a time was coming that the whole company was going out from where we were, about fifteen or twenty miles out. We would be there for a few days.

I had heard about how it could be, how the VC had popped up out of a bush and killed that guy named Shreck with a Thompson machine gun. I had heard about how a guy named Panucci got it in the head. Some guy in second squad told me, "I was right next to him, man, I heard a splat. Man, I looked and all that blood starts coming out." I had heard about the mortar round that came down on second platoon and wounded about six guys, all in one squad. Some guy named Sarver had stepped on a mine, it ripped his leg off and wounded some of the guys behind him.

I had heard about the almosts—how the bullets had hit all around Bright when Shreck got killed, and how the VC had third platoon pinned down for hours.

It was time.

It was still dark in the tents; the candles were being lit, and soon their flames began to flicker. Outside the tent, thick grayness spread over our hill and the rest of the sagging tents. The echoing call came: *"Reveille, reveille, squad leaders, get your people up. Let's go. Reveille."*

There was a chill on my back as the cool morning air hit my bare shoulders. I was sitting on the side of the rack, trying to wipe the sleep out of my eyes. I lit a cigarette and began to look around for a shirt.

"How much time we got?" Bright was asking as he sat up and began to light a cigarette.

" 'Bout an hour," I said slowly, then said, "Get Lee up."

"Lee, Lee, it's reveille," Bright started whispering.

I yelled over Bright's whispers, "Lee, get the fuck up. Get McCabe's ass up and the rest of your people. Rayburn, Rayburn, get up now. You and Bright go down and pick up chow. Come on, let's go."

McCabe and Rayburn came back a few days ago, so did Grunwald.

Rayburn was subtly crazy—didn't say much, and when he did it wasn't too fast. He had long brown hair that hung over his forehead and down to his sad eyes. When he had his helmet on, if he could find it, and that hair was hanging down, he looked like some comic-book character. Last time I saw him, he was with the dead and wounded. He was not either.

McCabe was the oldest of all of us; he was twenty-three or -four. Been to college; smart-ass, too. He was still a private after three years. He started his shit his first day back. You say right, the motherfucker goes left. You say stop, he's on his way. Shit.

Grunwald's ass was back; I hadn't the slightest idea where his mind was. That VC put a hole in his leg, but I thought his head got fucked too. I didn't think he was ready to go back out there, but he was going. I hadn't been there yet, but I had to watch him when we got there.

I felt like a kid with the other squad leaders—they were older, in their late twenties or maybe in their thirties, been in ten years and all that.

The platoon sergeant, Wiggins, is just Wiggins. He ain't changed none since first sight.

The lieutenant, Fargo, is from Mississippi someplace. Chews a little tobacco here, but at worst, he ain't bad.

Most of the guys are just guys, like back over the way. Typical crazy white dudes, fun-time homeboys, some Puerto Ricans. They bounce back and forth, some white, some black, but we all got into the same shit. Mr. Blackjack's here, even got some song sometimes, somebody got a tape recorder, play some stuff that makes you want to get the fuck out of here.

There's a lot of Mexicans, some crazy, some ain't. First squad leader, Sergeant Ituarte, he's Mexican, Indian, or something, but he's more lifer than anything. Been in ten, going for twenty. I didn't know, he didn't know; or maybe he did, maybe that same shit that told Arthur had already told him to forget about getting past ten.

We were going out by chopper, flying to someplace they called Death Valley because of all the booby traps and mines that were found there. Bravo Company had been out in the same area the week before. A guy stepped on a mine; he and another guy got killed, a couple others got wounded. They killed about six VC, caught them out in the open. The word came down yesterday that we were going out to search the area again.

I wanted to think. I wanted to brace myself, look at things. I had only been here for about a week, hadn't been fired at yet, seen anything yet—no dead bodies, just noise in the night.

I put my boots on and was standing now, looking at my watch again, trying to see how much time was left. We were told we would eat first, then move down to the helipad. It was 0515, about forty-five minutes or so before we would start to the chopper pad.

I looked at Grunwald. He was still sitting on his rack. His head was down, and as he sucked on his cigarette, the smoke rose and floated around his head.

I spoke quietly. "Grunwald, come on, let's go, start getting your gear ready. We're not going to have a lot of time after chow gets here."

Without lifting his head from the smoke, he said, "Okay, I'll be ready. I got my stuff ready."

I grabbed a towel and some soap and went outside the tent to the water can and washed up some. The cool water felt good on my face and made the morning and me start to feel alive. I thought about shaving, then thought if I was going to die today, why make the morning miserable? I hated shaving with cold water.

As I stood drying my face off, I could hear the shouting going on in the tent. I knew Rayburn and Bright were back with the chow. As I went back into the tent, I could see the chow boxes lying in the center of the tent and everybody grabbing at them.

"Come on, man, I'll trade you."

"Oh fuck, man, I got three of the same damn shit."

"Who got turkey and wants to trade for beef?"

"Who wants this ham-and-eggs shit? I'll take anything."

"Fuck you, man."

I was smiling and shouting, "Just take eight boxes, separate the shit later. Eat now, we only got a half-hour." Then I was yelling, "Bright, save me your Winstons, I got some of those Viceroys, I'll trade you."

Once the fighting over the chow and the trading was over, the sounds of cans being opened began. Grunwald was eating but still hadn't said much. Lee said, "Hey man, Sergeant Wiggins says that when we get back, two guys can do some R and R, party time."

Bright asked quickly, "Who's going first? How they going to pick who's going first?"

Lee laughed, chewing and shouting at the same time. "I'm going first, who the fuck you think! You ain't old enough to get in bars anyway."

"Fuck you, Lee," Bright shouted back.

I had found out just in some talk that Bright was only seventeen. In a few weeks or so, he and another kid, Little Man, some kid in second platoon, would be sent to Okinawa until they turned eighteen. Then they would be sent back.

I sat listening to the breakfast talk, sometimes breaking in and reminding everybody to hurry up. When I finished eating, I got a cigarette to pass the minutes away. I didn't want to think, but I did. Maybe nothing would happen, maybe nothing would happen out there. Maybe nobody would get killed, maybe I would not get killed. Maybe Bright or Lee, or even Grunwald, would get killed. Then I was thinking, *Fuck it.*

I sat quietly for a while and smoked the cigarette, then stood and spoke just loud enough for my words to get over the breakfast talk. "Okay, saddle up. Let's go, outside in five minutes. Check your weapons. Let's go."

I put my ammo belt on, slung my heavy pack over my shoulder, then grabbed my rifle and helmet and stepped out into the gray morning air. I held the rifle up, pulled the bolt back, and looked down into its oily chamber. I took my finger and stuck it down into the grooves of the chamber and wiggled it around, feeling for dirt or sand. I shouted back into the tent, "Come on, third squad, outside, let's go," then took the gray ammo clip with its copper-colored bullets and jammed it into the rifle.

We would keep the rifle bolts open and the triggers locked until it was time to hit the landing zone. Then we would load. The bolt would spring forward and jam the first bullet into the chamber.

I shouted again, "Come on, third squad, let's go. Lee, come on, get them outside. Grunwald, get a move on. McCabe, get your ass moving."

They were coming out of the tent now, the dark green ammo belts hanging heavily from their waists, their shirts, already stained from sweat and rain, hanging loosely from muscled chests and shoulders. Some packs were loosely carried, just over one shoulder. Grenades were being stuffed into big pockets and bandoliers of extra ammo hung from necks like big green necklaces. Their helmets sat awkwardly on their heads, some set to the side, others set far back; none were buckled, their straps swinging loosely. Rifles were slung over shoulders or held dangling from one hand. Cigarettes were being lit; gray smoke settled in the gray of the morning.

We were winding down from our hill, following the brown twisting path that led down to the mess tent and then to where the choppers would land. The other squads and platoons were coming down from their hills and tents. The shifting sounds of ammo belts and heavy packs swaying, the thumping sound of footsteps, and a quiet sound of silence gave cadence to our way.

As we neared the bottom of our hill, the paths seemed to converge, bring the squads closer together, and then the platoons. I had not seen all the guys in the company. Their faces were strange but their looks were familiar. The clothes were faded; black boots had been scraped raw and now were the same color as the ground, rough brown.

The machine-gun squads were coming in too. Their long black heavy guns rode their shoulders, and their long strands of bullets hung down from their necks, glittering in the early sun.

The words were being passed from the platoon sergeants, their voices cracking commands through the thin hot air.

"First platoon over here."

"Let's go, people."

"Third platoon, here."

"Move it out, people, let's go . . ."

As we moved closer together, the shouts back and forth between the squads flowed steadily under the sergeants' yells.

"Hey man, what's happening?"

"Hey man, where's that five?"

"Hey, heard we got some new guys."

"Hey man, I heard Spence got it."

"Ski, ya get any pussy down the ville?"

"Knock it off, people."

We settled into lines around the chopper pad, and soon a few fingers pointed toward the sky as the puttering sound of choppers could be heard. Silence had fallen in the ranks; last cigarettes were burning hot with quick drags.

The time was coming. I knew it would be here soon.

I stood looking around now, looking up into the sky, watching the green choppers circling. I looked behind me; the faces were there, just there. Grunwald was staring ahead, further than any distant hill. Lee had that half-smile on his face, but his eyes were still. Bright was fumbling around with some chain on his neck and looking off to the side. Then he quickly lowered his head and stared at his hands; I saw the cross sticking out between his fingers. Rayburn just stared with his blank Sad Sack look; his helmet sat low over his forehead, making his face just his eyes. He stared ahead silently. McCabe's face was always distant. His blue eyes shifted back and forth. His eyes came to mine and settled. I gave him a quick nod. He returned it. Doc was in our line; he was one of the corpsmen. He didn't smoke but always had a mouth full of gum, which he chewed quickly.

We became submerged in the loud puttering sounds of the incoming choppers. Shouts could barely be heard, and words were lost in the hot dusty air the choppers were blowing all over the place.

Our chopper had landed; dust and dirt were flying. I heard a faint yell from Sergeant Wiggins: "Third squad, move out."

I turned and shouted behind me, "Let's go."

I was running to the chopper, my face turned to the side, my arm up, trying to keep the dirt out of my eyes as I ran. I stopped when I reached the door and could see inside.

it, what the fuck? A thousand thoughts fucked, then tickled my mind. Two years of training, getting on and off these choppers, sitting, fastening seatbelts, closing the door, then up. *Shit, this damn thing doesn't have doors, seatbelts, doesn't have no damn seats either.*

The chopper gunner was holding his machine-gun barrel up to the sky and beckoning me aboard. I jumped on, then turned and helped each guy behind me climb in. Then I swung around and sat on the floor next to the door. I looked around quickly as the chopper thrust upward. I needed something to hold on to. I grabbed on to a netlike thing hanging from the wall.

The chopper was climbing, its engines droning. I was rubbing my face and eyes, trying to get the dirt and dust off so I could see. Then I turned and looked down to see the tops of our tents, our mud-brown hill, then just blurs of brown and green as we passed.

The air rushing through the open chopper felt good. The droning of the engines settled down some as we leveled off from our climb, but their vibrations still shook the ride. It seemed like everything was trembling in this time. My thoughts were huddled under the loud hum of the engines. I tried to still the time, tried to slow things down.

The moments did not slow, they only expanded.

I turned from the door. I was breathing slowly, looking down at my hands, seeing them wrapped around my rifle. I stared for a while, then slowly looked about to the faces around me. Grunwald sat in the rear of the chopper; his head was down and he was fumbling with his rifle straps. Bright was using sign language, trying to tell Lee something. Lee wasn't listening. Rayburn was just staring; he looked like he was sleeping with his eyes open, or dead already. McCabe had taken his helmet off and was playing with his hair. Doc sat chewing on his gum; his mouth seemed to chew, then stop, then chew again quickly. The door gunner sat on a stool; he had lowered the gun and now seemed to be hiding behind his mirrored sunglasses.

The loud humming sound of the chopper ground against my thoughts. I looked over my shoulder and out into the open sky, it was a pretty blue, light blue with pretty white clouds here and there. The cool air was blowing in my face. Everything seemed so beautiful and peaceful. Looking down, I saw vibrant greens, so many shades of greens, lights and brights, darks and thicks. I could see sketches of rice paddies below, their brown pencil-thin mud dikes edging through patches of sunlit water. It was a big beautiful quilt of the earth, with paintings of little people dressed in black and straw-yellow hats to give life to the beauty. It was easy for thoughts to fly away, to go where they wanted to, just to keep going.

I hadn't wanted to think, but I was. I turned from the door and looked back into shadows of where I sat. My neck was strained from looking over my shoulder and it felt good to lower my head. I sat staring down at my hands and the dark gray metal of my rifle, and all of the greens and blues went far away.

The door gunner began to shift in his seat. One hand had moved up to his ear and was pressing on the radio set. I knew the time was coming. He took his hand from his ear, then the sharp sound of his fingers snapping could be heard over the humming of the engine. As we looked toward him, he jerked his hand up and made it into a fist, then stuck his thumb up. Quickly he shifted in his seat and grabbed his gun with both hands.

It was time.

I yelled over the engine sounds, "Get ready. Lock and load, lock and load. Stand by."

I took my hand and pulled on the rifle bolt, then freed it, letting it fly forward and jam the first bullet into the chamber.

The chopper began to circle and swerve downward. I grabbed the net on the wall and began looking out. The greens and browns were spinning; the chopper was banking its curves. The door gunner began blasting his machine gun, and the weapon's report added to the tremendous vibration in the chopper. Everything was shaking; the shades of greens and browns beneath were coming closer. I could see the ground, the grass fluttering and the water rippling from the winds of the chopper's blades.

My mind was racing, passing thoughts. I could only feel feelings, not think of them.

The chopper slowed, hovered, then quickly lowered to the ground, only to jolt and bounce upward again before it settled, quivering and shaking.

"Let's go, let's go," I shouted, then swung around and jumped out the door. The ground was wet and muddy. My feet sank deep into the mud, but I was looking around, searching the treeline.

Behind me the loud puttering sounds of the chopper were still pounding against my thoughts. Quickly I looked over my shoulder, shouted, "Let's go," and started running through the mud we had landed in. Each step seemed precious, something I wanted to hold on to. I wanted to stay in each step's time, but I ran faster. I was running to the brown rice paddy dike ahead.

As I neared the dike, I spun around again, yelled, "Let's go. Spread it out, spread out." I couldn't hear anything, almost couldn't hear my own shouts. The other squads were landing, and a steady puttering roar kept pounding through the scorching air.

I reached the dike and dove to my knees behind it, then flung my rifle over its top and searched every shadow I could see. I watched and waited before turning around and shouting over my shoulder, "Third squad, over here. Set up here, spread it out, spread out." I was pointing and shouting, trying to be heard over all the noise. Everything seemed fucked, all over the place. I yelled again.

"Goddamnit, spread it out. Bright, get there. Lee, Rayburn, take that side. Grunwald, get a move on. McCabe, get down, damn it. Spread the fuck out. Doc, you can stick with me."

I spun back around, looked at the treeline, waited and watched. I was trying to still myself. I breathed slower, but my mind kept racing and trying to stay ahead of what may be ahead.

Soon the shouts and yells could be heard clearly as the choppers began to climb back in the sky. I was beginning to feel the wet muddy water seeping through my boots and pants. The water was cool, but the sun was becoming hot and burning down on my neck. I could speak now without yelling, but I only whispered.

"Lee, Rayburn, move down some, spread it out. Keep down till we get the word to move out."

We stayed still behind the dike. It seemed like the same long hot moment kept passing before Sergeant Wiggins came splashing through the water.

"Third squad, listen up." Wiggins was kneeling a ways off and whispering to me. "We're going to form up over there and start down that path. When we form, your squad, take point. Down that path about three hundred meters is a clearing. Hold up there, keep it spread out. Wait for the word. Set tight."

"Okay," I whispered back, then turned and whispered to the squad, "Stand by to move out."

I had turned some so I could rest my back against the dike. The sweat was rolling down my face and dripping onto my shirt. I wiped the sweat from my face. The heat was all around. I looked across the paddy, where I could see the other platoons beginning to form into columns. I looked back at my squad. Rayburn was kneeling quietly in the mud, whispering to Grunwald. Then I thought about that guy named Panucci, who got shot in the head while he was right next to somebody. I swung around again and looked toward the treeline and its dark shadows. All the greens and browns, trees and bushes, and their shadows were still.

I lit a cigarette and sucked the smoke in, then pitched the match into the water and watched its last little puff of smoke vanish. I could hear the word coming down the line.

"Move out. Let's go—we're movin' out."

"All right, let's go," I said, loud enough for the squad to hear, and then I pointed to the path and said, "McCabe, move out to the path, take point. Lee, follow up McCabe, keep it spread. Bright, move in behind Lee. Rayburn, Grunwald, fall in behind me, keep it spread. Let's go. Move out."

I could hear each step I took as my feet slushed through the mud. I was on the path now; the ground was hard and the shade was heavy and deep. We moved slowly and quietly. Distant sounds of birds could be heard as we moved further along the path.

I kept looking around. I tried to time and space my looks from up front, where I could see McCabe easing up the path, to the sides of the path, where the thick bushes and tall grass stood hard in the heat. Then I would look at the ground, search its little rocks, sticks, and the weeds between the rocks and sticks. Then I would look in the tiny shadows of the rocks and sticks lying on the path for skinny wires, shiny metal. Then I'd look ahead and step slowly, hoping the ground would not explode and tear my leg off.

The path brightened up ahead and soon McCabe stopped and signaled that the clearing was ahead. We were crouching now as I turned behind me and whispered, "Pass the word back, clearing up ahead."

Soon Wiggins came up. His face was sweaty. He looked ahead to where the clearing lay, then whispered to me, "Keep going, keep it spread out. When you get across the clearing, move in some. Should be a path on the other side. Move up that path some. Then hold up."

We were in the clearing now. To the left was a large open valley, to the right a shallow gully, then thick bush and trees. Ahead, on the other side of the clearing, was the mouth of a wide path. We kept moving. Our steps quickened. My finger was on the point of the trigger.

McCabe had reached the other side of the clearing and moved into the shadows of the path. Lee followed, then Bright. We kept moving.

The air shattered above my head.

I could hear the sharp slashing sounds of the air being ripped apart, then distant popping sounds and the slashing sounds again.

"Get down. Get down. Snipers, snipers!" The shouts were all around.

I could feel all of me. A sudden surge of energy and force in me had thrown me to the ground, then stilled me, frozen me. The sharp slashing sounds kept bursting through the air, then the thumping sounds of bullets hitting and chopping at the ground behind me.

I was crawling now, away from the thumping sounds.

The slashing sounds kept coming. I kept crawling and looking up the long shadowy path, searching for the snipers, listening for their popping sounds. I had clicked the safety off the trigger and now was aiming up the path.

Then it was silent. Not even the birds sang.

I whispered, "Anybody see where it came from? Anybody hit? Answer up."

I looked up the path and could see McCabe and Lee lying and aiming their weapons. Bright had whispered that he was all right. I heard Grunwald and Rayburn answer up. Then I heard Wiggins's voice calling from the rear, "Anybody hit up there?"

I whispered back to Rayburn, "Pass the word back, third squad's up."

Soon I heard Wiggins's voice and the word being passed up the column: *"Move out, move out."*

I was standing now, bracing myself for the air to be ripped open again and the pop-pop sounds to shake the stillness. I took a deep breath, then said, "Okay, let's go. Keep it spread."

5

THE RAIN

When the rain came, it didn't stop, it just kept pouring. I remember sitting inside the tent looking out and watching a million raindrops fall and the gray misty fog beyond. There was a puddle just in front that I remember staring into, watching the little circles form before another drop would splash them away.

Days and weeks had gone by, but just one night. The same night, dark and on the lines, dark and on the patrols, dark.

Sleep was only rest, not peace and not enough rest to slow things down, take a look back, feel what you were, or sometimes just feel.

I heard some squishy sounds and looked up, then said, "Where the fuck ya going? It ain't chow time yet."

Vernon stopped out in the rain, turned, smiled through the mist, and said something like "Swimming."

He stood with his poncho on, and his helmet. The raindrops were bouncing off his helmet and rolling down his poncho in small streams. There was no difference between his boots and the ground, they were both just mud.

"Ya look like you're fuckin' swimmin'," I shouted.

"What ya doin'?" he shouted back.

"Just waitin' on chow. Then I got a patrol and the fuckin'-ass hill tonight."

Vernon came in from the rain and we talked for a while. Quick little feelings would come, but went away like the circles in the puddle. And I watched the bright skirts, smiling faces, vanish. The echos of song would go away too. I didn't like to look at home, see Mom and the others. I didn't know whether or not I'd ever see them again, and I knew how they'd feel if they didn't see me again, and all that shit hurt.

Vernon left, and I probably lit a cigarette, but I know I thought about the nights.

It had been a night ago, maybe two, but it was raining too. Everything was wet, black and gray. I was shivering from the cold rain falling and trying to wipe the water from the face of my watch. Slowly I'd take my hand and stick it inside my shirt, rub my fingers against my skin, then quickly take my hand out and rub my fingers over the face of the watch. Then I would hurry and look to see if I could see the little green hands on the watch. I knew the small hand was on four, and when the big hand reached six it would be time to go back.

It had been raining hard all night; gray cold streaks of water poured down through the dark onto the muddy path beneath us and into the soaking bushes where we lay. The ground beneath me was soggy and muddy. If I moved or squirmed, or even shivered from the cold, I could hear my own squishy sounds beneath me.

The monotonous patter of raindrops pattering down on my helmet was not loud enough to keep me awake, alert. I was tired, and the nights had been long and without sleep. Some of the days had been without rest, and now this night was heavy on my eyes. I could not keep my eyes open. I tried looking into the darkness; I tried to watch the path beneath us; I tried to be ready to fire into it when they came by, if they came.

We were waiting for them to come through the dark, try to sneak by our killing trap, but they knew we were here waiting for them. And now they were probably waiting for us.

It was time to go back, or close enough. I tried to snap my fingers, but they were too wet to make a sound. I was whispering now. "Pass the word, pass the word. Stand by to move out. Pass the word."

As I whispered, I shook from the chill. I tried to still myself and listen for sounds, any sounds other than the pattering of the rain. I was easing myself up now, and coming to my knees. I could feel the water rolling down my back. I was shaking as I looked around, peering into the dark gray.

"Let's go. Keep it quiet, I think we been spotted," I whispered.

We began shifting and stirring in the dark. Low-hanging branches of bushes were snapping as we rose beneath their thick leaves. My whispers were now sharp hissing sounds.

"McCabe, take point. Watch it, I think they're on our ass."

McCabe came crawling through the dark. As he passed, I whispered again, "Watch it, man, they're close."

I kept my eyes on him as he crawled and then started sliding down the little muddy hill to the path. I waited for the night to break open with the cracking sound of gunfire. Then I heard McCabe whisper, "Clear."

I whispered quickly, a little louder now, "Okay, let's go. Hurry up. Keep it spread out down there. Spread it out down there."

I slid down the hill and crouched in the dark, pointing my rifle across the path and into the dark of the clearing. Except for the rain and our own sounds, the path was still and quiet.

The long night had teased us. Four hours we had lain in the rain, waiting for them to come by. They had come, but not close enough. We had heard them, their sudden footsteps splashing in the mud and water beyond our sight, beyond and too quick for us to aim.

They had fooled me, teased me, horrified me. I had heard the loud squeal of a bird cry, a taunting call. I had tensed when I heard it, then calmed when it was just a bird, then frozen in the cold rain when I realized it was not a bird. Birds don't fly in the rain and night.

They had come close to us, maybe crawled and slithered through the night until they were close enough to throw the grenade. They had thrown it into the dark. It landed behind us, far from where we lay, but close enough for its thundering sound and flash of burning light to break open the night and shake us deeper into our mud and hiding places.

Now we were on their path, in their trap.

We were all down from the muddy hill and crouching on the path. I was counting now, making sure we were all here. Then quietly I went to each guy, all five of them, and whispered, "We're going back. Keep it spread out. Anything moves, spray the fucking area, don't wait."

I could hear my own footsteps as I moved to and from each guy. Now we all moved quietly and slowly as we started back. The muddy steps seemed to last forever. The rain was just there, falling and blurring my vision. Sometimes when I'd look back I'd see Rayburn and Grunwald, then sometimes I couldn't see them at all but I could hear their footsteps coming.

We kept moving, only stopping when the sounds of the night came too far out of their darkness. We'd stop, hunch, aim, and listen, then move on.

A sharp whisper came quickly from ahead. "Halt, who's there? Who's there?"

I heard McCabe whispering, "Third squad. Third squad coming in."

We moved past the wet dark face that had said "Halt" and into the clearing where the rest of the company lay in the night. We waded through the dark until we found our platoon, then I found Wiggins and reported in.

I moved back with the rest of my squad and whispered, "We got an hour. Get some sleep, we'll be moving out in about an hour."

I tried to find a hard spot on the ground, then settled for anyplace that wasn't just a puddle. I got my poncho out, crawled under it, and used my pack for a pillow. I pulled my rifle in close.

Sleep came quickly.

It was still dark and wet. The rain had slowed to a hard drizzle and I could hear the whispers poking into my sleep: "Moving out, let's go, come on, we're moving out."

I hurried and folded my poncho. My helmet still lay on the ground, and the hard drizzle fell over my face. I tried to wipe the water off my face, to wake quickly, but I was still tired, almost dazed. Everything seemed dark and slow.

When I stood, my wet clothes were sagging from my body, still heavy with rain and mud. I could see the company forming, hear the commands being whispered. "Second platoon, over here. Third platoon, here—let's go, people. Squad leaders, get your people moving."

Slowly the company was forming into a long snakelike column of dark gray shadows moving in the night. Shadowy shapes of helmets and shoulders, rifles, packs, and dark wet faces passed in the rain.

I heard Wiggins calling, "Fall in, first platoon. First squad, second squad, third squad bring up the rear. Let's go, people."

We joined the column and we were moving now. I was still in a daze. I was so tired and wet. The rain was just there, always there, didn't make a fuckin' difference. We moved out in the same direction that my squad had set the ambush up in. We were on the same muddy path. It was still and quiet as we passed the ambush site and moved on.

The night was beginning to weaken some; the dark gray was becoming lighter and fading into the mist. I kept my eyes focused on the guy in front of me, moving with his movements and stopping when he stopped.

Now the night was thick again, dark and thick as we started up through a canyon. The path was rocky and slippery as we started our climb. The water was rolling down over the rocks and making dripping and splashing sounds and leaving faint echos. We kept moving and slipping up the path.

The night screamed; the little echoes ran.

Sudden bursts of machine-gun fire came streaking down on us. Bullets cracked the air, smacked and smashed into the canyon walls, bounced and ricocheted into the air. I could see their long burning orange streaks flying through the air. I could see the fire flashes from above. The loud tapping of the machine guns wouldn't stop.

"Get down! Down! Get down!"

I was down now, down hard on the rock path. Our machine guns were firing back at the flashes above. Everything was shaking and vibrating from the fire. Then all was quiet except for the sound of spent shells rolling down over the rocks, clanging like fallen coins.

"Anybody hit? Pass the word, anybody hit?" The shouts came quick.

I was on my knees looking about and asking, "You guys all right? Answer up."

Now I was passing the word up. "Third squad okay."

I could hear the shouts and yells from up ahead.

"The fuckers hit my pack. Look at this shit—right through."

"You lucky it didn't go through your ass."

"Anybody hit back there?"

"Hanner got one in the pack, that's all."

The word came down to move out and we started up the slippery path again. I was awake now and saying to Lee, next to whom I had dived when the firing came, "Man, that was close. Probably those same fuckers from last night."

We moved on with a steady uphill climb. The morning was breaking through, the night was vanishing, the rain had stopped. When we reached the top of the hill, the morning sun was there, the greens and browns were strong in the morning light. Far off from our path, the distant hills and valleys seemed quiet. Walking was easier.

Quick crisp whispers came down the column. "Hold up, get down. Keep it down, stay quiet."

The hand signals were pointing to the left and down over the hill. Whispers fell beneath the silence.

"What's up?"

"VC, down over the hill, 'bout a squad of 'em."

"Stay down. Keep it quiet."

I had crawled up to the edge of the path and then into the weeds, from where I saw one of the guys from second squad crouching and pointing.

"Where are they?" I whispered as I looked down over the hill.

"There, right there on top there," he whispered, still pointing.

I could see them—about ten, twelve of them, maybe more. They were standing on top of a smaller hill. I could see them talking and gesturing, I could see their dark green ammo belts wrapped around their black pajamas, their rifles and machine guns held loosely in their hands. They were amid the small green weeds and bushes. Beyond them, the hill sloped down into a green valley.

Behind me I could hear the quick, quiet whispers being passed up and down the column. "Guns up, machine guns move up front. Hold your fire. Stay down."

I was whispering now—"Third squad, come up"—and signaling to stay down and move in beside me.

I kept whispering and signaling. Then suddenly our machine guns opened up and the yelling started.

"Fire! Fire! Fire!"

Everyone was firing, rifles popping off, automatics blasting, machine guns chopping. I spun around and crawled further into the bushes and looked down over the hill. The guy from second squad was firing away. I could see the VC hill being kicked and cut up with bullets. Pieces of dirt and bush were flying through the air; little white puffs of smoke seeped out of the cool dirt from the hot bullets digging into it.

I brought my rifle up and aimed at the hill, looking for the black pajamas, searching in the flying dirt, bushes, and bare spots, but they were gone. Perhaps dead and lying in the bushes, or alive and hiding, but I could not see them.

"Cease fire. Cease fire. Hold your fire."

Quickly I asked the guy from second squad, "You see them? Where they go?"

He whispered back, "Fuckin' asshole waited too long—they took off. Maybe guns got 'em on the other side. They assed out, or got in a hole."

I lit a cigarette and spread the squad out and listened to the word being passed up and down the line. There was a lot of confusion; the other platoons were being shifted back and forth from their positions. The captain and other officers were huddling, their field radios blaring. Soon the word came down to stay down, the jets were on the way to bomb the hill.

We were sitting, smoking and keeping our eyes down on the VC hill. Except for the blare of the field radios all was quiet, but now the roar of jets could be heard. There was a sudden pop as one of our grenade launchers went off, and the distant boom of its smoke grenade exploding on the VC hill followed. A cloud of yellow smoke began to mushroom on top the VC hill.

"Get down. Stay down. Keep your heads down."

The jets came in high, three or four of them, then circled like hawks. Now they were swooping down on the hill, diving and dropping their bombs, which flip-flopped through the air, then smashed into the hill.

Everything shook and shook. I buried my face in the ground and threw my hands over my ears. The ground was shaking, almost bouncing up against my face. The bombs kept hitting and breaking the hill apart. I could feel the hot force blowing through the air like a burning wind. The sound had gone beyond sound, I could not hear it, I was in it. It was everywhere, pounding against my skull, in my skull, in my mind, breaking my thoughts apart and into little pieces of feelings I couldn't understand.

I was pushing my face deeper into the ground. Dirt was flying through the air, then a sudden loud thump behind me made me hold my breath. Then everything stilled, leaving the ringing in my ears and the humming of the planes above.

I raised my head and looked up into the sky. The planes were circling high. I looked at the VC hill. Hot smoke and fire covered its top; what bush was left was burning. Around me the silence was rigid. I turned to check out the rest of the squad, and that's when I saw a small puff of gray smoke coming from the ground a few feet away and re-membered the loud thump I had heard. There, lying on the ground and still smoking, was a foot-sized chunk of black, ragged, twisted bomb fragment.

"Fall back. Fall back. Hurry 'em up. Move back, move it."

We were moving back down the path quickly, almost running. Then the shouts came again, to get down. The roar of the jets came back and the bombs started falling again and again.

We kept down until the planes flew high in the sky, then vanished.

It was quiet, but only for a moment before the shouts came and we moved back up the hill. I could see the VC hill again; it was pitted with big burning holes. Then the chopper gunships came flying over the hill. They flew in fast and low, dipping their noses to the ground and firing their rockets and machine guns down into the burning hill.

I lay in the bushes and watched.

I was thinking about the VC who were down there, then I was think-ing about the hot bomb fragment that fell back on us. I lit a cigarette. My hands felt weak, and for an instant I stared into the flame of the match. Then I flicked it out and looked back at the burning hill.

THE BLUE SHIRT

I t was one of those days, times, that kept bouncing back and forth between shit and laughs. Some guy named Scooter, in Bravo Company, was right down over the hill guarding some farmers from the VC while they planted rice. One of the farmers lobbed a grenade in his hole, blew his legs all to hell. He bled to death before they could get him up to sick bay.

Shit is silly. Same people you supposed to be fighting for are fuckin' killing you. Some other shit been going on—two guys in third platoon tripped a booby trap right over the hill, but they just got some shrapnel in their legs, they're just up in sick bay.

The VC hit the airstrip the other night; two or three planes got blown and a couple guys got it. The VC got fucked too, left about ten dead. It's been hot as hell too—ain't rained in weeks, just been hot.

We've been getting beer rations at night, but that shit's hot too, no ice around anyplace. Everything's hot—the water, the food; that shit that ain't supposed to be hot, like canned peaches, is hot.

I was drinking some of that hot beer; some of the other guys were playing cards. Grunwald and Rayburn had been grumbling at each other all day.

"That's mine," Grunwald was shouting.

"It's not, I had this," Rayburn was solemnly swearing.

"That's mine, Rayburn, you're takin' my shit."

"I had it first."

"Fuck you, Rayburn."

Rayburn got quiet. Grunwald threw something down and reached for the entrenching shovel Rayburn had. Then the funny shit started. Both of them were pulling on the shovel from opposite sides and yelling about whose shovel it was.

"Jesus fuckin' Christ," I yelled, "knock the shit off. If I told either one of you to use the fuckin' shovel, you'd shit."

They kept picking at each other for a while. Then they must have forgotten they were pissed, because they got to talking and laughing about something else.

Everybody stopped what they were doing and watched the truck stop down on the road.

"New guys," someone yelled.

I looked down and smiled. I laughed and said, "Shit."

There was Franko, Felter, and Tig, some guys from my old outfit. Tig had sense, was a good guy. Franko and Felter together did not have the sense one of them should have.

I went out of the tent and stood there. Franko saw me and didn't smile. He did not want to be here, I knew that already. He was big and dark, and he had told me a long time before, "Man, I ain't fightin' no white man's war."

Felter, at least, was pretending he wasn't crazy. He waved and smiled. Had half a grin on his face. I knew the other half. Felter couldn't keep his mouth shut. Life and all the shit that came along with it was the biggest joke to him. You could have just found out your dick would have to be cut off, and Felter would do some shit, make you laugh so hard your balls would bust.

I was laughing at him just coming up the hill and trying to look sane. If I had known, could have known, had thought about it, I would have yelled, "Felter, go home, go home! My God, go home, man!"

I got three new guys in the squad. Mitchell, some young kid right out of boot camp, okay kid. Copeland, another corporal, from Louisiana; Copes cool, long-legged, long-talking, but okay. And Glickman, from Philly. Most guys are a little crazy, but Glickman had some problems for the talking doctor to listen to. Glickman was strange-acting, didn't fit in anywhere.

Franko and Felter went to second platoon. I was glad.

In a few days we were out again, and it was hot, and so was I.

"Keep down. Spread it out some. Sssh, be quiet," I was whispering as I peered through the bushes at the seven or eight people or VC standing in the clearing on the other side of the creek. I could see them talking and gesturing to one another. I was looking for their weapons.

"Keep down, damnit. Wait till we get the word," I whispered again as I heard someone moving beside me.

The sweat was rolling down my face and into my mouth. Everything seemed to be glaring in the sun—the green leaves on the bush, the grass and bare ground leading to the creek. Even the people on the other side of the creek seemed to glare and shrivel up in the heat.

Earlier, maybe even the day before, it had still been hot as we waited in the hot sand. Beyond the sand was a small mucky rice paddy, and beyond the rice paddy I could see and almost smell the village.

I sat in the sand now, leaning against a piece of fence that seemed to come and go from nowhere. It was too hot to talk, we could just mutter back and forth.

I heard Mitchell's kid country voice asking me, "You think anything will happen?"

I only muttered, "Damn, Mitch, I don't know."

I wiped the sweat from my eyes and wondered how in the hell McCabe could fall asleep in this fucking heat, but he sat leaning against a sand dune with his eyes closed and his head bobbing.

Lee had his bayonet out and his leg all twisted up so he could cut the strings hanging from the cuff of his pant leg. The strings were meant to be tied around your boots, but Lee never did tie them, so they dragged behind him all the time. I wondered why all of a sudden he got the notion to cut the fucking things off. Rayburn and Grunwald were sitting right next to each other and talking about cars, some Chevy. I was ready to shout at them to spread it out, but it was too hot to yell. Besides, they'd only move apart an inch. Then I'd have to yell again.

"Move out. Stay on line. Let's go, let's go." The word was coming across the sand; we were moving into the village. It felt good to stand as I stood shouting, "All right, let's go. McCabe, wake the fuck up. Rayburn, Grunwald, stop fuckin' each other, spread it out. Spread it out, stay on line."

We were moving toward the village and were in the rice paddy now. The cool mucky water felt good as it seeped through my boots and began to cool my feet. I kept my rifle high and my eyes on the hedge-row just before the village.

The hot air cracked and sizzled. The hot bullets hit far to our front. I looked toward Wiggins and he signaled to keep moving. We moved on to the other side of the rice paddy and into the hedgerow. The village was only about a hundred yards away. The word came to hold up, so we settled in the hedgerow.

Further in the distance were the sounds of automatic fire. It ceased but started right back up. We knew it was the sound of our guns blast-ing. We just sat and waited. It was cooler in the hedgerow.

Soon the word came down that third platoon got two VC coming out from behind the village. A guy named Gilner shot one of them—the bullet hit right under the VC's arm and went into his rib cage and came out his back. The other VC dropped his bag of rice and started running. Gilner fired and missed, but some guy named Vergio fired his automatic and hit the VC three times.

In a few days we would sit around and listen to how the VC had come out of the village and down a path and almost stood still when they saw Gilner and Vergio coming. Then we would listen to how Vergio went and cut the fucking ear off the VC he shot. He still had it, wrapped up in a piece of towel. We would look at the ear lying in the towel, looking like a piece of rotten meat. We would tell Vergio, "Man, that fucking thing stinks. Get it the fuck out of here. Burn the mother-fucker, pitch it."

Vergio would just sit there and smile.

We were moving into the village. The pigs were squealing and old ladies with wrinkled faces and black sticky teeth were squatting in front of some of the huts. Some of the kids sat or stood near the old women. Most of the kids just had ragged tops on and were butt-naked. They saw us coming and ran closer to the women.

The shouts and yells had already begun and could be heard over the squealing of the pigs and the cries of some of the kids.

"*Spread out. Check it out. Check behind there. Watch out for booby traps. Get those fuckin' people out. Turn that shit over.*"

I was yelling, "I'm going in—cover me, Mitchell," as I burst into a hut and saw an old woman sitting on the edge of her bed. I stopped yelling when I saw her; she looked old and sick. Her long hair had long turned gray, and her skin was tarnished and wrinkled.

I slowed to a time ago, took quiet steps to Ma-Ma's room, saw her frail and sitting on the side of her bed. The stroke had twisted her, made one side of her face sag, numbed her hand, made her drag one of her feet. I leaned to kiss her goodbye and felt her arm trembling as she tried to get her hand to me, to hold me, touch me before I went.

Mitchell was yelling something, but his words were far away, like the trains going by. A sound so close, but not close enough to wedge itself between feelings.

In the pieces of moments going by, in the midst of dying particles of passing time, I was home.

I heard Mitchell calling and then shouts outside. I sighed and gestured to the old woman, then quietly said, "Come on, Mama-san, you got to go outside."

Mitchell came in and I shouted to him, "Get her out."

I started looking around at the baskets, vases, little bowls of stuff all around. On one of the tables were some pictures inside small frames. They were just family-type pictures in small picture frames, but they seemed so out of place with the rest, which looked like prehistoric stuff. Somehow I kept the pictures in my mind, and I was careful not to break them as I started turning everything over. I tossed the bed upside down and stuck my bayonet into the floor, looking and feeling for holes and things hidden in them. I turned the big baskets over and sifted through the stuff inside them. Then I took a quick look around, sighed, and left.

Outside, the other squads were searching other huts. People were being herded into groups; some of the children were crying, others were just staring up at us as we passed them, shouting and yelling.

"Mitchell, get him, grab his ass! Grunwald, help Mitchell. Get his ass searched. Get that motherfucker!" I shouted as I saw a man coming out of a hut. He was a young man, his face hard, his eyes glaring.

Mitchell reached for him and he jerked away.

"Mitch, get his ass. Get him searched," I shouted, lowering my rifle as I neared.

The man was shouting at Mitchell, then at Grunwald. I yelled at him, *"Shut the fuck up!"* I approached him slowly, keeping my eyes on his. He stared at me, then started shouting something.

"You VC motherfucker!" I yelled. I grabbed him by the shirt and pushed him back into Mitchell's arms. He was squirming, trying to jerk away from Mitchell and Grunwald as they tried to tie his hands. I jammed my fist up into his chin and shoved him further back.

His eyes were on mine, and I could see the fire in his mind as

Mitchell and Grunwald pulled him away. I shouted to Mitchell as they took him away, "Take him up to CP, tell 'em he's a VC suspect. Mark him."

We threw the whole village upside down, searching the huts and digging around the area looking for holes under piles of hay. We found a few young women hiding, some with babies or young children in their arms. When we were done, we started moving out of the village with about twenty or so males who were suspected of being VC.

As we left the village and moved down the path, the air cracked open again. The shots were coming from the village and hitting near the rear of the column. We just kept moving. Some of the guys in the back of the column yelled back to the village, "Fuck you too!"

Sometimes it's hard to remember how long I've been here. I know it's not long, not even six weeks or so, but keeping track of time is a waste of time. Here you are the time; when you move, it moves. The quicker you run, duck, the quicker it moves. But when you wait and watch, it moves slowly, if at all.

I was hoping the people, or the VC, across the creek wouldn't leave, wouldn't see us and run. They seemed at ease; I knew they had not heard us yet.

The sweat was still just rolling down my face. I kept wiping my eyes and looking to see if I could see weapons. Weapons could be anything, not just rifles or machine guns. Weapons could be grenades or bombs hidden in their baskets, or sharp punji sticks they had carved and carried hidden in bundles of wood.

The sun kept burning.

"What the fuck are we waiting for?" McCabe whispered.

"Keep quiet," I whispered back, and then looked over my shoulder to the radio guy who was with us. I could hear him saying, "Roger, Alpha two, okay." He nodded to me, and I knew that second squad was in place to cover us when we moved into the open.

"Okay, let's go, keep it spread out," I whispered.

We crawled out of the bushes and started across the clearing toward the creek. We were walking slowly, easing our steps, trying to sneak up on them, or get as close as we could before they saw us.

They could see us now.

We were running at them. Everything was blurry, the ground became green and brown blurs. We shouted, *"Don li, don li—stop, stop."*

They stood looking across the creek at us, then started backing from us, turning and running out of their small clearing toward the bushes and trees beyond them.

I slowed, lowered my rifle, and fired over their heads. Everyone was firing. The people were ducking, screaming, and waving their hands in the air.

Our fire slowed and I saw him.

I had seen the bright blue, seen it stick out of the greens and browns; now I saw it moving away. I saw him, a young guy with a bright blue shiny shirt, almost irridescent. He was backing slowly from the rest of the people and then darting to the bush.

"Don li. Don li!" I shouted. I brought my rifle to my face and pressed my eye to its sights.

The blue shirt kept running.

I could see it bouncing and darting at the end of the rifle sights. It kept moving, but it was still there, dangling on the end of my rifle. It had become a fuzzy blue blur with greens and browns around it.

Everything was silent. I couldn't hear anything—the pounding of my heart was no longer sound, just a count of time.

The blue shirt kept moving, dangling, bouncing, becoming a part of the greens and browns. Then it jumped, flung through the air as my rifle shook.

I kept my finger on the trigger until the rifle shook too high, then lowered my aim and fired again.

I could no longer see the blue; everything seemed gray, still, forever. I had seen the blue shirt fall into the bush, but now I could not see it, I just felt it.

The people were screaming. I stood silently. I heard a shout: *"Cease fire!"* It was mine.

The people were coming to us now, their faces strained, their hands high in the air. They came to the edge of the bank on the other side of the creek, then began to wade into the water. The creek was deep and running swiftly; they had to swim. I watched them swim, grabbing on to one another, reaching for branches to pull themselves up. One old man was swimming with one hand still stuck in the air.

"Get them out, help them out of there," I yelled as they neared.

We pulled them out of the creek, made them stand. We didn't listen to their moans and gestures as we searched them, reached into their wet pockets, jerked their shirts up, tugged at their waistlines, spun them around and pushed them to the ground.

I could hear the sounds behind me now as I edged my way down to the bank of the creek and looked across.

"Ya get him?" Mitchell called to me.

"I seen him go down in the bushes," I shouted back over my shoulder. Then I stood silently and tried to listen over the shouts behind me and the sounds of the water flowing in the creek.

I tried to see blue, but I couldn't. I listened for moans, but it was quiet. I turned and started back up the bank.

Inside, I became two mes, then four, then eight, then a million. I was coming apart.

I shouted, "Get those people tied and down to the CP."

I looked back over my shoulder and across the creek, then turned away again.

Maybe he wasn't dead? Maybe he ran? Maybe I got one, yeah, killed one of the fuckers, blew his ass away. Maybe he was lying over there just fucked up, blood coming out of him, thinking about being dead.

Fuck him.

Maybe I missed? Maybe I should swim across the creek, look for him, look for what I didn't want to see?

Maybe every fucking thing.

Everything, nothing, all the same shit.

Maybe he's still running, all dead, going to keep on running and haunting me. Poking at me in the night.

"Okay, let's move out. Keep it spread," I shouted, taking one last look over the creek.

Fuck it.

7

SUNDAY

"*H*ey, Franko, what's up?"
   "Nothin'."
   "What ya doin', man?"
   "Nothin'."
   "Did ya win?"
   "Shit, yeah. Got me seventy-five dollars off that dude. Goin' ta git me some more too. Shit, he thought he was slick. Ah gits all in that boy's ass. Hey, ya remember that silly motherfucker, ahh, Wells—ya know who Ah'm talkin' 'bout, useta go with y'all up ta W-town, ya know?"
   "Yeah, Wells, from Kentucky someplace."
   "Yeah. Right after you left, Ah got that motherfucker's whole paycheck, got all his shit. He was talkin' his shit, too. Ah gots that boy's money."
   "Shit, Franko, ya ought to be a millionaire. What ya do with it?"
   "Man, Ah hads me some, but Ah blows it. Ah was shackin' up with this fine honey Ah meets in D.C. Ah stayed there, never did go home. She say, come on with me."
   "Ahh, man, ya bullshittin'. Ain't no bitch in her right mind goin' to ask your ugly ass to come home with her."
   "Swear to God. Swear to God, man. Swears it."
   "Man, you didn' even go home, ya spent your whole leave in D.C.?"

"Man, pussy is pussy. Shit, if it's there and it's good, ya know Ah ain't leavin' for shit."

"Ya must have left for somethin'—ya here, motherfucker."

"Man, them motherfuckers almost had to come get me. Ah gits in about a week late and they want to send me to the brig. Ah say, go ahead, shit, send me to some brig. I'll go to some brig, stay in some brig. Yeah, keep me in some brig and takes this Vietnam shit and shoves it up they's ass."

"Man, ya bullshittin'. What happen then?"

"Had this captain, he say, Allen, we need some men over there, big strong mens, and all that shit. Then, that's why he say he wasn't givin' me no time, says if Ah keep straight, it will come off my record. It ain't no big thing, Ah'm gittin' out of here, ya watch me. Ah swears, ya watch."

"Yeah, okay."

"Man, Ah swear ta God, man, ya watch."

"Man, this ain't no North Carolina and sneaking out the gate."

"Ain't supposed ta be here in the first damn place. Johnson into that oil, now he wants to git him some rubber too. That's what this shit's all about, get him some rubber. See, he don't need it, but—and this is the shit—he don't want that other white man to get it and the yellow man to keep it."

"What other white man?"

"Khrushchev, who ya think? All them motherfuckers want shit. Communism ain't nothin' but the other white man, ya know, like good and evil, 'cept this is evil and evil. Ain't no good shit about it. See, they git this shit, then they wants some more. That's what all this shit's about. That freedom shit, that's just for TV. People watch TV likes that freedom, likes lookin' at John Wayne, Daniel Boone shit. Theys be wantin' ta die for some freedom, but that freedom shit ain't real. Ya go try and gits some freedom, try it. Try and gits ya some. Ya white, ya might git some, a whole lot if ya gots some money. Ya skin like mine, ya ain't gittin' shit. Ya got that light skin, but ya ain't gittin' none of that freedom either. Ya can come here and die for it, but ya ain't gittin' none."

Franko kept on talking, and I kept listening. Franko was out of his mind, but he could touch stuff, knew some things—knew of the African sailors who came to South America long before Columbus, knew of the art and culture they left, knew of black kings and kingdoms when Negroes were still Negroes.

Franko could be one way and think the other. He had those big hands that could hide all his cards in them, hold them so close to his self that you didn't know he had cards at all.

I would see Franko in a different time, away from the rains and mud, fires in the night. I'd say, "Hey, good to see you," then, "Check you out later," and never see him again, but I knew he was all right, I knew that. He was in a long line in the Philly Naval Hospital. It was the line of guys who didn't connect within, the line of guys who lost their cards, but I knew Franko was just hiding his.

When I got back to the tent, Bright was sitting and talking with Lee, then blurted out, "You should have come."

"Huh," I said, and shrugged.

"To the services," Bright said.

"Oh."

"Yeah, the chaplain's real nice, he gave a good sermon. He said a lot of things . . ."

Bright went on about the chaplain. Him and that cross could be a pain in the ass sometimes. I was older, but not old enough to be his father.

"Hey man, that's good," or something, I said.

Lee was saying nothing; he just sat with half a smile on his face. He could be that way. We'd talk sometimes, talk away from here, back to Cincinnati, Pittsburgh, and high school.

I counted on Lee but couldn't say, "Hey man, you're like me, but I can't say that. I can't say, Hey, before we're this shit, we're home, same song, same dance, same mamas, same slanted shacks somewhere." I had to say, "Let's go, Lee, spread it out. Move out. Take point." I didn't know whether or not he knew that, but I couldn't tell him.

I hadn't thought about it until Bright mentioned the chaplain, but it was Sunday. Talking with Franko, I was back to W-town, then it was King and the Klan, WHITE ONLY and COLORED signs, back doors to dirty restaurants on dark highways. And it was freedom—whose?

This side of our hill was home now. The other side, out there, was never Sunday, never a day, just time.

Not too much time had gone by, your time with its long days and sleeping in the nights. Come Sunday, all the shit stops when Jesus comes and asks what you been doin'.

I was getting older, I could feel it, but I was still trying to smile young, laugh like before. But I was thinking old, different, carrying too much in my pack, and I didn't want to carry anything at all, sometimes not even my own life in the night, and everybody else's too.

"Hey, Vern, ya goin' to chow? Wait up," I yelled as I saw Vernon coming out of his tent with his mess kit. I hurried, grabbed my rifle and mess kit. When I caught with Vern, we started talking about little stuff.

"You hear from that girl you were telling me about?" Vern was asking.

"Which one, that girl I met in L.A. or that one back in Pittsburgh?"

"Pittsburgh."

"No, she's in school in Philly. I didn't even see her when I was home. I just got some letters from my mom. My little sister wrote one too."

"How many sisters you got?"

"What the fuck you want to know for?" I heard Vernon laugh as I went on to say, "Two—one's nine, and the baby's just three."

"Ya got any brothers?"

I sighed and didn't want to slow my words, but I guess I did. "Yeah, well, yeah, got four. One, Macky, was stationed back at LeJeune, down with Sixth Marines. I saw him once back there. Georgie's in jail someplace, reform school, all that shit. Nooty, that's the oldest one, I ain't seen. There's a younger one, Richie, I guess he's about twelve or so. My old man, I mean my real father, I ain't never met. I mean, I used to see him, but that's when I was a kid, didn't know who the fuck he was. You know how that shit goes. He's from Texas. Fuck it."

I don't know what Vernon was saying, or asking. I was walking and staring down at the weeds, rocks, along the path. I wasn't looking for booby traps, maybe just looking for who I was.

Macky, Georgie, and Nooty, playing cowboys and Indians in the weedy lots, chasing trains we couldn't catch.

Macky, Georgie, and Nooty's daddy coming by, saying hi.

A thousand years ago and me sixteen, wanting answers to who I was.

I didn't think much about my real father. If I saw him, it was in the quick, quick glimpse of tiny memories of me standing aside while he came to see Macky, Georgie, and Nooty.

If I thought of him, or could not stop thoughts, the thoughts would be too big and empty, and I'd turn away.

If I died here, he wouldn't even know it. But he was a ghost already.

After chow, things may have slowed, maybe some talk time, thinking time, but if things slowed, it wasn't Sunday's way, just the time. The night would come soon. I spy, stick 'em in the eye, who's not ready, holler I. One two three and some more peekaboo shit. Looking for the green man in the green, the brown man in the mud, the gray man in the mist, and the dark man in the dark. And he's watching you look for him, knows you're coming, he's laughing at you, saying *Hee, hee, hee, try and see me. I'm here, over here. I see you.*

"Get down."

Hee, hee.

I'd still think of Arthur sometimes, see his face, the look in his eyes. A letter from Mom said he had a big funeral, little picture in the newspaper. I don't know what I said when I wrote back, but I didn't tell her they didn't bury him deep enough.

I can hear song.

Somebody in the tents above got their tape recorder playing. It still feels funny to look out, see all the green, the mud-rutted road, sagging tents, and hear Diana Ross and the Supremes filling the air with love.

Sometimes I'd wish I was in love or something, but that got me to thinking home shit. Wishing I'd done this, done that, wishing I had made a move on that Karen Owens. Maybe it was best this way, then I could keep her in my mind, make it a movie love. Me coming home, her there, wet beaches and moonlit water glistening on her face while fire lit her eyes. All that, then the little raindrops and the little muddy fucking circles with their mucky little bubbles ever bursting.

I knew most of the guys in our platoon and some of the guys in the other platoons. We weren't much different, I guess to strangers we'd all look alike. Green clothes, faded and stained with mud and sweat. Sometimes we'd add our own things to our looks, maybe a red or green handkerchief around our necks. Our helmets were our own; some were green, others had faded so much they looked white in the night. You could find all kinds of little things written on them, anything from "I Love Pussy" to "God Bless America." The black rubber bands around the helmets were used to stick stuff in, like matches, cigarettes, spoons, little can openers, or weeds and leaves if you wanted to look like a bush.

We wore chains around our necks with little tags that hung from them. The tags had tape on them so they wouldn't clang together when we moved. If you pulled the tape off them, you'd see an imprinted name, seven little numbers all together. One little blood-type letter, a little USMC, and the name of what God you belonged to. If you got killed, one of the little tags got stuck in your mouth.

You were what you could not see, only feel. You watched others in order to be, looked at them to see yourself. You knew they were watching you, you could feel their feelings touching you.

We could change from day to day. Sometimes we could all change together, be all pissed off at the same time. Then sometimes it would be a circus all day. We could joke about everything that happened. We caught a prisoner one day who had something wrong with his balls. He had on these shorts, and his balls were hanging down to his knees. When he was trying to run, he was using one hand to hold his balls up. We joked about that all day. We got sniped at; I dove down in the mud. It wasn't mud. Big water buffalo had gone by. Guys thought it was funny. I didn't. I said, "Shit," and for the first time I was right.

I wrote a letter home. It was quiet and a good time to write, and time to think of things to say, but I think I just settled for a few words after all.

I didn't look at my watch unless I had to, but I saw the sun beginning to set. I turned and shouted back into the tent.

"Third squad, listen up. We got a patrol from 0100 to 0500. Down to the ville, around it and out to that bridge, then back in along the beach. Get your shit together now. Grunwald, go check out a radio—make sure you get one that works."

The usual moans and grunts came from the tent. I would look away, but I always listened. I could tell their sounds, put them into words in my mind. It was not the bitching I listened to, but the fears I listened for.

It would be dark soon. I got my watch out and looked at it. I could get five hours' sleep before going out. Sleep wasn't like it ever had been, home sleep and horns blowing, some fool playing his hi-fi all loud. Road sleep, and the hum of the engine soothing your mind. Good old home sleep, good dreams; you could crawl deep into your sleep, wiggle around in it, stretch out and enjoy the black waves of the night. See the smiling faces smile back, laugh at the jokers in the dark. New day was coming. Good day, going to W-town day, going home day. Going to see Karen day, see her in that tight skirt that makes her ass look like a peach that came to life and danced to song.

Home sleep was a bridge to tomorrow. This sleep here was the only way back to yesterday, but it was better than staying here all night.

I sat for a while smoking a cigarette, then walked out into the early night and climbed the hill to the CP tent and dropped my letter in the mailbag.

At least *it* was going home.

8

THE FUNERAL

The squad and I were exhausted.

The last few weeks had been long and hot, one fucking thing after another. Bravo Company was out on an operation. We covered their hill and ran their patrols and ours too. Then, when they got back, we went right out. Lost another two guys in third platoon—both of them stepped on a mine, got torn up pretty bad. We killed six VC and took a bunch of prisoners, so-called VC suspects. My squad was credited with one kill. None of us was certain who had hit the VC; we just saw him flop in the air and fall.

We weren't back an hour before I got the word to bring the squad down here. We are down at the dock—that's what we call it. It's a short stretch of beach where the Navy's flat-bottomed boats, barges, can come in one at a time.

It's a pretty place.

There's a little village about a hundred yards away. The beach is sandy, and there's a little hill that surrounds it; that's where most of the holes are dug. We have a semicircle of positions around the beach, about eight holes. We have a roadblock across the wide path coming from the village and going down to the beach. We're spread pretty thin, but there's really nothing new about that shit.

The rest of the company is three or four miles away, up the shore and up in the hills. In a way, it's not all that bad being down here. It's good to get away from the company for a while, get off to ourselves. It can be like a little vacation, if the shit's quiet.

Wiggins gave me five or six extra guys from the other squads to help cover the area. They even sent down one of the corpsmen, the biggest one. Doc's about as fat as a hog and even wiggles when he walks. Talks a lot, too. He's from Louisiana; he and Copeland get along just fine.

If we're not out in the sands, we're sitting in the main tent. Guys who ain't on watch are hanging around waiting on the chow to come down. The radio guy is trying to get the company on the radio to find out when the chow is coming.

Doc is pissed. He's yelling over the radio operator's voice as he's trying to make his call, "Ya can't get the bastards yet?" Then he goes off on us: "Damn son of a bitches, they were supposed to send that damn jeep down here an hour ago. Get my ass the hell out of here. Shit, what the fuck are they doin' up there? I'm supposed to be going back up battalion."

"What's wrong, Doc?" I was teasing. "Don't ya like us anymore?"

"Never did," Doc blurted out, and kept shouting. "You assholes're fuckin' crazy. I ain't no damn grunt, can't be chasing ya damn fools all over the place. I got too much time in for this shit. Y'all're more fucked up than an elephant with an alligator stuck up its ass."

Doc had us laughing.

I was picking. "Doc, look at it this way. You ought to feel at home. You got the ocean right here. You can take ten steps and be in it. You got one of your Navy fuckin' boats down there. What else you want?"

Doc got to shouting, telling us about ourselves so fast his stomach was shaking. "What else I want? I want to get my fat ass the fuck out of here and as far away from ya turtle-fuckin' cocksuckers as I can get."

Copeland was sitting there laughing and had to pick at Doc too. "How much more time ya got to go 'fore ya gettin' out this time?"

Doc stopped shouting about what nice people we were and got to answering Copeland. "I got two more years, then I'll have my ten in. Then I'm gettin' my ass the fuck out."

"Oh fuck, Doc," Copeland laughed and shouted, "you're a fuckin' lifer. You'll be in for the next twenty years. I'll be back in Louisiana 'fore you. I'll be back there suckin' up some cold brew, sittin' someplace with some pussy on my lap. You'll still be doin' pecker checks."

Copeland stopped yelling and started pointing out of the tent. "Oh shit, what the fuck's that?"

I turned quickly and looked out to where he was pointing. I could see an old beat-up pickup truck approaching our lines at the roadblock. I saw Glickman up there, surrounded by a bunch of village kids.

"Glickman! Glickman, stop that fucking truck!" I yelled out of the tent as I grabbed my rifle and jammed a round into the chamber. "Doc, stay here. Copeland, come on," I shouted, rushing toward the roadblock.

I was walking fast and pointing my rifle high but leaning it toward the truck. I shouted to Glickman, "Get those fuckin' kids out of there and stop that truck!"

The truck was nearing the long pole stuck across the ammo boxes. I began running and yelling over my shoulder, "Cope, cover me."

The truck slowed, then stopped in front of the poles. I slowed to a fast walk and went up to it. I kept my rifle high, but my eyes were on the Vietnamese in the front of the truck. I tried to see their eyes, their hands.

"Glickman. Glickman, check out the back, look in there good."

I stopped near the truck and lowered my rifle. I kept my eyes on the Vietnamese. One of them was getting out the truck. I yelled and pointed to him, *"Don li, Don li."* I put my hand up, signaling for him to stop.

"Glickman, is it clear?"

Glickman nodded his head.

"Is it clear, Glickman?" I yelled again, not satisfied with just a nod.

"It's empty, nothin' in it," Glickman faintly said.

One of the Vietnamese was shouting from the truck, talking fast, then slowing his words and trying to say something in English. I beckoned for him to come forward, then shouted over my shoulder to Copeland to go up and check out the guy still in the truck.

The Vietnamese was coming forward and pointing down the beach to the ship, trying to say, "We have truck, we have truck for boat, yes? We pick up boat, yes, okay, okay?"

As he came closer, I quietly clicked the safety off the trigger and eased my rifle a little lower in his direction. I was watching his eyes and trying to watch Copeland at the same time, as he searched the inside of the truck.

"It's clean, ain't shit here," Copeland finally yelled.

Calmed, I quickly put the safety back on the trigger and went up to the Vietnamese and tried to make out what he was saying. Then I turned and yelled to Bright, who had come out from the tent, "Get the ship's OD and tell them they have a truck here."

I let the Vietnamese man talk and gave him a cigarette and lit one myself. He was saying, "Zue, Zue number one. We have truck, pick up boat, yes?"

Soon a Navy officer came up from the ship and said it was okay for the truck to pass. The Vietnamese said a few, "Zue number one, zue number one."

As soon as the truck moved on, I tore into Glickman. He had gone back to his position and was standing there, still surrounded by the kids.

"Glickman, Glickman, what the fuck are you doing? What the fuck do you think this shit is? I told you to keep those fuckin' kids the fuck away. Didn't I? Didn't I? Ya didn't even see that fuckin' truck comin'. Now get those fuckin' kids away from your position, now."

Glickman had a sour look on his face. I waded through the kids and got up in his face. "Ya got a problem?" I shouted.

Glickman looked off in a different direction but muttered, "What do you want me to do? I told them to go, but they won't. What am I supposed to fuckin' do?"

"You're supposed to keep the kids out of here and away from your position. How many fucking times I have to tell you, huh? I'm tired of fucking around with you."

The kids had backed away some and stood looking up with their big brown eyes. Now they were asking from where they stood, "Hey zue. Hey zue, zue buy zoda pop? What zue name?"

I started gesturing at them to go away and shouting, "Dee dee, you dee dee. Come on, dee dee."

I stood there until the kids moved away, then turned to Glickman and shouted, "Now keep 'em away."

I turned to leave.

"Fuckin' bastard," Glickman mumbled.

I spun around. "What the fuck did ya say? What the fuck did ya say? Private, what did ya say, huh? I been tellin' ya all day about these kids. Now get your ass up the tent. Get up there, get a move on, private."

I turned and shouted to Copeland, "Cope, take his watch for a while. I'll get someone up to relieve ya in a bit."

Glickman followed as I went back to the tent. I told him to wait out front while I went inside.

Doc asked what was going on. I told him about Glickman fucking off as I hurried and grabbed a shovel off one of the packs.

"Glickman, get in here."

"What's this for?" he asked.

"You're goin' to learn how to take fuckin' orders. You're goin' to learn to do what you're told. You're supposed to be on watch, ya didn't even see that fuckin' truck comin'. Now take this shovel out back and start digging. And don't stop until I tell you to. And something else, private—I'm not your fuckin' bastard. Now get your ass out there."

Glickman left with the shovel.

I turned to Bright and told him to go up and relieve Copeland. Bright started whining, "I just got off watch. That ain't fair."

"Bright, get your ass up there now. Right now. And keep those kids away. And if I come up there and see those kids, you're goin' to be out there with fuckin' Glickman."

Bright grabbed his rifle and left the tent, stomping his feet.

Doc started. "Ya all fuckin' crazy."

"Shut up, Doc. Glickman's out there playin' with those kids. That truck could have come through here shooting your ass full of holes. And you'd be out of here a lot quicker than ya want. When they hit the airstrip last week, or whenever the fuck it was, and fucked those planes to hell, and fucked a few guys too, one of the bodies they left behind was one of those kids that sold the *Stars and Stripes* down there. They found a map on the little son of a bitch. It had every gun emplacement on it. That's how the fuck they got in. Ya can't trust this shit."

It was quiet in the tent for a while, then I asked the radio guy if he had heard when the chow jeep was coming. He answered, saying it would be about an hour. I grabbed my rifle and said I was going to check the lines, and left the tent. I wanted to check the lines, but I wanted to get away for a while, take a walk.

The midday sun was baking everything—the sand, the air, everything was hot.

I went to the roadblock first, where Bright was sitting on the ammo box. He turned when he heard me coming, then turned away when he saw me.

"Hey Bright, set tight for a while. I'll get someone up here to relieve you in a bit."

As I turned to leave, I heard Bright call, "Did you check and see when I could go see the chaplain? Remember I asked you last week?"

I stood silently for a moment.

"Remember I asked you? You said you'd check on it."

"Listen, soon as we get back, I'll check again. I'll tell Sergeant Wiggins that you asked again. I'll tell him that I'm sending you up, then you can just go ahead. Okay? Just try and stay loose."

I turned and walked up the hill toward the rest of the positions. I was worried about Bright. He seemed to fit better with the kids who tried to sell us soda pop and begged for cigarettes. At least once a week he wanted to see the chaplain. Sometimes I'd see him sitting with his head down. One time he quickly turned away, but the tear had already fallen.

I checked the rest of the line.

Some of the guys were sitting in their holes, shirts off, helmets on, rifles ready. Some, like McCabe, were sitting like they were at a Sunday school picnic. Shirts off, helmets off, pant legs rolled up, sunglasses on, and rifles propped on sandbags like fishing poles. I stopped and talked to each guy. I told McCabe to keep his ass awake, it wasn't the picnic he thought it was.

When I got back near the tent, I could hear Doc's mouth going. I saw Rayburn poking at something on the ground and Doc and Copeland standing around. Glickman had stopped digging and stood watching.

"What the hell you guys doin', shootin' crap?" I shouted as I tried to see over Rayburn's shoulder.

Doc was shouting, "That's one of them bamboo snakes. Them things can kill ya real quick. Look at that son of a bitch."

I looked beyond Rayburn's stick and saw the snake crawling and hissing in the sand.

Doc was yelling, "Kill the son of a bitch!"

Rayburn stepped back from the snake some and asked me, "Is it okay to shoot it?"

I thought for a second about the noise it would make. I didn't want the guys up on the hill getting alarmed, so I said, "Use a pistol."

Rayburn stood looking at me, then slowly said, "I don't have a pistol."

"Here, use mine," Doc yelled. He took out his forty-five, saying, "Watch it, it's got a round in the chamber."

I blurted out, "What ya doin' with a round in the chamber? That damn thing goes off, that's your leg."

"I ain't worried about my leg, I'm worried about my ass. And I don't care what nobody says, I keep that thing loaded all the time," Doc said.

Rayburn took the pistol and moved closer to the snake, aimed, and fired. The bullet hit the sand beside the snake. The snake hissed and wiggled. Rayburn fired again. The snake kept hissing and wiggling.

We were laughing.

Doc was saying, "Why don't ya try and throw a rock at it, Rayburn?"

I took the pistol from Rayburn, saying, "Watch—I'll show you how to shoot."

I moved in closer to the snake. It was wiggling through the sand, trying to get away from us. I leaned over, pointed the pistol at the snake's head, fired, and hit the end of its tail. I handed the pistol back to Rayburn as the snake wiggled around in the sand with its tail dangling.

"Here, Rayburn, you use this damn pistol of Doc's. Fucking thing shoots crooked."

"None of you fucks can shoot," Doc shouted.

Rayburn finally hit the snake, but not without Doc's supervision.

After shooting the snake, we went back into the tent and started joking around again. I told Glickman to go on back to his position and keep the kids away. Things quieted down some, but the chow jeep did not come. We had enough chow to last to evening chow, but most of the guys had eaten the best of their rations and had only what they didn't want left over. Last radio check said the chow jeep would be down mid-afternoon. Doc was still pissed.

Some of the time passed. I went to check the lines again. When I came back, I saw the jeep pulling away and a couple guys standing behind the tent as if the snake had come back. As I neared, I could see something wrapped in a poncho and lying on the ground. Then I saw the blood seeping from the poncho and the feet sticking out of the end of it.

"What in the hell is this shit?" I asked.

Flies were already buzzing around in the blood.

The radio guy was telling me, "They brought him down on the chow run. He's that VC the second platoon shot, that one that was wounded. He bled to death up in sick bay."

"Well, what the fuck is he doin' here?"

The radio guy said, "Amtrac is coming over, they're goin' to take him out in the bay and dump him. They stuck a lot of rocks in there with him."

I stood for a while looking at the body, then went into the tent. The chow boxes were there, and so was Doc.

"What are you still here for? I thought you were leaving," I asked Doc.

"Fuckin' new guy ain't here yet," Doc hissed, like the snake.

"Where's he at? Maybe he ain't comin'." I had to pick.

"They're goin' to keep his ass up headquarters for a few days so he can get used to things. My first day, they sent my ass down here with you assholes, shit."

"Well, Doc, look at it this way. You got beach, good chow, it's not rainin', and it's better than them fuckin' swamps you and Copeland crawled out of, down there wherever the fuck y'all from."

"Where the fuck you from? Fuckin' Pittsburgh, steel mill city? So much smoke, ya can't find your dick to take a piss."

I laughed and said, "Shit, Doc, ya probably can't find your dick now, and it's not because of no smoke."

Doc really started flying off.

I ate and had a few cigarettes, picked at Doc a little, and went out of the tent. The body was still there, bleeding in the sand. A couple guys who were coming to pick up chow were standing around poking at the poncho with sticks, trying to peek at the dead face beneath it.

I could hear them saying, "They got rocks all stuck in there."

"This is that gook O'Malley got."

"No it ain't. O'Malley's was dead. This one died up in sick bay."

I stood off from them, listening but mostly remembering the three or four VC running through the rice paddy, jumping over the dikes, with the second platoon behind them shooting all over the place. I remembered one getting hit just before he reached a dike; the bullet knocked him over it. He tried to get back up, then just fell in the water. The others didn't get much further.

I couldn't remember any just getting wounded, unless it was one of those people running out of the village that we and third platoon were firing at. If it was, then this guy just might be some dead farmer who should have run the other way.

The big green amphibious tractor had come floating through the water and now came rolling over the sand with seawater still dripping from its treads. The guys on top of the thing were shouting over the humming of its engines.

"You guys got that dead gook here?"

When the amtrac guy saw the wrapped-up body, he jumped off the top of the tractor and began guiding it up closer to the body. The amtrac stilled, its engines lowered to a slow humming idle of *putt-putt-putt*.

The amtrac guy stood looking at the body for a while, then yelled to one of the guys still on top of the tractor, "Gimme a hand down here!"

Another guy jumped off and went to the body's feet, asking, "Who shot the bastard?"

The radio guy answered, "One of our platoons wounded his ass a couple days ago. He bled to death up in sick bay."

The two amtrac guys bent over to lift the body. It sagged in the middle from the weight of the heavy rocks inside. Blood started pouring out the side of the poncho.

"This is a fuckin' mess. Shit," one guy said, and dropped the head of the body back to the sand. "Throw those ropes down," he shouted to the guy still on top of the tractor.

They lifted the head and put it into a loop of the ropes, and put the feet in the other. They dragged the body across the sand until it was closer to the tractor. Blood was now flowing freely from the poncho. When they began pulling the body up the side of the tractor, the poncho burst open as it scraped against the sharp metal tractor treads. Some of the rocks, wet and red with blood, fell to the sand.

"Just tie it here," one of the amtrac guys yelled.

The tractor backed into the sea with the body dangling from its side. I watched as it went out about a quarter of a mile. I was surprised that I could hear the thumping splash when they dropped the body into the water.

We stood around talking for a bit, then went inside the tent. Night was coming; the grayness of it had already come.

I grabbed my rifle and went to check the lines. Glickman was on watch again. He sat staring off into the distance. He turned as I neared, then looked back out at whatever he saw.

"How's it goin'?" I asked.

He shrugged his shoulders.

I sat on the sandbags and lit a cigarette, then just sat for a while. Glickman was silent.

In a time far from here, further than across the sea, far into the years and into a me whom I did not know now, I'd be in a newspaper office, and I'd be working there. I'd ask someone what he was doing.

"Hi, Sandy, what are you working on?"

"I got to put this whole list of names into the computer."

"What names?"

"We're running the names of all the men from Pennsylvania who got killed over in Vietnam."

"Huh?"

"It's to go along with the Vietnam Memorial's unveiling tomorrow."

"Oh. Can I see the list?"

I found your name, Glickman. I wish we could have talked tonight. I'm sorry for all the shit today. Every day.

When I finished checking the lines, I came up along the beach to the back of the tent. The last light of the day had faded; only a glimmer of its ever being dimly sprinkled the sea.

I neared the rear of the tent, then slowed as I noticed the blood-stained rocks still lying in the sand. I stopped and stood for a while, looking out to sea and remembering long black cars, people crying, red flowers.

I looked back from the sea at the bloodstained rocks and thought of the body out there somewhere beneath the water. I bowed my head, just slightly, and muttered, "God bless that man, whoever he was."

Then I felt foolish and went back into the tent.

9

ANTS AND EGGS

"*Hold up.*"

The word came down the column to stop. We started wiping the sweat from our eyes and faces, then looked for a low-hanging branch that might have some shade under it.

"How much further?" Mitchell was asking, reaching for his canteen.

"I don't know," I muttered as I wiped the sweat from my eyes.

"What we stop for?" Bright asked.

"I don't know. Just set tight and take it easy on the fuckin' water. Don't bunch the fuck up. Damnit, Grunwald, get the fuck away from Rayburn. Keep it spread out."

We were moving again.

We had moved out of the night and had been moving all morning. Now we were on a small path, if a path at all. Thick bushes and vines made walls, and we tried to squeeze through the cracks. We were climbing, then maybe for a moment took a few steps down a gully. We went down only to go up again.

"Hold up."

The word came down the column again. We stood for a moment, waiting for the word to move, then found a place to sit when it didn't come.

Copeland lit a cigarette, and without taking the sweaty look off his face blurted out, "What the fuck is goin' on? That second pla-

76

toon up there's fuckin' around. Shit, we'll be fuckin' around here forever."

I didn't say anything; it was too hot to talk. Soon the word came down to take a break and watch where we stepped—second platoon had found a booby trap. We sat wherever we could, took our helmets off, sipped some water, and lit our cigarettes.

Copeland was sitting there, still hot and miserable, and he just started talking. "This shit is for the birds. When I get my ass out and somebody mentions walkin', I'm goin' to take a bayonet and stick it up their ass. Shit, I could use a cold beer and not that shit they pass out."

He was quiet for a moment, then got that country grin on his face as he looked at Mitchell. "Mitch, tell me, ya ever get any leg? Ya ever get close enough to smell it?"

Mitchell gave Copeland the finger, then said, "Next time I do, you can smell my dick."

Copeland laughed and said, "Next time will be your first time."

Bright jumped in and asked Copeland, "When's the last time you had some? You're the one that's always talking about it. I bet you ain't ever had any."

Copeland turned to him. "Bright, shut up. Ya don't even know where a pussy's at. You probably think it's behind the kneecap."

"Fuck you, Copeland. I had more than you'll ever get."

"Knock it off, you two," I whispered as their voices began to rise. Then I looked at Mitchell and asked, "Hey, Mitch, did ya ever get any?"

Soon we were on the move again. The word came down the column to stay spread out and watch where we stepped. We were going downhill now, heading for a village to search. We had been sniped at earlier, a few miles back. The rest of the morning had just been long and hot.

Second platoon had point, third platoon was to the rear of us. Our platoon was in the center of the column. We'd probably move up and take point after chow.

Being back here in the center could get boring, but it was easy walking. You didn't have to worry that much about booby traps or being the first to walk into an ambush. Up front you had to stay with your mind, couldn't daydream, sneak home, think about what you had done or wanted to do when you got there. Up front on point you wondered whether or not you'd ever get home. Then sometimes you didn't think at all. Your mind would stay in everything around you, waiting and watching for things to move, to blow up in your face. Sometimes you got so tired of pushing bushes out of your way and picking thorns out of your hands, trying to get a mouth full of just air, you didn't give a fuck about going home, staying here, fucking again, or what a TV was.

Sometimes it would be easier just to kill yourself in your mind up there. Then you wouldn't have to worry that much about getting killed; you were already dead. God is something else around here. Sometimes he's here, you think, then sometimes you don't want him around fuckin' with your mind. Thou shalt not this and that—seems like that shit don't work here. That stuff is okay for hot churches and fans, people singin' and shakin' hands, but here we don't count. Maybe to ourselves and one another, but the stars in the sky and the sun and moon and all that shit is just there. Mickey Mouse and assholes with fat bellies can get fucked; nothing that is not here is here.

"*Get down. Down. Hit it, stay down.*"

The *pop-pop* of gunfire broke open up front, then we could hear our automatics going off and the shouts: "*Move up! Move up! Get on line and spread it out.*"

The air fizzled, then cracked open. The ground shook and then screams came through the air.

I shouted back to the squad, "*Stay down!*"

The screams kept coming.

"*Oh shit, help. Oh god.*"

"*Corpsman, corpsman, corpsman.*"

"*First platoon, move up, move up.*"

"*Let's go, third squad!*" I shouted.

We were up now, crouching as we quickly moved up the path. I could still hear the screams. Then we moved through second platoon and I could see two or three guys squirming on the ground. The smoke was still in the air. I tried to see their faces, but I couldn't, and I kept moving.

Everything was green and thick, and we kept moving through it. I could see Wiggins pointing ahead, but I could not see ahead. I moved on. Wiggins neared, whispering, "Spread your squad out. Hold up here. You got the left flank, watch it. We think there's about a squad of 'em, maybe more, about fifty meters up."

Wiggins moved away.

I was whispering now. "Cope, you and Mitchell, Bright, and take

Glickman—move down to the left. Keep down, and spread it out. Lee, take McCabe and Grunwald with you. Move over to the right. Rayburn, move up, stick here with me."

I heard Wiggins whispering, "Third squad, move out, stay on line."

"Cope, move it out, stay on line. Lee, move out, stay on line. Rayburn, get that M-79 ready, but don't fire unless I tell you to. Too many fucking trees."

We weaved through the bush.

Except for our own sounds, it was still and quiet. Everything ahead became silent as we passed. I clicked the safety lock off the trigger and waved the barrel of the rifle back and forth.

We moved into the area where the VC had been, but only silence was there. We moved on.

"Hold up," the word came.

It was silent. Then the sound of choppers filled the air. I tried to see in my mind who was wounded back there, but I couldn't.

After the wounded got out, we moved on in a column again and down into a valley, then along the side of a wide creek. Sometimes only weeds and tall grass separated us from the openness on the other side of the creek. We walked in the emptiness along the bank.

We were quiet.

Finally we moved away from the creek and started up a small hill that had a small grassy clearing on top.

"Hold up," the word came. We stopped, and I was telling the squad to spread out when the next word came: "Chow down. Got a half-hour. Spread it out."

I was hot and hungry, and mumbling to myself that it was about fucking time. Then I yelled over to the squad to spread out, eat, but keep their eyes open, take it easy on the water.

When I got the squad spread out, I noticed a small mound with a big flat rock on top, and I hurried to take the four or five steps to reach its top. After looking around the ground for any loose dirt or pieces of weed covering little pins sticking out, I decided this would be a perfect place to eat.

I took my helmet and pack off and laid them beside the rock, then unbuckled my ammo belt and let it hang from my suspenders. I laid my rifle down and just stood for a moment, taking some slow deep breaths and wiping the sweat from my face with my shirtsleeve.

I heard Wiggins passing the word, "Send one man from each squad down to the creek to fill up canteens. When we move out, first platoon will move up to point. First squad will have point, second squad right flank, and third squad left flank."

I caught Wiggins's eye and held my thumb up so he'd know I heard him, then I yelled over to the squad, "We got left flank when we move—must not be too far from that village. Check your water, give your canteens to Lee. Lee, go down to the creek, but wait for whoever else is going down."

I heard Vernon calling my name.

"Hey, Vern, ya havin' fun?"

Vernon stood there smiling, with little bubbles of sweat all over his face and his pistol belt hanging from his waist like some movie cowboy's.

"You going down to get water?" I asked, then said, "Hold up, Lee's goin' down. Were you near that booby trap that went off?"

"No, it was up some from me."

"That one guy really looked fucked."

"Who?"

"I don't know, I couldn't see his face. Small dude, black hair."

"Oh, that was that new guy, the one that was hollerin'."

"Yeah, shit, I'd be hollerin' too."

"Doc said it wasn't that bad. Buckley got most of the shit. He was the one that tripped it."

I knew Buckley, had heard his name being called around the tent area: "Hey, Buck, ya in? Ya playin' man, huh?" I remembered he was from Johnstown, Pennsylvania—wasn't Pittsburgh, but it was close enough to get a little talk in. He had said he'd come to Pittsburgh a lot to see the Pirates play, even seen one of the World Series games a couple years ago.

"What did Doc say about Buck—did he say he was goin' to make it?" I asked Vernon.

"Doc said he didn't know. He said Buckley and Woods were pretty bad. He said they might make it."

"Shit."

Vernon, Lee, and some other guy went on over the hill to get the water. I hurried and reached into my pack and grabbed two or three cans of chow I had stored away. I knew they were there, I had been saving them—one of them was my favorite.

I took the cans out of the pack and set them on the rock. The large can would have cocoa mix, cookies, chocolate candy wrapped in silver paper. None of that shit in the big can tasted like what it was supposed to be. The candy would melt and look like just what it tasted like. The cookies wouldn't melt, even if you set them on fire. The cocoa was good for changing the taste of the water or covering up that iodine shit we had to put in it.

One of the small cans would have a clump of dried bread, dried up and as hard as the fuckin' rock I was sitting on. The other small can contained what I was saving, my favorite—chopped ham and eggs. All in one can.

I was the only one in the squad, or maybe the whole company, who liked them and could eat them. When you opened the can, you could smell them, easily smell them. I thought they smelled good, although they did look like a can of dog food. They reminded me of a can of Rival dog food. You could open the can, hit the bottom a few times with your hand, and it would all come sliding out in one big round can-shaped hunk of meat.

I opened the cocoa first and made a little cup out of the empty can. Making the cocoa was easy; you just poured the mix in the can, filled the can with water, and stirred. The hard thing was trying to make the cocoa strong enough, so you wouldn't have to taste the water.

I opened the can of bread, picked that thing out, and set it on top of the rock. Then I opened the can of chopped ham and eggs. I took a little sip of cocoa to wet my mouth, then took my spoon and carefully sliced down into the can and got a big spoonful. I liked ham and eggs, because when you ate them, you could taste eggs in them. Once in a while there would be something that tasted like ham.

I grabbed my rifle, then stilled.

The sound of gunfire came through the air again, and again. Wiggins's shout came quick: *"Third squad, check it out. Move it."*

I yelled, *"Let's go, come on."*

I knew when I heard them that the shots were coming from the creek. Vernon's sweaty face flashed in my mind: Lee's face had never left it.

We moved quickly down the slope and into the clearing that lay before the creek. I could see Vernon and Lee lying in the grass near the water's edge, their rifles and pistols kicking up in their hands. The other guy was close by, firing too.

"Let's go."

I kept running toward them, keeping my eyes searching across the creek, looking into the tall grass, the shadows beneath the trees. My run slowed to a fast crawl. I edged my way closer to Vern and the others. I still couldn't see anything except the tall grass on the other side of the creek, but I started firing into it and seeing chips of its green flung into the air.

"You guys all right?" I shouted after I fired.

I could see Vernon nodding his head. Then the air filled with gunfire. Our machine guns had moved up behind us and were firing over our heads and cutting down everything on the other side of the creek. Then our grenade launchers started blowing the shades and the shadows away.

The shooting slowed, then stopped, and the still came, and then the wait. That wait that you wait on to settle into sounds, your sounds, your mind saying, *The shit's over, it's cool, you ain't even here.*

I yelled over to Lee, "How many of them were there? Did ya see 'em?"

" 'Bout two or three of 'em. They popped up over by that tree, had carbines, started firin'. Motherfuckers shot all up between my legs. Man, shit."

I saw Vernon stomping around and looking at his feet and legs, then rubbing at his face.

"Hey man, you okay?" I called.

"Yeah, bullet kicked a stone up into my face or somethin'."

I was up, near Lee, who was still muttering under his breath and staring across the creek. Vernon kept rubbing at his face, and when he stopped his hands were still shaking.

We stayed down by the creek until the canteens were filled, then backed away and left it silent.

When I got back to my little hill, I was hot and sweaty again. I stood wiping the sweat from my eyes, then looked down at my rock.

"Goddamnit, fuck!" I was yelling. "Ya rotten bastards . . ."

"What's wrong?" someone asked.

"Shit, every fuckin' ant in Vietnam is in my eggs."

"They'll probably taste better."

"Fuck you, Copeland."

"Just wait a while—soon as they taste that shit, they'll leave."

"Fuck all y'all."

I stood there staring down at my eggs. Then I saw the fucking ants swimming around in the cocoa. There were even a few climbing around on top of the hard bread—they must have been the dumb motherfuckers. They damn well couldn't crawl into that shit.

I reached down and picked up the can of eggs and shook it some, trying to shake the little zigzagging red things off without shaking the eggs out. Fuckin' ants kept stickin' to the side of the can, and the ones inside didn't give a fuck about what I was doin'.

I sat down on the rock and held the can in my hands, then started rubbing the ants off the side with my finger. This worked some, but those little fuckers were smart. They'd climb onto my finger, then on the next rub they'd climb back on the can.

Shit.

I took my finger and started pressing down on them until they popped. Some of them were hard to catch, kept zigzagging all over the place. As soon as my finger would get close, they'd take off. Some I had to squash twice.

In a while I had the side of the can clean of ants, or just about. The ones already in my eggs still weren't thinking about me. I started trying to pick them out with my fingers, but they had too many places to hide. I took my little plastic spoon and tried to dig them out, but I found myself flicking more eggs than ants.

Shit.

I took the spoon and started scraping it across the eggs, trying to get just the ants on the spoon and leave the egg stuff in the can. This shit wasn't working. These little red things had two little round parts with something like a little red string holding them together. When I scraped them, some of the little red strings would break. The front part of the fucking ant would go one way and the back part would still be zigzagging around.

Fuck it.

I took the spoon and just started jamming it up and down in the ants and eggs. I sat there, just jamming and mixing the ants and eggs together until the eggs looked like they had little pieces of red pepper in them.

I picked up the can of cocoa and tried to dip the swimming ants out of it, but I was dipping more cocoa out than ants. I took my spoon and started a whirlpool.

The first taste of the eggs wasn't that bad—it certainly didn't taste any different. The cocoa wasn't that bad either, same old nasty taste. I sat on my rock and ate the ants and eggs and drank the cocoa.

The other ants were swarming over the chocolate candy and trying to gnaw the hard-ass bread.

They could have that shit.

10

THE LANTERN

The rain had been pouring out of the sky for days again, maybe weeks. Our hill had become a mountain of mud, and the paths running between the tents were thick streams of mud. The rice paddies beyond our lines had flooded over their dikes. Everything was soaking. Snakes came out of their holes and floated one way as we waded the other.

We had just come back from a patrol and were inside the tent getting the mud and water off our weapons. It was about midday.

"*Squad leaders up. Squad leaders up.*" The word was being passed through the tents.

"Fuck, shit," I muttered, wondering what was up now—more shit? I flung my poncho over my shoulders and began climbing up the muddy path to the lieutenant's tent. Wiggins was already there, and first squad leader Sergeant Ituarte was in there too. The second squad leader, Sergeant Langford, was new—well, maybe been there a month or so.

I liked Langford; he was colored, older, in his thirties. He had three kids he was always talking about, when we got to talking about home. I remember Ituarte was married and had kids too. He was from Texas. I could never really figure him out. Sometimes he'd seem all right, then sometimes he'd seem distant to me. Maybe it was because I was just a corporal and he was a sergeant. Maybe because I was just a kid to him, one of those who came in right after high school and got the fuck out when their time was up. Didn't want to do ten and twenty.

The lieutenant was chewing on his tobacco and doing the general bull, like who was fucking up, who needed a haircut, what's going on around us that we should know about. He was going over the distant gunfires of the night. "Two-four got hit again on the other side of the airstrip. Battalion thinks it's elements of that VC regiment that regrouped after getting their asses kicked on Operation Starlite. Battalion thinks they're probing. We got to stay alert, keep our people up. We can't afford to get caught with our pants down."

He was still chewing on his tobacco as he reached for his map case. "Now we got one. Captain just gave me the word, the platoon's going out this afternoon right after chow. We'll have a machine-gun team attached to us. We're going up to this island. We haven't had anybody up there yet, so . . ."

He pointed to a spot on the map and tried to say the name of it. Then he said, "It's about fifteen miles up. Battalion thinks there's a large VC force staging there. Aircraft have been getting a lot of fire from there every time they fly over. Now we're going up by amtracs at 1900 hours, we'll get there about 2000."

The lieutenant went on to tell us that the rest of the company was on standby. If we got hit, they would be flown in by choppers, but if the rains were still too heavy, we'd have to hold until they could get there by sea. We'd be gone for three days.

"When you goin' to come over and visit?" Langford asked as we left the lieutenant's tent.

"Visit for what?" I said with a laugh.

"Nigger, so I can whip your little ass in some cards. Get all that money you got hid somewhere."

"Shit, if I come over on that fuckin' hill of yours, there'll be some ass-whippin', but it ain't goin' to be mine."

"See, that's what's wrong with you young dudes. Talk the talk but won't walk the walk. That's all y'all do, is talk. I'll tell ya what, when we get back from this shit, I'll give ya two to one on every hand and still whip your butt."

Langford was still going on about whipping my ass in cards, then spit in the mud and got to saying, "Man, we been bustin' ass every motherfuckin' night. The day before yesterday, we ran four fuckin' patrols. Then, get this, the lieutenant comes sneakin' and checkin' the lines, then gives me hell 'cause my whole squad's asleep. Shit, what they 'xpect, up all day on silly shit. Gunny callin' for workin' parties all fuckin' day, then we out in the shit all night. I tell ya, man, the shit is getting thick. Two-four got their fuckin' ass kicked up on Starlite—shit, fifty fuckin' guys dead and two hundred wounded. What's that sound like? Taylor was tellin' me, he heard they landed H Company right in the middle of the VC headquarters. The whole fuckin' company just about got wiped out. Ya hear that shit, and they're tellin' ya they know what's goin' on and land the fuck in the VC headquarters and didn't even know it."

I got to thinking. "Man, I got seven guys—at least you have a full squad. I got seven guys and they took two for mess duty. Shit, I don't mind that much about being here—shit, that's the way it is, no fuckin' choice. But I don't want to get my head blown off behind some shit. Last night we had to patrol with them fuckin' ARVNs—they are fucked up. Man, we had to check this house out where this VC supposed to be livin', or hidin'. We tryin' to sneak up on it, and these assholes are out there with all kinds of pretty-colored umbrellas, talkin' and holdin' hands like a bunch of faggots. That's the shit that pisses me off. You run a patrol, you don't just have to worry about the VC, you got to worry about those assholes too. Last night, down by the ville at the end of the road, we almost got fucked. Those bastards had an ambush set up, wasn't even marked on the patrol route. We could have walked right into it. The only thing that saved us was their first man was asleep. When we walked up on him, the son of a bitch woke up and started screamin'. I think we scared the shit out of him. We started yellin' 'Americans!' Tell ya the truth, man, I was ready to blow his fuckin' ass away. I didn't know whether he was fuckin' VC or what. And if ya shoot one of 'em, ya probably get court-martialed. Shit."

Langford and I went on talking for a while and got to talking about playing some cards, drinking some beer, when we got back. I slipped back down the hill and went into the tent.

"What's up?" Grunwald asked.

I got the squad together and told them about the island. We'd land, move inland, set up a perimeter; then we'd have an ambush from 2400 to 0500.

No one said too much. I didn't either—wasn't too much to say. As fucked up as we could be, we could all count. Our platoon, with its three squads and even a machine-gun team, would only be about thirty-some guys. And thirty-some guys on an island full of VC could add up to a lot of shit.

I knew we had been lucky. No one in the company had been killed since I had come. Maybe about ten, twelve guys had been wounded. No one in the squad had been hurt. The shit had always come close. Two-four wasn't that far away—only a mile, if that. Bravo Company and the guy who got killed in the hole were only on the next hill; we could see it easily from our own. And in the night, sometimes you could feel yourself, knew you were near/passing through/rubbing up against something that stayed dark even in the day.

Chow came and went, then the time came and got us.

I lit a cigarette, stood, then quietly said, "Saddle up, let's go. Outside. Make sure ya got all your shit. Each man make sure ya got a shovel, we might have to dig in."

We started down the muddy path to the road. The rain had stopped. It would do that sometimes: stop, still itself, go where it went for a while, shit and take a break, then come back. You'd forget it had even left.

Soon the platoon had stretched out into a long column on the march. Rifles were slung over shoulders, machine guns rode atop. Packs were just slung and hung from backs. Helmet straps just dangled and swayed with each step.

When we reached the beach, the amtracs were waiting. Wiggins got to shouting and pointing. *"First squad, first tractor. Second squad, second tractor. Third squad and guns, get that tractor. Squad leaders, get your people on."*

We climbed on the big green monstrous-looking tractors. They were bigger than tanks, with big iron tractor treads on both sides. On the ground they stood about eight feet high, but when they went into the water, only about two feet of the things remained above the surface. I was always amazed the fucking things could float.

The tractor engines started up, and the big monsters slowly backed into the water, turned, and started out to sea. We found a place to sit on top of the tractor, took our packs and helmets off. The ocean was rather calm. The sound of its waves was soothing, and looking out to sea was easy, felt good.

We were talking some, but mostly we were quiet, not because we had to be quiet. I think it was the ocean, the cool breeze blowing, the silence in the gray of all the sky.

Sometimes I'd pray. I don't know why, I just did. I wouldn't make words, a lot of them, just say "God" in my mind and then just try and feel it. Maybe see church, Reverend Harris up there clapping his hands, talking about Jesus. Different-colored faces, close faces; different songs, one lingering melody.

I know I said, "Hey, Mitch, you bring your fishin' pole?"

Mitchell smiled and brought his eyes, and his far look, back from the sea. Then he asked me about Christmas, about maybe being able to take leave and meet his girl in Hawaii. She had written him and said she'd come there if he could get there. I just said I didn't know. Christmas seemed a million miles away.

"Is that it?" someone asked, pointing.

"How the fuck I know, I ain't the fuckin' tour guide," someone else muttered.

I looked ahead. I could see the dark gray mass in the distance. It seemed to be just part of the sky, but it kept getting closer while the sky stayed where the fuck it was.

I lit a cigarette, figuring that by the time it burned out it would be time to go in, and by the time we settled in it would be too dark to smoke. I leaned back and rested on the hard iron of the amtrac and just watched the island get closer, its gray turning into faint greens and browns and the shadows between them.

I didn't have to yell when I gave the word to saddle up, get ready, lock and load. Soon the clanging sounds of rifles being loaded and ammo belts being tussled with filled the silence. The tractor's engine began to rev up and roar. We had been floating parallel to the island; we could see its palm trees looming over its beach. The shadows beneath the treeline had thickened into darks and blacks.

Quickly the tractor turned and started speeding toward the island. I kept watching the treeline and waiting for the sound of gunfire to crack the air open.

"Listen up, listen up." I was talking fast now. "When we hit, we got the left flank. Lee, you take the left, keep your people spread out. Guns, you follow up in the center. Rayburn, you keep close to me. Copeland, you take the right, make sure you hook up with second squad. Keep it spread out."

Suddenly our tractor slowed, jolted, then stopped. Its engines began to roar, then sputter, as it lunged forward again, only to stop and still in the water.

"*Fuck. Oh shit. Fucking thing's broken,*" someone shouted.

The island was seventy, eighty yards away. The other tractors moved on toward the beach. Our tractor engine was still puttering, but we weren't moving. The driver popped his head out of his hatch and said, "Y'all got to walk from here, I'm stuck in the mud."

"You're what?" I shouted.

"I'm stuck in the mud."

"Shit, damnit," I muttered, then looked toward the beach and the waves and water all around us.

"Okay," I shouted, "test the water. Someone see how deep it is."

I kept looking ahead toward the beach. The other squads were landing. "I'll do it, I'll see," I heard Rayburn mutter.

"Okay, hurry up," I shouted.

Rayburn stood, stripped his gear off, and started taking off his shirt. It was the only time he had volunteered for anything that I could remember, except for mess duty.

He was stripped down to his waist now, and stood on the side of the amtrac. He then raised his hands in the air as if he were an Olympic diver, jumped high into the air, spread his arms out wide. It was a swan dive. It was a nice dive, but the water was only a couple feet deep.

When Rayburn hit the bottom, his legs seemed to stick straight up out of the water for a while before spreading open like a pair of scissors. In a bit, he stood, with mud all over his arms and face, saying, "It's not deep."

"No shit, Rayburn. Ya want to try it again?" The yells and laughter started.

I looked at Rayburn standing in the water with mud all over that sleepy look of his and forgot where the fuck I was. I couldn't stop laughing and could not remember when I had started.

Copeland said, "Hey, Rayburn, ya get any clams stuck in your ass?"

Other guys got to yelling, "Hey, Rayburn, ya see any submarines down there? Ya oughta try divin' for fuckin' pearls, Rayburn. Hey, Rayburn . . ."

The island had disappeared in the laughter.

The other tractors were on the beach; I could see the rest of the platoon running along it. I could see Wiggins standing and angrily waving for us to get in. I think we were messing up the war.

Rayburn had already climbed back on the tractor and wiped the mud off his face. I was shouting now, "Come on, let's go, hurry up." And laughing a little.

We jumped in the water and ran through the waves. I looked back to see if everyone was off the tractor. Rayburn was the last one to get off and was running to catch up. Copeland turned and yelled, "Hey, Rayburn, why don't ya swim?"

Finally we reached the beach, soaked from the chest down. We ran up the sand and moved to the left of the rest of the platoon, and it became quiet. We moved slowly, crouching as we moved. Soon we had made our way into the treeline and its shadows.

"Watch it, watch it. Keep it spread." The shouts were muffled as we moved through the bushes and trees.

"Watch where ya step," I whispered when I saw the punji sticks sticking out of the sand. They were all over the place, sticking out of the shadows and silence. They gave their message, quietly.

We formed into a staggered column and began to wind slowly through the trees and bushes, moving inland. The night was falling quickly; already distant trees and bushes had begun hiding in the dark. We were moving along a path. A man and a woman stood watching. The woman approached us, smiling and extending her hand as if asking for something. She came to me, trying to say something, to ask for something. Her eyes were glassy, jerky, as if she were drunk or high. She kept smiling, silly-like, witchy-like. Like she knew shit she didn't even know she knew. Couldn't tell you what it was, but wanted you to know.

The man kept a distance from us, let us pass and take his half-assed smile with us.

The whole island seemed dreary. The trees and bushes were spread thin as we moved further inland. Soon we met the night and settled in its darkness. We had circled into the trees and the whispers had come: "Spread out. Get the gun set up, set up here. Two men to a position. CPs in the center. Keep it quiet, stay down."

Probably I sat for a while, perhaps leaning against a tree and staring out into the night. I know I was thinking about that woman, how weird she was, and that man just standing there, with the smile on his mouth but not in his eyes. And the punji sticks sticking out all over the place on the beach, just waiting. Seemed like they knew we were coming. One thing for certain, the motherfuckers knew we were there.

We kept quiet.

I could see down the path we had just come up. I kept staring until I heard my name being called. I turned and quietly eased my way through the darkness to the CP. The lieutenant and Wiggins quietly whispered, drawing the ambush site in the sand. I could barely see the little stick in the lieutenant's hand, but I could easily see the dark path coming into my mind. I could hear his whispers. "Go back down the way we came up. Keep to the right. A little ways past where we landed, there's a wide trail. Set up on this side of it . . . ."

When I got back to the squad, I passed the word, then said, "Okay, get some sleep, we got about three hours."

Sometime in my sleep the rain came again. I could feel the cold drops thumping, then soaking into my back.

When I was awoke, the night was darker. The silence seemed to push on me, make me lean away from it. I had heard my name being called and had said okay, then got to my knees and wiped the water from my face. "Third squad," I whispered, "come on, get your shit on. Let's go."

In a moment I was saying, "Okay, gather around. We're going down that same path we came up. We're going to try and stay off to the side of it. About a half-mile down there's supposed to be a wide path that goes up into a village. We're going to set up on this side of it."

I watched their faces. What I could not see, I could feel.

"I'll take point," I said.

I had to—at that moment I had to go first, lead the way. I don't know why, only that it had nothing to do with their faces, nothing to do with the VC, that silly-looking woman, punji sticks. None of that shit. If Arthur was out there waiting, it had nothing to do with him, even if he was calling my name.

"All right, let's go, keep it spread out."

I stepped out into the night, took about ten steps, slowed, looked around, then raised my hand in the air for the next guy to follow and moved on. The night became darker the further we moved away from the rest of the platoon. All I could see was dreary dark, twisted and curly shapes out ahead. I had taken the safety off the trigger and was holding my rifle low, with its barrel pointing ahead.

I could hear my own footsteps sliding across the sand. I would turn from time to time and look back, make sure we were still all together but not bunched up. Then I would quickly turn, slow, and peer ahead.

Slowly I moved my head back and forth, looking and listening. I would stop if I could not make out a shape or form ahead. I'd stop and stare, turn away, then quickly turn back to see if it moved, if it was only pretending to be a bush.

Ahead the darkness had thickened—ahead was never far, only what you could see, hear, but I could hardly see now. I was reaching out with my hand, feeling into the darkness, feeling my way through the thick bushes and branches, hearing the little crack of a branch sound like thunder in the night.

I kept moving.

The thickness thinned and I could see again. I raised my hand, slowed, then stopped and looked around.

"Okay, set up here. Spread out. Lee, take the left, move down some. Cope, take the right. Grunwald, you and Mitch move up by Cope and them. Rayburn, stick close to me."

We settled into the darkness along the path. Beyond the path it looked like there was a clearing or rice paddy. Beyond that, I could not see. The darkness we had fought was now our only ally. We hid in it. The ground was wet and cold; the rain just kept falling.

I don't know what I thought of. Sometimes it may have been the cold rain and my chills and shivers. Maybe I thought about the time, whether it had moved. But mostly, probably, I did not think thoughts, words, that went beyond what I could see or hear. Beyond the dark and the rain. I kept my mind in the night until the light came.

"Hey, you see that?" A whisper came through the rain.

"Shut the fuck up. I see it. Stay down," I whispered back.

On the other side of the clearing was a slow, swinging light, just slowly swinging and swaying back and forth in the darkness. A flashlight or a lantern, just swinging and coming toward us.

I was staring, watching it move, trying to see into it, see beneath it or around it, but all I could see was its glow. And it kept coming.

"What is it? What's that?" someone whispered.

"Shut up. Don't fire. Wait till it gets closer," I whispered back.

I kept staring, waiting. Forty, thirty yards—across a street. Quietly I raised my rifle and eased its sights toward the light, but my mind raced. Got caught up in shit. Suppose this, suppose that. Some poor fool just out in the night. Some woman looking for her kid. A million I don't knows, and one thou shalt not.

"Jesus fuckin' Christ, who in the fuck . . . ?" I muttered, watching and waiting.

"Hey man, it's comin' over here." The whisper came fast.

"Shut up. Let it get closer."

I put my eye to the sights of the rifle and aimed it into the glow of the light. Everything was becoming silent in my mind; the pitter-patter of raindrops stilled and got the fuck away from me. I could feel only one thing in my mind, and that was coming closer.

I eased the trigger back to its pressure point.

I heard a cough, then another and another. Mitchell was coughing, trying to muffle the sound.

"Shut up. Shut up."

Mitchell coughed again and again.

"Mitchell, shut up. Shut up."

The swaying light stilled, then shook and bounced into the darkness. Its glow dimmed and died, and the night was quiet again. I could feel the raindrops, and their monotonous pitter-patter filled the night again.

A moment of raindrops fell, maybe more, maybe beyond count, and then the bullets came streaming through the night. I shuddered, sank further into the ground, but looked, searched and listened.

"Stay down, stay down. Rayburn, come on, I'll cover you. Fire two rounds over there."

I crawled closer to the path, looked up, then waved to Rayburn and whispered, "Fire two rounds right over there, I'll cover."

I looked ahead as far as I could see and listened to every sound I could hear. Rayburn crawled by, then edged his way out toward the path. I watched and listened. I could feel Rayburn's moves, feel him coming to his knees and feel the silence before his grenade launcher broke open the night. I saw the darkness beyond flash light, then heard it crack open.

I watched, aimed.

I could hear Rayburn loading, the quick clanging sound, then a loud *pop*, and the distant dark flashed light again.

I was crawling now. I passed Mitchell, whispering, "Stay down." Passed Grunwald, whispering, "Cover me," and then to Copeland.

"Where are they? Did you see 'em?"

"Over there somewhere."

"Where?"

"Out there, over there somewhere."

"Shit."

I watched and waited, but only silence came, then the chill of a thought. Quickly I turned to Copeland and whispered, "Fuck this shit, we've been spotted."

I got to my knees and whispered, "Listen up, listen up. We're going to move. Keep low, let's go."

We stayed low as we moved down the path about thirty or forty yards. When we stopped, I could still see where we had been. We set up a small circle and then lay deep in the dark.

The time was like the dark: if it moved, it was still the same. It was quiet. If the rain fell, it fell into the silence and did not shatter it.

I could not hear anything. Then the only thing I could hear was the gunfire tearing up everything where we had been. It had to be machine guns; they just kept firing, the sound wouldn't stop. And when it did, I could hear branches still falling around where we had been. I raised my head and looked out. Little white puffs of smoke floated from where the hot bullets had hit.

"Stay down, keep quiet," I whispered. I kept shaking. The silence, the stillness, the darkness, became one. Then it and time just stood still.

I waited.

"I see somethin', I see somethin'," Grunwald called quietly.

I turned and crawled to him, peered where his finger pointed.

"See, right there. I saw 'em right there."

I stared.

"They were right there, I saw 'em."

I lay beside Grunwald for a while, then whispered, "Fire if ya see them again."

I turned and was crawling away. Grunwald's automatic burst into fire. I spun around and came to my knees, firing into the darkness beyond Grunwald. My rifle shook in my hands, and fire poured out its muzzle. I kept firing at what I saw, didn't see, what moved, didn't move. Then I fell to the ground and crawled to Grunwald.

"Did ya get 'em? Ya get 'em?" I whispered, searching the darkness.

"Yeah, I got him, I got him."

"Ya see him?"

"Yeah, see? See? See by that tree? See? See?"

I stared into the darkness beneath the bushes, listened for any sounds, anything moving, moaning. I knew they were there, waiting and looking for us. I saw them move when I fired. I could see something now.

"Ya still see him?" I whispered.

"Yeah."

"Okay, we'll wait."

I lay staring and watching everything I could see. I lay still, making the time pass, pushing it through my mind. I watched it move, lighten the dark, slow the rain.

I had to know.

I just had to know. I whispered over my shoulder, "Lee, Lee, swing around. Cope, you and Grunwald cover us. Mitch, come on. We're going out—take the right and stay back a bit. Cover me."

I stood peering into the darkness. I waited for the silence to break open, but it was quiet. The first steps were useless; the darkness ahead did not come any closer. My finger eased on the pressure point of the trigger. My steps were soft, almost gliding. I could feel each raindrop hit my back. I looked at everything I could see. Thick forms of blackness remained still.

"Ya see anything?" I could hear Mitchell whisper near me. I shook my head and kept moving. Searching the ground, waiting to see whatever it was, dead, dying, ripped all apart.

I searched.

"Mitch, stay here. Cover me."

I moved on further, looking into the bushes, looking down on the ground for dark puddles of its blood in the rain.

I stopped.

Something far away, further than I could hear, called. I knew I had gone too far. If it was lying cold in the night, it would have to stay. I was moving back, backing away from its darkness.

"Come on," I whispered to Mitchell. "Come on, let's get the fuck out of here."

We moved back and crawled into the dark, but I could still see the light from the lantern in my mind.

I should have killed it.

11

THE PARTY

Franko was sitting there with sweat bubbles rolling down his face and dripping on the cards he was hiding.

"Come on, man, whatcha goin' to do? You passin' or what?" Henderson asked Franko, but Franko said nothing.

I had peeked at my cards, seen the six of something and the nine of something else, and already said shit.

Franko was still looking. I shouted, "Motherfucker, ya ain't got but two damn cards. Come on, man, ya goin' to pass?"

Franko looked at me, gave me one of those slick, sly smiles, then said to Henderson, "Gimme one."

Henderson flicked a card over to him, a big fat-ass queen.

I laughed and shouted, "Ya busted, ain't ya, motherfucker?"

Franko gave me that same slick-shit smile and fucked around with three cards for a long time before he asked for a fourth.

I heard Bright shouting, "Hey, Lee. Lee. Hey, Lee's back."

I turned, looked out the tent, down the hill, and saw Lee coming up. He looked funny with his dress uniform on, but he was just as raggedy-looking as the tents he was passing. That uniform looked like he had slept or fucked in it all week. Seemed like he had been gone a month instead of a week, but when anyone's gone he's missed.

I looked back at the cards in my hand. They were still the same old nine and six. Fifteen, and I needed twenty-one.

"Ya want one?" Henderson was asking me.

"Yeah," I said, then said "Shit" to myself as I saw the deuce coming my way. Fifteen, two, fucking seventeen. That ain't winning shit.

"Fuck it," I said. Then, "Gimme one down, let me look at the shit slow, then go on and see the next man."

Lee came into the tent and the shit started.

"Hey, Lee, how's that pussy down there?"

"Hey man, ya get that shit for me?"

"Yeah, Lee got some pussy, motherfucker's still smilin'. Look at him."

"Hey man, how's Bangkok? Is there anything to do down there?"

I looked up at Lee and said, "Hey man, welcome back. Did ya have a nice time?" Then I tried to peek at the new card in my hand.

I heard Copeland's mouth going. "Ya bring back what ya promise? Ya ain't got down there and forgot about us?"

I heard Lee say, "Man, I ain't thought about this place. Put y'all out my mind. Started to come back."

I was still trying to peek at the card in my hand. I said some quiet yeahs, then I saw the other deuce. At first I thought it was the same one I'd just got. I was thinking, "I got nineteen, what's that faceless card Henderson ain't showed yet? I hope he bust his ass out."

Henderson was dealing, been dealing and winning. I watched him count the numbers off those cards, then slowly get himself one more.

"What ya got? Ya better have twenty-one. Better have," Franko taunted.

Henderson was still looking at his cards and still had the same look on his face when he laid his cards down. Big red king and two goddamned fives popped in my eyes. Shit, mother luck says fuck me.

The piece of table we had shook. Franko smacked his cards down, shouting, "Ah got ya, got ya. Ya can't beat the big man. What's wrong with you? Think ya can takes my money. Ah gots twenty-one."

I watched Franko grab my money.

Henderson got the cards and got to shuffling them. He gave me a quick look, asking, "You in?"

"Yeah."

Lee was still being questioned about his R and R and was still telling guys he wished he had stayed. Then he sort of sighed and asked Bright, "So what's goin' on? Did I miss anything?"

Bright said, "No. We went out once, ya know, out there by Hill 22. Oh, Brooks got shot in the hand down Scully Wagg, he was just standin' there and a couple snipers started shootin'. He got one of his fingers off."

I heard Bright talking and shouted over my shoulder to Lee, "Hey man, we're going down at 1500. We got to relieve second squad. We'll be there for three days, ya better get your shit ready."

The cards came and went, none of the ones I was looking for. In a while I told Franko how ugly he was and threw in my last hand. Copeland had a big smile on his country face when he leaned over and whispered in my ear. I said, "Yeah, what the fuck."

The outpost was called Scully Wagg, a silly fucking name for a little rocky mound along the beach. It was about two miles away, a forty-, forty-five-minute walk. We usually took our time getting there. Once we were there, there was nothing to do. There were no holes; the ground was rock-hard, so we'd just sit or sleep during the day, put one man on watch and try to catch up on all the sleep we didn't get. All in all it was a pretty place, with the sea a few steps away.

"Outside, let's go."

It was hot again. The shade from the tent was only a shadow now that Franko's mouth was popping out of it. *Shit*, I was still thinking, *down fifteen bucks—shit.*

"Come on, let's go, third squad."

When Lee came out of the tent, he looked like he was going on R and R again. He had his rifle, pack, and all, but he also had a green plaid suitcase.

"Lee, what the fuck?"

He gave me a quick grin.

"Man, what the fuck ya got in there?"

Bright was beside him with a big smile on his face and blurted out, "Lee brought back some new sounds. We got Speer's tape recorder, we're goin' to listen to 'em down there."

"Shit, fuck, get a poncho and wrap that thing up. Lieutenant will shit if he sees us lookin' like we're going on a fuckin' picnic."

On the way down to the outpost, we passed second squad coming back. I saw Langford and shouted ahead, "Hey, Franko's waiting for you, they got a little game going. Y'all have any more shit?"

We slowed, stopped, and talked for a while. Lee was the center of attention among the guys in the other squad. They wanted to know about the price of pussy in Bangkok. I was asking Langford about the sniper.

"Ya see any more shit?"

"No, it was quiet."

"Yeah, I hope it stays that way."

We were on the way again. As we neared the outpost, I let my eyes wander. We'd come down to help search the area where Brooks had been hit. We'd found the shallow hole the sniper had dug and fired from.

We flung our helmets and packs to the ground, then each guy was claiming his own little bare space and spreading out his poncho. Rayburn hurried; his pack, helmet, and shirt went flying off.

"Can I go swimming?" he asked quickly.

In my mind, I looked around. I could still see the distant treeline where the sniper had fired from. I could see Rayburn in the water and us getting hit. I could see shit that didn't have a name, words and all that—dead-tomorrow-fuck-today shit.

"Yeah, take somebody with you. One in the water at a fuckin' time."

There were no trees up on the bare rocks of the outpost. Just standing there and trying to cool off was a waste of time. The rest of the guys were trying to cool off too. Looking back, I guess we were always hot, in our own little hells. I'd look at the sea, and my thoughts would only go to the shore, then turn around and come crashing back in my head, showing me the shit that was right in front of my face.

It was too hot to do much talking; even Copeland kept his mouth shut. Glickman was off in his strange shit, sitting and staring at stuff that wasn't worth looking at, like the ground. Grunwald and McCabe went swimming with Rayburn. Mitchell was writing that girl another letter. Lee took about half the time he needed to fall asleep. Bright was talking to me, but I wasn't listening.

I wondered where the kids were. About four or five kids from a distant village would always come down and sell us soda pop. They ranged in age from about five or six to thirteen or so. A cute little girl named Phau would come; she was about seven or eight and had long black hair, big brown eyes, and copper-colored skin. She would always stand back from the rest and just stare, and smile if you looked at her. She reminded me of my little sister.

Bright knew all the kids by name, and they knew his. He would find things to give them and find more things to talk about than they could with their three or four words of English. I wondered if they had come earlier. There was a curfew in the area; anyone out in the night would be shot.

Sometimes I'd look at my watch, but most of the time I'd look at the sky, see where the sun was, or at night the moon. Evening was coming. The hours passed slowly, miserably, in the sun.

"I'm goin' to check the area."

I felt like walking some, maybe just getting the fuck away from everything, maybe walking the fuck on home. I grabbed my rifle, leaving the ammo belt lying. I just grabbed a couple ammo clips and stuck them in my pockets. I would circle the area before it got dark. I knew I wanted to check the area across the gully. Then I'd come back along the beach and get Rayburn and the others. It bothered me that the kids weren't around—the local people always seemed to know when the VC were in the area and kept their distance from us.

I was in the shadows of the treeline now, moving slowly, listening and watching. I knew exactly where the hole the sniper had fired from was. I waded through the bushes and branches carefully, looking for fresh footprints, trying to see black through the green, see movement in the stillness. I could see the hole; it was empty. The sharp punji sticks we had stuck in it were still there. They were our message to the sniper. We just wanted to tell him, *We know where you are, motherfucker.*

I was this now, a part of its days and nights. I had taken the safety off the trigger so that there would be nothing between me and this, so I could completely be a part of this moment. I knew what I was doing—couldn't say it, stick it in words, but I could feel it, knew it. I knew if the sniper was watching me from a different hole, watching and waiting for me, I was teasing him, daring him, daring this.

The green of my clothes had faded long ago from rains and sweats. The black of my boots was scraped away to the color of the sand and mud. My hands were hard, sometimes swollen with pain from thorns that had scratched and cut at them. I didn't know whether I had faded with the clothes, changed. Because I didn't know who I really was back there, up the way. Or had I been scraped away to a real me, what I really was underneath all that? And this—now this, this wasn't ever going away.

"Hey, Rayburn, you guys come on up," I yelled, going back to the hill.

The squad was beginning to settle in for the night. We gathered around, asking Lee about his R and R. He was talking now, smiling and saying, "We just walked around during the day. They got hotels, nice rooms where you can stay. Soon as you walk in, girls come up. If you want, they'll spend the whole time with you, or ten dollars for the whole night. Down where we were they had a couple of flicks you could go to. Had old movies, cowboy stuff, and *West Side Story* was playing. Had all kinds of places to eat. We went to a restaurant, they had American food, you could get anything you wanted. Me and Spence picked up these two girls, they're all over the place. They could speak some English, but you couldn't understand them too much. I had this one named Monica."

Bright quickly asked Lee, "How old was she?"

Lee paused, looked at Bright, then said, "She was too old for you. What you want to know for? She was eighteen, nineteen. How should I know?"

Bright shut up, and Lee got back to his talk. "She looked good. They'll do anything you ask. They go home in the morning, but they come back. Spence had this girl named Susie—she was pretty, but a little fat. But he kept her the whole time. He said she really knew how to do it . . ."

The night was nearing; the distant greens were turning gray. Bright asked if we could play the tape recorder now, and Copeland slowly reached in his pack and brought out a bottle of liquor. Then he looked at me with a big grin on his face.

I looked around. It would be dark soon. I knew no one from the company would be down.

Fuck it.

"Wait," I said. "Wait a minute. Let me call in first. Then third squad's going to have a party."

The yelling started. "All right, party time. Yeah, party time."

I got the radio from Grunwald and stepped a few feet away, then yelled, "Settle down till I call in. I don't want the whole fuckin' company down here." I held the radio up and pushed the little button.

"Alpha one. Alpha one. Alpha one, this is Scully Wagg, over."

Soon I could hear the garbled voice on the other end of the radio. I reported in. "Area all secure. No enemy contact."

Laughter gave way to the hum of the tape recorder, then the loud sound of sudden song.

Ain't no home for me . . . Except my girl's arms . . .

Mellow yells of "All right, yeah. Yeah, man" harmonized with the music.

The cap on the bottle of liquor came off. Copeland became the bartender, and everyone gathered around with their makeshift cups. The smell of liquor seeped into the air. Spam, stale hard bread, crackers, and cookies popped out of cans. The song was with us, in us.

Say you love me one more time,
Say it again nice and slow . . .
Let me hear it one more time,
Say you love me before I go . . .

The music played and the talk of long ago felt good. Mitchell had taken a few sips, was quiet, but now he was talking. "I met my girl in Bensonville, she's going to be a nurse. She's real nice. If I make it, we're getting married as soon as I get back. I'm not going to wait until I get out. Man, I can't wait."

The liquor was feeling good. I could feel it oozing into me, like live, swaying bright skirts in the night. Pretty colors came into my mind; I watched them become reds of lips, browns of big eyes, and rainbows of smiles.

Copeland was drinking slow and talking slower. "Man, I tell ya, ain't nothin' better than to get you a good ole honey. Get you some good booze. Find you some quiet spot on the beach and just fuck all night. I met this honey, we went up to this lake. Man, it was like heaven. Man, the only thing we did was fuck, sleep, and fuck again. Man, I tell ya . . ."

Someone asked, "Hey, Rayburn, you still hear from that girl in San Diego?"

Rayburn quietly looked up and said, "She used to write, but she stopped. I guess she said fuck it."

Copeland had to say, "Well, Rayburn, you are kind of ugly."

Rayburn laughed and put his head back down.

Bright got to talking about his girl, and Lee told him, "Bright, shut up. You ain't got no girl."

"Yes, I do. How you know what I have, huh? I don't tell ya everything. Her name is Judy . . ."

McCabe just started talking, not to me or anyone, just talking and staring into the night. "Fuck this place, fuck this shit. I haven't heard from my old lady. She can get fucked too. She waits till this shit happens, then she pulls her shit. She wants a fuckin' divorce, she can come over here and get it. I don't give a fuck anymore . . ."

I could still hear McCabe's voice somewhere out there in the dark, but I was listening to the whisper, the pleading, a love coming into my ear. She sang softly, and I could see her face, her eyes.

When I look in your eyes,
I see my love in your heart . . .
My love will be with you,
No matter how far we are apart . . .

I was talking now, thinking of McCabe. "Yeah, I had this girl, went together all through high school. We were down in Panama, playing jungle shit, and here comes a Dear John letter. That's a bitch. You're out there in the middle of nowhere and out of nowhere comes that shit. Man, fuck it . . ."

That's what I was saying, but I could still feel me and her, just us. If I said love, let myself say it or think it, she'd come dancing into my mind, stepping on my heart. I could smile and cry at the same time, but I'd do neither.

The songs played and the talk continued. I looked away into the night, wondering if the sniper was out there, crawling to his hole.

"All right, all right," Bright was shouting as the liquor wiggled in his head. The sound of song was strong; its beat was drums in the night. We began to sway with its rhythm.

Dancin' past the midnight hour . . .
Yeah baby, let the night catch on fire . . .

Bright and Lee were up, their bodies swaying in the dark.

"Do it, Lee," we shouted as Lee broke into dance. We sang and clapped our hands. Now we all stood, dancing and singing, moving with a will that was free, loosened by the hot, melting liquor. We were dancing and twisting freely in the night.

It felt good, so good. The sniper was gone, the sweat, rain, mud, thorns in the night were all gone. Never there; now it was what we wanted it to be. Just a party.

The squad was asleep now, the night was quiet, but I could still hear the music. I sat leaning against a rock, my rifle lying across my legs. I watched the shapes in the night, watched them and watched them. I was waiting for the sniper to move.

The party was over.

12

PATCHES OF FIRE

Pencil, paper, and candlelight, and Dear Mom, I just got your last letter. Just writing to say I'm okay. Things are going fine. Don't worry, I'm all right. How is everyone doing? How's the kids? How's Ma-Ma? Tell them I love them and think about them. If you see Ronnie, tell him to write me and let me know what's going on. I'm going to have an allotment sent home. Just save the money for me, or if you need some for something, just go ahead and use it. I'll write again next week. Don't worry, I'm doing fine. Love, me.

Everything was changing.

I could see Arthur standing off in the night.

One day we just got on trucks and went someplace else. We moved to the other side of the airstrip, out in the sands. Dug our holes deep, made bunkers, and put mines out in front. We became something else too. We were the same guys, same company, but now we were in a different battalion.

Everything was changing—lots of new guys. I was transferred into machine guns. Vernon was in my team, next to me all the time with the gun. We settled into our new holes, but the days and the nights would not settle. The days seemed to be longer, and some nights lasted forever. Fire would light up the night and flash in our faces.

Our tents were set far back from our holes; they were bigger than the ones we had had before but still had their sagging tops. Behind the tents ran an old railroad track, weeds and grass covering the rusty rails. The train tracks had been bombed and in some places were all twisted and curled, sticking up out of the weeds. Behind them was a highway, or what was left of one; only chunks of cement remained. Beyond the broken road was a high barbed-wire fence. Near the fence two, maybe three skeletal remains of planes sat, with their wings twisted and burned.

We were always on alert. The VC were attacking in strength. The word was they were getting ready to hit the airstrip. They had been probing our lines, hitting here and there, firing, then backing off into the night. A few nights would go by, then they'd come again. Maybe the same place, maybe someplace else on the line, but they'd come and we'd wait.

I was having a lot of time to think. Sitting behind the gun at night could be easy time sometimes. The gun would have a five-hundred-round belt of ammo sticking in it, and we had another two or three thousand rounds of ammo in cans nearby. The area in front of the bunker was flat and open, and anyone coming across that open field would get hell, then death.

Sometimes thinking wasn't about being shot at, it was just about sitting in that hole and thinking of what the rest of the world was doing. I didn't want to die there—I wanted to buy a car. I knew what kind I wanted, a new Chevy Super Sport. I wanted to travel the highways again. I wanted to roll into the night, then turn a corner with one finger on the wheel. Then I wanted to take the car to the limit, everything to the limit. I wanted to stretch time out.

I could have all kinds of thoughts, but sooner or later I'd see the long black barrel of the gun sticking out into the night, the long strand of bullets hanging from its side. Then thinking could sneak into feeling, and I'd be afraid to turn my head and see if who I thought was standing there was really there. Slowly I'd turn and look for Arthur.

I had taken some pictures and money I had and sent them home. I made sure to write home. I never wrote about what was happening where I was, never mentioned the shooting and all that stuff. Somehow I just felt it was important to write now to my family and casually sign with love.

The feeling was strange. It was about the time that was coming this time. This kind of time was like living in a spark; I had the feeling the spark was out and I was just living in its dying glow.

The rumors had been flying: we were moving north, any day. A large VC regiment with elements of North Vietnamese units attached had come into the area beyond the distant hills.

I guess we were just waiting.

There was just me and Vern and two other guys, Steve and Hutnik, with the gun. I didn't know Steve or Hutnik too well; I'd seen them a lot but not spent time in the holes or nights with them.

Steve was from Maine or someplace by there. He was a little quiet— not fucked-up quiet like Glickman, just quiet a little. He was about nineteen, been in a year. He was okay.

Hutnik was younger, looked younger, but tried to act old. He was eighteen but still had kid pimples on his face. Looked like Bright a little, same kind of look and same blond hair. Sometimes I'd have to get in his shit, wake his ass up when he should not have been asleep. Just for stuff like that, he'd get pissed and get that kid look all over his face like Bright.

The platoon sergeant was a guy named Watts, a tall, thin guy but down to earth. He had been in for about eight years, and said that as soon as his time was up, he was getting the fuck out.

For the most part we sort of kept to ourselves, stayed by or always close to the gun. Back in the States, I had always liked being in guns; it was like being a specialist. The machine gun could fire five hundred and forty rounds a minute, and you could kill a lot of anything, quick. The flip side of all that firepower was, you knew that as soon as you opened up, the motherfuckers would be on your ass, quick. They even told us back in the States that the life expectancy of a machine gunner in combat was some of that minute shit. Say your prayers, get your pussy before you get there.

Our bunker was like a little house. It didn't leak too much when it rained. Had a window for the gun in the front, a little side door, a side window too. Outside, it was all covered with sand, looked like a little sand dune. It was like the Hilton to us. Fucking rats liked it too—some of them moved in. I used to watch them scoot this way and that way. Got used to their little sudden sounds in the night.

Behind the bunker about a hundred yards or so, artillery was set up. Every night the guns would go off and the ground would shake as if it were trying to get you off it. The rats would start their get the fuck out of here drill and start running all over the place.

It was December.

November had left only a rainy Thanksgiving in my memory. The other things—the patrols, ambushes, sudden fire—I still can't pick apart. But I remember December coming and bringing thoughts of Christmas. I didn't like to think about it or talk about it, but Vernon did. So we would talk about Christmas sometimes.

Vernon didn't say it, but he seemed homesick. Sometimes I'd see him writing, but mostly he just stared at the paper with that silent look that could speak the loudest thoughts. I didn't bother him; I'd find something else to do, look at, think about.

Sometimes Vern could get in some deep shit, start talking about America and freedom and this was right, this was wrong. He had written a letter to his hometown newspaper. He had been upset about the news of the war protestors, and he just wanted to tell folks that fighting for freedom was always right.

I remember saying, "Yeah, man," then changing the subject. I didn't like to talk about that. I didn't like to think about it either.

I was down in the tent area when the final word came down. We were moving out the next day. All weapons—machine guns, rockets, everything—were to be test-fired. Extra ammo was to be picked up at the supply tent. All personal belongings were to be put in sea bags. All sea bags were to be locked and marked with name tags. Squad leaders were to make sure sea bags were marked.

After going over all the details for the next day with Watts, I grabbed my rifle and started up to the bunker. Going up through the sand seemed to take longer than usual. It was that passing-through-space shit again. That space between things, not distances. I guess mostly it was passing through what you knew, what you were, and leaving it all behind again.

Squeezing through the door of the bunker didn't take long. Vernon was sitting behind the gun, reading a magazine or something.

"Hey, Vern, I just got the word from Watts, it's tomorrow. The whole battalion's going up."

Vernon kept reading, then in a moment turned and asked, "What time? Did they say how long?"

"After chow in the morning—I guess before noon. They didn't say how long. The word is a bunch of ARVN got fucked today. The VC ran all over their ass up there. Watts was saying they got some antiaircraft guns and hit a lot of choppers going in to help the ARVN."

Vernon was quiet for a bit. Then he got this smile on his face and asked, "You think we'll be back before Christmas?"

"What fuckin' difference does it make? Shit, I don't know. Hope so. What's today's date?"

It took us a while to figure out the date, but when we did, I laughed and said, "Shit—December seventh, Pearl Harbor Day." We laughed a while about that; then Vern, or maybe me, got quiet. We still said things, but I don't think they were things we were thinking about. I was thinking of Arthur.

The night came. The first part of the night was still. Then the flares started shooting up into the sky, distant machine guns rattled, and the outgoing artillery started roaring overhead. Some sleep here and there; then first light would peek over the horizon and see if it was okay to bring the rest of its ass.

It was morning now, a couple minutes into the day, and we were moving about quickly. A new company had moved in to take our positions on the line. We were all back at the tent area, getting ready. Packs were being filled with extra ammo and food, all kinds of stuff. Extra grenades and ammo clips were being tossed around like baseballs.

Little special things we did were being done.

Little screws on weapons were being tightened. Ropes and cords were being cut into little pieces to tie bayonets to legs so they wouldn't bounce when you ran, to tie extra food and stuff on your ammo belt so if your pack came off, you'd have enough stuff on your belt to keep you going. If you smoked, at least one pocket would be filled with cigarettes and matches. Extra cigarettes and matches would be kept in cellophane, so if it rained, you'd have some that were dry.

The little tiny things, sometimes secret, were being done.

Quick glances at little crosses and quiet sighs filled a cornered moment. Putting Mama's picture away someplace safe. Adding words to last pages of last letters, telling that some love always will ever be.

It took a while, but I finally got all the ammo and food stuffed in my pack. I turned to Vernon, saying, "Come on, man, let's get the gun test-fired."

Vernon had the gun on his shoulder as we went across the sand and out in front of the lines a bit. Some of the other guns were already firing into a small ditchlike hole. I always liked the sound of the gun being fired. It had a rhythm to it, and when it blasted its rounds, you couldn't help but feel it.

Vernon held the gun and started firing. He let go about thirty or forty rounds into the hole. The sand splattered, and gunsmoke floated in the air.

"Vernon, check that fuckin' pistol of yours. See if the fuckin' thing shoots—ya ain't fired the thing since ya got here."

I took the gun and Vernon got his pistol out. I joked, finding some laughs, and said, "Hey, Vern, wait until I get away from you before you fire that fuckin' thing. I don't want to get blown up too. That thing don't look like it's been fired since World War Two. Do you know how to shoot it?"

Vernon turned, smiling and saying, "I'm a good shot with this. Watch, I bet I hit the hole every time."

Chow went quick, and we were back at the tent area. I was ready but still doing things, checking this and that. I had changed clothes, put on whatever I had that was clean. I had on my green sweatshirt with the cut-off sleeves under my shirt. It would help cushion the pressure from the ammo-belt straps. But maybe I put it on because it was from home, only dyed green. It was from a time I was leaving.

If I want, I can go touch the faded green sweatshirt now. It is in a time away from here, so far from here that I don't dare look at it or for it. It is in a drawer, one of the only two things left from that day.

"Outside. Outside, everybody outside. Get 'em outside. Fall in. The Captain's got something to say. Come on people, outside." The shouts came through the tent.

We left our gear inside and fell out of the tent and into a classroom formation. We were sitting when the captain came out. Someone yelled, "Attention!" but before we could get up the captain waved us back down and began speaking to us.

"Okay, men, listen up. We got a battalion of North Vietnamese and a regiment of VC up in the valley. About ten, fifteen miles west of Tam Ky. They are damn hot. They have just overrun two South Vietnamese Ranger battalions. We're going in. The operation is called Harvest Moon. We think these are the same VC that two-four went against in Operation Starlite. We can anticipate a well-armed and disciplined force. Reports indicate that they have bunker complexes, antiaircraft weapons, and heavy machine guns. We have already lost a few choppers . . ."

We had about an hour before the trucks would come and take us to Tam Ky. From there, the captain said, we would be flown in by choppers. Most guys were just sitting around, waiting.

I may have been quiet, saying things like "Hey, Vern, make sure that . . . ," "Hey, Steve, Hut, make sure ya got that . . . ," but still having quiet thoughts, finding things to think about, catch onto, ride a moment, get away from myself.

I heard Felter's mouth going. I sat and watched him for a while, watched his face smiling and laughing. Felter was a million miles from all the shit, just going on about some Beatles record. In my mind, I could see and feel us back in the States, in our old outfit. I could see him falling out for inspection, all fucked up. Him laughing at all the silly shit, making the rest of us giggle inside, see the joke too.

Now I wish I could have whispered, "Hey, Felt, this shit ain't no joke. Go home now, man, go home."

Felter was like Arthur—he was dead, couldn't do anything about it. Only thing was, Felter didn't know it, or maybe he did and just didn't give a fuck.

"Let's go. Saddle up, saddle up. Movin' out, outside . . ."

I was standing now. I took a deep breath before saying, "Let's go, guns. Get your shit on. Make sure ya got everything."

I reached down and grabbed my ammo belt and slung it around my waist, then put the heavy flak jacket on. Quietly, I took an extra ammo clip and slipped it into my shirt pocket, the one above my heart. It just might help to slow down anything that was going into it. I heaved my heavy pack onto my back, grunted, and said, "Steve, Hut, get those extra ammo boxes. Make sure ya got the spare parts. Come on, let's go."

We were moving out of the tent. Swishing sounds of water in canteens, clanging sounds of bullet belts gave a rhythm to our time. Outside, we began to form up into platoons and squads. We stood loose and easy, rifles and guns slung over our shoulders, helmets sitting loosely on our heads or dangling from the ends of free hands.

When the word came it wasn't a shout, just a "Let's go." We turned to the right and started moving down past the tents and out onto the broken road. The trucks were pulling up. It did not take long to climb up on them.

I could see from the top of the truck just how long the convoy was. I could see the other companies further down the line coming to their trucks. Soon the engines started turning over, and the last shouts of "Everybody on, stand by, stand by" died under the sounds of the trucks.

At first we just crept along, moving and then stopping and starting up again, but soon the ride was steady and the road widened. We sat back in the trucks, most of us with our helmets off, taking advantage of the breeze. I had taken my pack off and stood looking over the side of the truck at whatever we passed. I lifted my rifle and casually pointed it out; already we seemed to be an easy target.

In a while we passed through a village where the young girls were beautiful and wore bright colors, greens and reds. They stood watching the trucks go by. Some waved and answered our calls of "Hey, sweetheart, ya want to go for a ride? I'll be back, just wait right there. Hey, baby, what's your name?"

The village was big and clean, with shops, street corners, and buildings. It was not like the villages we searched in the fields, the ones out in the middle of the greens and browns. Nameless to our minds, sameness to our eyes and noses. Their people were all one face.

We moved through the village and out onto the road again, and the noon hour was left behind. Somehow I could always find the far colors of the land so beautiful, so peaceful to my passing soul.

We began pulling into Tam Ky, which was like a little city, with paved streets, streetlights, even policemen directing the convoy through intersections. Everything was clean, and the women were beautiful. We left our calls behind but kept their smiles in our minds.

We went through the city and pulled into a large soccer field that seemed to be guarded by the South Vietnamese Army. These guys always looked funny; they were very small people but had been given American helmets, which fell down over their faces. Some of them had this thing about wearing brightly colored scarfs around their necks— red, orange, yellow, all kinds of colors. They looked like little toy soldiers with big guns.

"*Stand by.*" The word came as we unloaded the trucks and formed into our platoons and squads. Each platoon took a little section of the field, then each squad took its space. We had taken our packs and helmets off and just sat or lay in the grass.

"*Stand by. Stand by,*" the word kept coming.

The rumors started having a party, dancing all over the place, but the word kept coming to stand by, and soon to chow down. Eating in the grass was like having a little picnic. Some of us were laughing and clowning around; some seemed to eat, then think of green grass in their long time ago.

Vernon was quiet, Hut and Steve had not said much either.

The word finally came down that we were not going in until morning. Evening came. I remember watching the colors in the far sky—I watched them fade. The night was easy: small talk, then sleep.

The morning came quickly, faster than the sun.

"*Let's go, people. Get 'em up, squad leaders. Get your people up. Pass the word, chow down and stand by.*"

The morning had a subtle haste in all its moments. Words were quickly spoken; things that were reached for were grabbed at. A quiet buzzing hum hovered in the air, then over the field and within us when it became choppers in the sky.

"*Saddle up, saddle up. Get your people saddled up. Get 'em in lines, choppers comin' in. Let's go . . .*"

As soon as I heard the choppers overhead, they began landing like a swarm of bees. I was yelling and looking back over my shoulder. "Stay close, stay close to me. Make sure we get the same chopper."

Everything was spinning like the chopper's blades. Sounds and shouts flew through the air. I kept my eyes on Watts, watched for his hand to move, to signal.

"Okay, let's go. Let's go," I shouted back to the squad, then I was running to the chopper, only slowing to look back, make sure we were all together. We climbed in and settled into our space. Quickly we climbed into the sky, then seemed to circle. The door gunner sat looking outboard with his hands on the gun. Like a flock of birds, we seemed to come out of our circle and soar off into the sky.

I could see green hills with gray morning mist bulging in the coming sky. Between them, in their valleys and so silently, dark satiny rice-paddy water sparkled through the gray mist.

I always looked inside the chopper at the faces near me. Sometimes they could be blurred, with quick-moving eyes, twitching and searching. Then other times, maybe just moments, the faces could still, become portraits. Wind-blown faces colored with fear and etched in silence. Shadowed lines would curve, soft browns become a face and never be browns again. Dark eyes would give and then leave a look, creating a time without moments. I'd turn from the faces and try to see my own, look at me. Then I'd turn away from me too.

No one said it was time. I knew, when the chopper started dipping its nose to the ground, then circling. The door guns opened up, and the report of the rapid blasting shook the inside of the chopper.

I shifted in my seat, leaned so I could look down, then turned and shouted, *"Get ready. Lock and load. Lock and load."*

I could see the tops of trees, then green grass and water waving and rippling from the chopper's wind. I kept looking down until the water splashed up as we landed.

"Let's go. Let's go!" I yelled, jumping out of the chopper and into the muddy water. I started running and looking around for a place to set the gun up, but I watched for quick flashes coming from all I could see. I listened for the breaking of the air or the cracking of gunfire trying to sneak in beneath the loud roar of the choppers.

"Come on. Come on," I kept yelling, and started pointing ahead to a wide rice-paddy dike. *"Vern, there. Set up there."*

I reached the dike and dove to the ground. Quickly I looked ahead, then turned and signaled to Vernon to set the gun up. Then I turned back and kept searching all I could see—the near treeline, its shadows, then the far openness of the rice paddy, the far greens of hills.

I could hear Vernon coming, then feel the thump as he hit the ground. Quickly I turned to him and shouted, *"Switch belts. Get a long one in. Cover that fuckin' treeline."*

I signaled to Steve and Hut, then shouted, *"Spread out some. Keep down."*

The choppers were still coming in, splashing in the rice-paddy water. Shouts and sputtering chopper sounds filled the air, but around me it was quiet. The shadows in the treeline were silent. I was trying to get my breath, wipe the sweat from my eyes, but I was still looking around.

"Shit."

I looked behind me and could not see third platoon, then I could not see Watts. We were to hook up with them, then move out with their column.

I turned to Vernon and shouted through the noise behind me, "This is fucked up. I don't see third platoon. They're supposed to take this side of the LZ. Shit. Maybe we're on the wrong side. Fuck it, we'll stay here."

"What do you think?" I could hear Vernon asking.

"It's too fuckin' quiet. I know damn well they know we're here." I could whisper now; the choppers were leaving.

Vernon was silent for a moment, then I heard him saying, "I think if they were going to hit us, they would have by now. What ya think?"

"I don't know, man, it's fuckin' quiet. Maybe they're still settin' up."

I kept looking at the treeline, then trying to see beyond the end of the rice paddy. I looked for a village, but I could only see more greens and shades beneath trees. Nothing moved.

I turned back to Vernon and took a deep sigh, then said, "Shit, this pack is heavy. Man, I ain't lookin' forward to runnin' all through this shit with this fuckin' thing on." Then I twisted so I could see Steve and Hut. They lay still, with their rifles pointing out beyond the dike. I could see some guys from second platoon moving in beside them, but I still could not see third platoon.

Fuck it.

I lit a cigarette and looked back into the treeline. Something wasn't right, but whatever it was, I was pushing it away. I was still, but my mind kept racing. I felt okay about what was out there; I felt it wouldn't come now, but I felt open. It didn't have a damn thing to do with the shadows in the trees, a burst of gunfire fucking with us. It wasn't about taking a chance. Maybe it was about not having one.

I heard Hut yell over, "I think we're movin' out."

I turned and looked over my shoulder. I could see the company forming into a column, then I could see Watts coming toward us, gesturing. I waited until he neared, then I could hear him saying, "Fall in with third platoon, they'll be movin' up in a bit." I stuck my thumb up so he knew I understood.

The company was passing now, trudging through the sticky rice-paddy mud and heading for the path on the other side. I relaxed as they moved past, then out in front of us. I could see third platoon coming by.

I got to my feet, took a deep breath, then just said, "Come on, let's go. The show's started."

I could hear the shouts from the guys in third platoon as they waved and beckoned to us to join them. "Come on, you guys. Welcome to Disneyland, wonderful world of fuckin' color."

We were on the path now, and on the move. On one side was an open area with scattered rice paddies. On the other side, small sloping hills with bushes and small trees hovered over our shoulders. From time to time bursts of distant gunfire could be heard, but we kept moving.

The sun was high; sweat was soaking my face. Every few steps I'd wipe my eyes, squint, and watch near and far again. We were passing through a small open area, and I could see the guys up front pointing to something on the ground. As I neared, I saw them. At first I just saw a different color, black, lying on the ground. As I got closer I could see the black and the red of blood splattered over the ground. Three or four dead VC lay along the path. One lay face down; the back of his black shirt was ripped open, and blood still seeped from its shreds. One of the others lay twisted, with his arms and legs tangled. We moved on past them, but not without leaving our shouts of "They dead? No, they just fuckin' sleepin'."

"Get down. Get down."

The gunfire came quickly from up in front of the column, then shouts followed—*"Move up. Move 'em up"*—as the bursts of fire kept coming.

I turned and looked back at Vernon, then at Steve and Hut, signaling to stay down, but now we were moving quickly, running up the path, then up into the hills. The path was steep, slippery. When I got to the top of a hill, I stopped and reached for Vernon's hand. The gun was heavy, twenty-five pounds, all day long. Two thousand rounds of ammo were in his pack with the rest of the shit. I yelled back to Steve and Hut, "Come on, stick close to the gun." Then I turned and ran to catch up. The hill was leveling off some, but the path was still sloping and thick with bush. We zigzagged through the bush but could not get around the thorns.

"Hold up. Hold up. Spread out. Stay on line."

I was kneeling, trying to catch my breath. Through the sweat in my eyes, I could see a shallow valley below and thick bushes on the next hill. I turned back to Vernon; sweat was pouring out of his face and dripping down onto the gun. Steve and Hut were panting like hot dogs. I could hear the word coming down the column: we were going into the assault. We were going down through the valley and up the next hill.

"Move out. Stay on line. Let's go."

We started down the hill and kept going through the sounds of gunfire. Sometimes you could see ahead, but most of the time the bush was thick and all you could see were the green leaves and brown branches that swung back in your face when you tried to push them away. The gunfire was coming and going, but you couldn't tell where it was coming from, except when our automatics opened up.

At the bottom of the hill was a clearing and a dry creekbed. I shouted to Vernon and the others to spread out and run through the clearing. I started up the embankment; the ground was slippery and steep. I struggled up as fast as I could, grabbing branches to pull myself up. I slowed, stared, then kept going. Three, four, maybe more dead VC lay twisted up in the thick, thorny bushes. One I could only see the legs of, but they were not moving.

It was hard getting the gun up the hill. I slid back down some and grabbed Vernon by the shoulder and started pulling; then, staying in my spot, I got Steve and Hut up. The top of the hill was thinner—the bushes were spread out, small trees were only here and there. We were on the move again.

"Guns up. Guns up," I could hear Watts calling.

"Let's go. Stay close," I was shouting.

The sound of our gunfire was all over the place.

I could see Watts just ahead. As I got closer, I kept yelling to him, "Where do you want us?"

He was kneeling and pointing over the hill. I flung myself to the ground, and when I heard Vernon coming up behind me, I twisted around and yelled, "Set up here, set it up!"

I looked back to where Watts was pointing. I couldn't see anything—no flashes of fire coming out of the treeline on the other hill. Then I saw movement in the far valley. Twenty or thirty VC were crossing a rice paddy and running toward the far treeline.

"Vern, there. See? There at the end of the paddy, see? Three hundred yards, ten o'clock, see?" I was rushing my words, then crawling closer to Vernon. His face was tight against the sights of the gun. He was shifting the barrel and twisting with his aim.

"Ya ready?" I shouted.

"Yeah."

"Fire!"

The gun started blasting, filling all the air around us with its cracking sounds. I looked at the rice paddy. The VC were splashing through the water and nearing the treeline, with bullets kicking up behind them.

"Up some, Vern. Get it up some," I shouted.

Three or four VC just dropped in the water. Some of the others turned and tried to help the ones that had dropped. Then they went down. Some tried to get back up, but they kept on getting hit. The others were racing into the treeline.

"Shift up, Vern, shift up, get in the treeline."

With all the sounds, the cracking and blasting of guns, there was still the far silence, the quiet twisting and jerking of the VC in the water.

"Cease fire. Cease fire . . ." The shouts came down the line, then the quick word followed, *"Let's go, move out."*

We got the gun up, put a fresh belt of ammo in, then went down the hill and up the slope of the next. The firing had ceased; the silence was still. Shouts became whispers. We moved slower.

"All shit," I whispered to Vernon, then signaled to Steve and Hut to spread out. From the distances this had looked like the rest of the hills, thick bushes and small trees. Now it was different. I could see neatly dug holes and trenches; I could see worn paths weaving from hole to hole.

I looked at Vernon. Like the distant hill we were on, his face had changed. His eyes had widened and seemed not to see what he was looking at. I shouted quickly, "Hey, watch where ya step!" I watched for his eyes to come to mine, but they didn't. I could have said lots of things, but I didn't know what to say or if anything was right to say. Vernon may have been just hot, tired.

We had never talked about killing—we joked about it, but we had not taken it apart. I'd push it away, bury the shit in my mind, put it with the blue shirt. Wouldn't talk about it.

"Hey, Vern. Vern, ya want Hut or Steve to carry the gun for a while?"

Vernon was silent, then shook his head.

"Hold up. Get down," the shouts came, and then there was a stillness. I could see a couple guys crawling up a small mound, their rifles pointing into a shadowed circle.

"What the fuck's going on?" I heard Steve asking.

"Stay down. Looks like a fuckin' bunker or somethin'," I whispered back, turning to the bunker. One guy scooted up to the hole, swung his arm as if he were tossing a softball, then quickly backed away and scrambled off the mound.

"Get down. Heads down."

It was silent. Then the air fizzled, the ground shook, and dirt came flying as the grenade exploded. I raised my head, pointed my rifle toward the mound. White smoke was curling out of the ground.

"Anyone in there?" Hut whispered over to me.

"Beats the fuck out of me. Ya want to crawl in and find out?"

Hut started smiling, but his eyes were big and tense. I spoke quickly. "Anyone in there won't be coming out."

We searched the hill and its holes. Someone found a bunch of rice hidden under a big flat rock that was covering a hole. We blew the rice up; it blew through the air. A couple more bunkers were found, but they were all empty. We blew them anyway. Then the word came to move out and we went to the next hill, but it was just a hill. We searched it all the same, then moved on.

The hills became smaller and flatter on top. The bushes were not as thick, and we formed back into a long column. Everybody was soaked with sweat, and everything was hot. After a while we stopped and spread out for chow. We stopped on top of a hill we had just searched. Someone had bombed the hill, or hit the hell out of it with artillery. It was full of shell craters, and most of the trees had been burned or ripped apart.

When we stopped, I didn't. I stood still, but it felt like I was still going. The sweat kept rolling down my face. I saw some shade under a piece of a tree and moved toward it. I got my pack off and just sat for a while before I started digging some chow out of my pack.

Vernon still had not said too much. I glanced at him; his face was just sweat and silence. Steve and Hut were quiet but getting their chow cans opened. I got some water, then got my chow out and ate quickly.

Vernon started talking.

"You notice anything strange?" he asked.

"Huh?"

"You notice anything strange—you know?"

I didn't know what Vernon was thinking about. I just shrugged my shoulders.

"There's no people around, anyplace," he said, and he waited for me to say something. I hadn't thought about it. The last people we had seen who weren't dead or running from us were back at Tam Ky. I thought about it for a second, then said, "Yeah, maybe the motherfuckers had sense enough to get the fuck away from here."

Hut yelled over, "Shit, Vernon, if you didn't have to be here, would ya?"

I smiled. Vernon got a smile on his face too, then said, "No, I mean, like when we were on Snaggletooth, remember?"

I knew what he was getting to. When there was no sign of people working out in the paddies or carrying shit around, it was a good sign that the area was filled with VC somewhere. I didn't want to think about that now. I tried to make a joke, laugh the shit off. I laughed and said, "Maybe the motherfuckers are out partying somewhere, ya know?"

Vernon laughed a little and we got to talking about something.

Soon the word came to saddle up, and the packs were slung back on. We were on the move again, searching hills, up and down. We got sniped at a few times but kept going. Distant gunfire would come and go. Sometimes it was heavy, and we knew one of the other companies might be getting fucked up.

I didn't know how long the day had been until it began to vanish and we moved on into its evening. The greens and browns started turning into their gray and black shit.

As night fell, we settled down on top of a hill, spread the positions out, and circled ourselves against the dark. We set the gun up on the side of the hill. In the late evening I had seen a large rice paddy that looked like a lake, and then it became dark and just part of the night. Below the gun, right down over the hill, bush, weeds, and small trees became anything you wanted them to be—crouching creatures, dead men coming back, some shit from long ago that always scared you.

I had taken my shirt off but kept my sleeveless sweatshirt on, and I was just sitting behind the gun with Vernon when I heard Watts's voice.

"How you guys holdin' up?" he asked, then said, "CO says everybody did a good job today. We got about twelve confirmed kills. We got about seven or eight of that VC platoon out in the rice paddy. Three-three got a lot of action in their area—they got about fifty confirmed kills, but they lost about ten guys, took about twenty wounded. This place is hot—keep fifty percent watch tonight."

"What's the word for tomorrow?" I asked.

"They're flyin' in another battalion in the morning," Watts said. He sighed a little, then said, "We should make contact with the main force tomorrow."

When Watts left, I went over to Steve and Hut's position. "How you guys doin'?" I asked as I found a place to sit for a bit. They had cleared out an area about ten feet from the gun and dug a shallow hole.

Hut just stared out into the night, but Steve asked, "What do you think?"

"I don't know. Watts says another battalion is comin' tomorrow. He says the word is we should make contact with the main force of 'em."

Hut looked away from the dark and asked, "Where the fuck they at?"

"I don't know, man. Three-three ran into some of 'em. They got about fifty of 'em, but they lost some guys. Watts said they lost about ten, twelve guys and had about twenty wounded."

Hut sighed and said, "Fuck," then turned back to the dark. We sat quietly for a while and whispered small talk, simple stuff that didn't mean a damn thing, shit you didn't have to think about, some things you could find some laughs in. Then I had to say, "Listen, if the shit goes down tomorrow, stay close to the gun. Keep your heads down—no silly shit, none of that hero crap. If I get it, Vernon moves up. Steve, you take the gun . . ."

As I moved back to the gun, I could still see Steve's and Hut's faces in my mind, then the faces of ten or twelve guys I didn't even know. Maybe didn't want to know.

Vernon was sitting up behind the gun, looking out over its barrel. He turned and seemed to shudder when he heard me.

"Just me," I whispered.

I sat beside the gun and just stared out for a while. The stars weren't out yet. Staring was just listening for what you couldn't see. I heard Vernon ask, "Ya think we'll be back before Christmas?"

It was small talk, but good talk. I laughed a little and answered, "Damn, Vernon, you over there thinkin' about Christmas? Shit, Christmas is three weeks away. I hope the fuck we're back." I think I was still smiling when I asked, "This your first Christmas away?"

"No, I was in boot camp last one," Vernon said. "I thought I might get home this year, but I guess not. I know next year I'm going to be there. I don't care where I'm stationed."

His voice lowered in the dark. He was silent for a moment, then asked if I had been home the previous year for Christmas. As I answered, I could see Christmas at home, but I was saying, "No, we were down in Puerto Rico, we were out in the fuckin' field Christmas Eve. I remember that shit. We got in late that night. Christmas Day it rained like hell. New Year's wasn't bad, we went over to San Juan. I thought I'd be home this year, till this shit popped up. Man, but this time next year, I'll be as short as hell. I'll have about a month to go, then goodbye to this shit."

Vernon asked, "You goin' back to Pittsburgh?"

"I don't know yet. Been thinkin' about school, but I don't know yet. I like traveling—I just don't know. I just want to get away somewhere, ya know, and just take some time and think without havin' to be here, there. Hey, what's it like in Florida, ya know, for Christmas? It didn't seem like Christmas down in Puerto Rico—damn hot and all."

Vernon laughed a little and said, "It's always hot in Florida. Christmas is Christmas—lots of parties. A lot of my friends went to school. They all come home, we party a lot. But mostly I just like to be home, be around my mom and them." He was quiet for a moment, then said, "Unless you're home, it don't seem like Christmas."

I heard myself say, "Yeah, man."

We sat quietly for a while, listening and looking into the night. Sometimes you could forget it was all around you, but you couldn't forget to look at it, keep staring at it.

Some days and years I can't remember, some moments I'll never forget.

"Hey, Vern."

"Huh?"

"You okay, you know, about tomorrow?"

"Yeah. I pray. I believe in God."

I thought about home, Homewood and Sundays. I could see things I didn't want to look at now, didn't want to feel. God and me had this thing, and sometimes it wasn't the same thing. Sometimes I'd want him around, thought he was here somewhere. Sometimes I didn't want him around, gettin' in my head and seein' the shit I was thinkin'. I wasn't thinking about it and wouldn't realize it for a while, but tomorrow was Sunday.

Vernon took first watch.

I pulled my poncho off my pack, wrapped my hand around my rifle, and covered us both up. I don't know when sleep came; it was probably quick. Sleep could bring things that weren't real, like peace and that kind of stuff.

When Vernon woke me, the night was cooler and darker. I asked if everything was quiet, then crawled up behind the gun. I took a grenade out of my pocket and set it beside the gun, then reached my hand out until my fingers could feel the trigger grip. I rested my hand on the gun's grip and looked out into the darkness. I could see down over the hill some, but only enough to separate the different shades of the night. I tilted the barrel down a little.

It was quiet.

I knew it was out there. I wasn't afraid of death, I was afraid of not living. Death was around all the time; in a way I guess we were a part of it. Living was distant, like distant things you loved and were but couldn't touch. I was afraid I would feel living again. I didn't want to die, but I didn't want to beg death, crawl from it and let it chase me for the rest of my life. I didn't want the flies in my fuckin' blood either.

The night weakened, and I watched faint rays of light glisten on the water in the rice paddy. It was pretty, the grays with the yellows, the darks with the blues. I waited for a while, then woke Vernon and checked on Steve and Hut and told them to chow down and be ready to move out.

The morning was quiet.

After chow, we just stayed at our little shallow holes waiting on the word to move out. I smoked a few cigarettes and tried to think of nothing. Vernon was quiet too. I didn't know what he was thinking, I didn't ask. I had this thing, I'd think about shit until it was time to get in it, then I'd just say, "Fuck it." Then try to feel what I just said.

Fuck it.

"Saddle up, we're moving out. Saddle up."

We slung the heavy packs back on, grabbed the gun and all the ammo, and joined the column with third platoon. We were moving in the same direction we had the day before. The bushes were thick again as we searched the hills, and before long the sweat was covering my face.

"Hold up. Hold up. Get 'em held up," the shouts came quick and loud.

I was kneeling on one knee, trying to get my breath and looking to see what was going on. I could hear distant fire, but it was far to our rear. The captain and lieutenants had gathered. I could see them talking and pointing; the field radios were blaring.

"Turn 'em around, turn 'em around. Get the point in. Squad leaders, get your people turned around. Move it."

"Something up," I heard Hut say. Then he shouted to me, "What's going on?"

I said to him and Steve, "When we move, keep close to the gun." I told Vernon, "Put the long belt in now, before we get moving. Sounds like the shit's startin'."

"Let's go. Let's go."

We started walking fast, then the word came to move faster and we started running. Everything began speeding. Shouts flew through the air, blurs of greens and browns sped the other way. We ran back over the hills we had just searched. The sound of gunfire filled the air and the thump of explosions shook our stride.

The sweat kept rolling in my eyes; everything was blurry. I kept looking over my shoulder, yelling, "Come on, come on!" I was slowing; each step became a push, a stretch. I didn't give a fuck about the thorns, couldn't feel their stings and burns anymore.

"Hold up, hold up. Spread out, get down."

I fell to my knees and signaled to Vernon to stay close, get down. Then I looked for Steve and Hut and signaled to them to spread out and stay down. We were on the same hill we had slept on; I could see the spot where we had dug the shallow hole.

The gunfire was heavy; machine guns were blasting, and rifles were popping down over the hill. I could see Watts and the lieutenant crouching and looking over the hill toward the big rice paddy.

"Guns up. Machine guns up," Watts called.

"Let's go," I yelled, and ran, crouching low to the ground. I kept my eyes on Watts, then shouted, "Where ya want us?" But I could tell by the look on his face that he didn't know. He signaled for us to hold up and get down.

There was no silence; everything had a sound. The guns were blasting all over, field radios blared, faint cries of "Corpsman, corpsman" filled the air. I kept down, looking and watching Watts, waiting for his signal, not wanting it to come.

"Incoming, incoming. Down, down . . ."

The air cracked open, the ground shook. Mortar rounds were hitting the hill. I was shaking. I turned to Vernon. Through the sweat on his face, his eyes just stared. I could see Steve and Hut; they were close together, almost covering each other as they lay on the ground. I was signaling now, taking my hand and waving it up and down, telling them to stay down.

Watts was pointing to me, signaling me to come up. I crawled, and when I was close enough, I could see his sweaty face. His eyes kept shifting back over his shoulder to the rice paddy below the hill. "Listen up," he said. "They got that company pinned down in the rice paddy. There in that hill over there, they got a lot of heavy stuff. We're going in. First and third platoons are going in, second in reserve. When the word comes, move down the side of the fuckin' hill, cross the path, hold up at the edge of the paddy. Keep it spread out down there. Wait for the word."

I crawled back to Vernon, then signaled to Steve and Hut to follow me. We crawled over to the bushes on the side of the hill. I could see down into the rice paddy and the path below. Bullets were splashing in the water and kicking up the dirt on the path below. Then I saw them, the guys in the other company. I could see them trying to fire over the dikes, see them trying to drag bodies through the muddy water. I could see bodies lying in the water and up against the dikes. Some were covered with ponchos; others were just lying still.

We were in a thick clump of bushes. I whispered, "Spread it out. Listen up, now. When we get the word, we're going down and across the path. We'll set up at the edge of the paddy. Move quick, man—keep the fuck spread out."

I took a cigarette out and lit it. I could see my hands shaking. Then everything was shaking inside of me, and I could barely feel the cigarette in my fingers. It felt light, like it wasn't there.

"Incoming, incoming. Down, down . . ."

Everything was breaking apart. The fucking mortars were tearing up the path below. Dirt and fragments were flying through the air, and the sound of water splashing and cries for the corpsman followed.

I lowered my face close to the ground. I could smell the dirt, see the little rocks and pebbles beneath my face, but I could still hear the shouts of *"Incoming"* and the cries for the corpsman.

"Jesus fuckin' Christ!" I heard Steve yell.

"Shut up, man," I shouted back.

I couldn't see Vernon's face, but I could see his hands over the gun;

they were quivering. Shit was going away—greens, dirt, smell, all that shit was going away and leaving me. I didn't want to be alone. All this shit around me—screams, shouts, bursting ground—and I'm alone.

Shit.

"Move out, let's go, move out. Get across the path," Watts screamed.

"Let's go, move down," I shouted. Then I stood and wove down through the bushes. When I was near the path I slowed, looked back at Vernon, looked over at Steve and Hut. A moment passed. I wanted to keep it.

"Okay, let's go. Let's go," I yelled.

I was running down the rest of the hill, out onto the path, holding one breath. I ran past moments standing still, through dirt and shit flying. I could see the blurry green of the grass and bush just ahead on the other side of the path.

It was green now. I was lying in the grass and looking back over my shoulder, yelling, "Come on, come on. Hurry up." I saw Vernon coming and was looking for Steve and Hut.

"Over here, hurry. Come on, damnit." I could see them running, coming to my side and then thumping against the ground. "Stay down, keep your heads down."

Through the thin grass and weeds I could see the distant hill and its quick sparks and flashes, then the big splashes in the water every time a fucking mortar hit. I looked at Vernon and caught his eyes staring at me.

"You okay, man, you okay?" I muttered.

"Yeah."

I looked around. I could see the other platoons staging, spreading out, getting ready for the move across the paddy. I checked out Steve and Hut, then looked back at the hill. There was nothing left to say. Beneath all the sounds, we waited quietly.

"Move out, third platoon, move out."

I looked at Vernon, then down at Steve and Hut, took a deep breath, and shouted, *"Let's go. Stay close to the gun."*

I got up, tightened myself inside, and started running out into the paddy.

The water was deep, sometimes coming up past my knees. They were on us already—their fucking bullets were splashing in the water around us. We just kept going.

As we got closer to the guys from the other company, I could see green boots sticking out from beneath ponchos. As I passed, I could see hands lying in the mud and the frozen stares on the faces that weren't covered. One guy, whoever he was, lay against the dike. His head was back, his face looking up to the sky. His whole chest looked like a swamp of blood. Another guy leaned against the dike with his hands folded in his lap. I thought he was alive until I saw his face.

We kept moving through the water, over the dikes, and into the water again. I could hear near cries for the corpsman. I looked to the side; some guy down the line was staggering, falling. I turned away and kept going, kept running through the water and waiting.

We reached a wide dike, got down behind it, and set the gun up. I searched ahead, shouted, "Vern, there at the bottom of the hill. See? Fire!"

I watched, looking for the bullets hitting. Vernon kept blasting. Incoming fire started kicking up all around us. We ducked, got down behind the dike, then fired again.

We moved to the next dike. Bullets were hitting the water like raindrops. I could feel every drip of time, every wet splashing inch of each step. I could hear it coming down, breaking the air above me. I could hear its quick wind-curling sound, the distant faint cry of *"Incoming."* I couldn't stop running, couldn't duck. Everything stilled, froze. It all became quiet; the gunfire, the yells and shouts, were far away. The only thing I could hear was the mortar round falling in front of me. The water splashed up in my face, but it was still silent. I kept running, bracing myself and waiting for the big cracking sound, for all the hot burning metal to blow up in my face. I kept running. Then I could hear the sounds of fire again, the shouts of *"Keep moving"* and the screams of *"Corpsman, Corpsman!"* I kept going, leaving one mortar round stuck in the mud. A dud? Or still waiting to explode?

Every fucking thing was loose, breaking up into little motherfucking pieces, dirt and blood flying in the same fucking air. I could hear guys getting hit, see them falling out of the corner of my eye, other guys reaching for them and dragging them out of the water.

I reached the next dike and started firing into the treeline. Vernon was hot on the gun; we were trying to tear up all of the hill, kill the sparks and flashes coming from it. The VC had a heavy machine gun firing down on us. Its rounds were chopping through the mud dikes.

We moved on.

We ran, skipped some of the dikes, and got closer to the hill. We could see into its shadows now. I was pointing, firing, and marking targets. Then shouting, *"Vern, in there. In there, Vern. Up some, yeah."*

Shit.

We both ducked as a zinging bullet went right between our heads. Vernon looked at me and sighed. One of us said, "That was too fuckin' close." Then both of us laughed—not that funny laugh, the other laugh. That one when there ain't nothin' funny, that one you can hide your real shit behind.

We moved up again, got closer. Vernon was on the gun, blasting. My eyes were on the hill, looking, firing, looking. It smashed into my face; my head shook and jerked back. Everything was hot, my neck was burning. I tried to breathe but couldn't. I started gagging and trying to turn to Vernon, but my neck felt ripped, as if it were tearing more when I tried to turn. I got my hand to my face and neck, then looked at it. It was full of blood. And the blood was still dripping into it. I looked down at my chest, and all I could see was blood.

I tried to yell, to tell Vernon, "I'm hit," but I couldn't. I kept gagging, crying in my mind, screaming in there. I wanted to change this, make it go away. I saw Mom, could see her eyes, her smile, wanted to see the kids. Wanted to be just me again. Not this shit.

Words came out. "Vern, I'm hit. I'm hit."

Vernon stopped firing and turned to me. His mouth flew open, his eyes widened and froze.

I pointed and muttered, "Keep firin', keep firin'."

He turned and screamed, *"Corpsman, corpsman!"*

Watts came splashing through the water and grabbed me and pulled me down behind the dike. He looked at me, whispered, "Hold on, hold on," then turned and also screamed, *"Corpsman, corpsman!"*

I could feel the blood running down my chest. I kept getting hot; my neck was burning. I wanted it to stop. I wanted to breathe, but I couldn't stop gagging. Watts was holding me so I would not slide into the water. He slid me closer to the dike. I could see his face now; he was whispering in my ear, then watching my eyes. I could hear him saying, "Listen. Listen carefully. Take your finger and press down right here."

He was taking my finger and placing it in my neck. He kept saying, "Keep your finger pressed down here. Keep it pressed down. You hear? The corpsman will get here soon."

He was closer now, leaning over my face and whispering, "Hold on, the corpsman will get to you. Keep your finger there. Don't move it, you'll bleed to death. I'm sorry, we got to leave you."

I shook my head. I had to tell the look on his face that I understood they had to move on.

"*Let's go,*" Watts yelled.

I watched Vernon grab the gun. He looked at me, then quickly turned and moved on. Hut and Steve looked over, then went over the dike.

I was lying deep in the water; only my chest and head were sticking out. My whole body started shaking and feeling hot. Each time I breathed or my heart beat, I could feel a gushing sound in my neck and I shook more.

It was time.

I couldn't wait. I didn't think I had time to wait.

"Dear God, please bless my family. Please take care of them. Bless my mother and Harry. Please bless Sherry and Stacy. Please take care of them, be with them. I have no regrets, come what may . . ."

As I prayed, I could see the faces of my home, the people in me who were so far away. I kept my finger pressed down in my neck. Everything seemed quieter, but the bullets were still smashing into the dike and zinging through the air.

I was trying not to shake. I didn't want to die, but I didn't want to shake. I was still hot, but the water was cold and I started shaking anyway. My finger could just feel slippery stuff inside my neck. I knew there was a hole there, I could feel stuff that felt like raw meat. My finger kept slipping. I knew it had moved from the spot. I tried to put it back, but I couldn't find the right spot and dug into something else inside my neck. Whatever it was, when I touched it, my whole face raged with pain and I shook more.

I didn't want to close my eyes, so I stared into the sky. It was pale blue with thin white clouds. The clouds seemed to be moving, just drifting by. I watched the clouds. I could still hear the gunfire, I'd flinch when the bullets hit the dike or zinged right over, but I watched the clouds. I guess I was looking for peace.

I heard the water splashing and leaned toward its sound. I could see someone coming. As he neared, he dropped to his knees and looked at my neck, saying, "Hold on, pal, we'll get you outta here, just hold on."

He spoke quickly, flinging a thin bandage over my neck. Then he took my finger and put it back on the right spot. He looked at me, sighed, and said, "Listen, we'll get you out. I'll be back. Hold on."

The corpsman moved on over the dike and into the sounds of the gunfire and the cries of "Corpsman, corpsman." I tried not to breathe too hard, tried not to think at all. I'd think of home, but I didn't want to think of home. When I thought of home, when I thought of how it was going to hurt them if I died, it hurt. It would hurt them so much, and they would cry.

I kept watching the sky. It was turning from blue to gray. I knew it was too early for evening; I didn't think noon had come yet. But the sky weakened from the blue and rain began to fall. At first it was just drops, then it just started pouring down. It started raining in my neck, and I had to turn from it. The water made the wound sting.

Time would come and bring its thoughts, and they'd bring fears. Then time would go away, but it would come back again, find me just wanting to live, but mostly waiting to die. I was cold and numb, and I thought the colder I got, the closer I was to death. As if life were the warm stuff and I couldn't feel it anymore.

The rain slowed, maybe even stopped, but the gunfire kept coming. I could still hear the shouts and cries for the corpsman. Then the sounds of planes and choppers, and artillery soaring through the sky. The dike shook with the blast. The gunfire slowed, then started back up again.

I wanted to talk to somebody, but not myself. I wanted Vern and the others to come back so we could get out of this shit. I knew they'd come and get me, wouldn't go back without me. But maybe I'd be dead. I wanted to say some things, but knew no one would hear me. I started to shake again, but I stilled myself. I did not want to die shaking.

I did not know and could not think about it, but as evening neared, the eleventh hour of this shit was passing. The rain came again, and everything around me turned gray. The gunfire died down, then burst open again. Then it slowed to almost sniper fire as night came.

I heard voices coming through the gray fog that was now creeping about. They came closer, and I heard, "Got one here. Here's one, he still alive?"

I raised my hand, trying to wave. I heard a voice saying, "Yeah, he's still alive."

Splashes and voices neared; there were guys coming. They looked like shadows in the fog, ghostly. They were strangers from a different company, but they said, "Hey, buddy, you all right? We got to get you out of here. We're fallin' back."

A big dark shadow came out of the fog. I knew who it was, and he came to me, saying, "Come on, man, Ah'm gettin' ya outta here wit me." Franko leaned over and reached for me.

I tried to move but felt numb and weak as I tried to get out of the water. I could hear one of the other guys saying, "Watch it, looks like he lost a lot of blood." Franko grabbed my shoulders and began pulling me.

When I stood, I was dizzy, weak, and shivering. I looked back over the dike and into the misty fog hovering about. I could barely see the hill or the treeline; all I could see was patches of fire burning through the dark gray fog. Closer, I could see the ghostly figures of the platoons and squads coming back through the water. Some walked, looking back over their shoulders; others were helping one another, or dragging wounded and dead in their arms. I could hear moans of pain and cries of "Hold on, man, I got ya . . ."

"Where's guns? Where's Vernon and them?" I asked as I saw someone from third platoon passing. The guy I asked just shook his head and said he didn't know.

"Anybody seen guns? Anybody seen Vernon and them?" I asked again as others passed. Someone passing answered, "He's dead—they got it back there."

I just stood, staring into the mist and the fires. I saw his eyes looking at me, and I wasn't there.

"Come on, man. We gots ta get out of here," I heard Franko saying, and I felt his hand gently pull on my arm. I turned away and began wading through the water. Some guy, some sergeant I knew, was being dragged. He kept shaking, gasping, and his arms fell limp. I was walking all right, and when I slowed, Franko was there. I had to keep looking back.

We reached the path where we had started, which was now filled with dead and wounded. I could hear the moans coming from the darkness. I moved closer to the group of wounded. A corpsman or someone put a blanket over me, then got me down.

I saw Glickman lying there in the rain and the dark. I knew it was him, so I moved closer. I stared. His face was all bloody, but I kept looking and then I could see him fight for a breath, shake some, then still again. I asked a corpsman how he was doing. The corpsman looked up at me and shook his head, then whispered, "He's pretty bad." Then he looked at my neck and pointed down the path, saying, "Battalion got an aid station down the path some. Can you make it down there?"

The path was dark, and as it curved, I could see into a small clearing I was passing. I stared only for a moment, then turned away. All I had seen was dead guys lying in the rain and muddy water.

I went to the other side of the path. A corpsman came out of the dark, looked at me, then looked into my neck. He whispered, "Man, we can't do nothin' now. We'll get you out of here in the morning." He pointed through the dark, then whispered, "You can get over there. Try and keep still, get some rest."

I heard guys moaning, and one guy was calling for his mother. I went and sat by a stump of a tree and pulled the blanket over my shoulders. I saw someone else sitting without a blanket, just staring into the rain. I knew his silence.

"Rayburn, Rayburn, you okay? Huh, you okay?"

Rayburn was silent.

"Hey, man, did ya get hit? You okay?"

Rayburn kept staring into the rain, but I could hear him saying, "Everybody got fucked. Everybody got fucked. They all got fucked . . ."

"Did ya get hit? You okay?"

Rayburn shook his head. He had not been hit, but I knew he was hurting as he hid in the dark with the dead and the wounded.

I just sat and shook from the cold rain. Sometimes I'd try to jerk myself back to feeling like me, but I couldn't. I'd get dizzy, feel I was falling over, could see myself sitting in the rain, but I wasn't in me. I was floating in different dark colors, and I didn't know who I was, what I was, and I couldn't get back to me. When I heard noises, I'd flinch and look around.

Shouts and whispers came through the dark. Guys who weren't wounded were out on the perimeter, along the path. I could see them passing, shifting positions, then they'd vanish into the dark again. Except for the rain and moans and whispers, it was quiet. A waiting quiet.

I tried to sleep, but I kept waking up and looking around. When I woke, I could still hear guys moving around, slushy footsteps in the mud. I knew it was late in the night. Sudden sounds and shifts, the pitter-patter of feet, came into the night, splashing and running. Automatics went off, screams and the cries of a child filled the dark air.

"Cease fire. Cease fire."

Screams and shouts kept coming.

"Cease fire. Get them over here. Damnit, that's a kid. Get her over here. Corpsman, corpsman . . ."

The quick movements and the shouts stilled, but the cries of the child lingered into the night.

I tried to take everything out of my mind so I could just be me, keep me going until morning and being alive. Sometimes I couldn't tell whether it was a raindrop dripping and rolling down my chest or blood. I didn't want to sleep now. I kept drifting into it, but I wasn't sure it was just sleep. I started shaking it away.

I grabbed for thoughts to hold on to, but I kept grabbing Vernon. I could see his eyes staring at me, I kept on seeing everything happening again. Round and round, it kept coming. I'd sneak away, run home, be sitting and talking, not thinking about this. Never been here, this shit never was. Then I'd be looking back down at the dark, shaking from the rain and pushing sleep away. Some kid out of nowhere crying, and her mama screaming.

The rain slowed, then stopped, but the air blew cold. Morning was nearing, and I could see around me. I can still see it. The ground was wet and muddy, and blood lay with the water and the mud. The wounded guys shivered from chills of many kinds. The dead were oblivious to the chill, to the blood still seeping from them, to the coming day. They still had yesterday on their faces—eyes still looking, some mouths wide open and still trying to call Mom, God, somebody. I didn't turn away; I couldn't, they were all around me. So I closed my eyes, but they were there too.

The morning was slow. Squads were going out to get the rest of the dead and drag them in from the rice paddy. We moved down the path to a small clearing where the choppers were coming to pick us up. The dead were being brought to the pickup point. They were lying right in front of me, some covered with ponchos, others just lying there.

The first chopper came in, and as it lowered, the wind from its blades blew some of the ponchos off the bodies. I looked down and there lay Glickman. His face was still and pale yellow; only his hair had the color of life as it blew in the wind. We covered him back up, along with the others. I did not see Vernon. They told me he was hit pretty bad—the left side of his head was blown off.

I finally got on a chopper, and as it climbed into the sky, I could still see guys moving the dead and wounded to the pickup point. Then I could see the rice paddy and the far hill. It was still smoking.

13

THE REFRIGERATOR

The sun had gone down; the night was nearing again. I was in a hospital tent in Da Nang. I'd been flying around all day, from a field hospital to a ship to see a doctor. Now it's Da Nang and the night again, and I'm cold.

I can hear the sounds of the guns going off up on the line. I can see the far lights of flares in the night, but it is only candlelit in the tent. Some of the other guys are asleep, or just lying and moaning from time to time.

A corpsman comes and goes.

"How you feeling?"

"I'm okay, Doc. I feel a little dizzy, but I'm okay."

"You need anything?"

"Ya got a smoke, Doc?"

"Yeah," the corpsman said. He took the cigarettes out of his pocket, got one out of the pack, and held it up to my mouth. My whole face was numb. The cigarette dangled and almost fell. I grabbed for it. The corpsman struck a match. I saw the fires; then it was a match and I lit the cigarette.

"You guys got it pretty bad up there?" the corpsman was asking.

"Yeah, a lot of guys got it."

"You were with Echo two-seven, weren't you?"

"Yeah, that's my company."

136

"How long were you guys pinned down out there?"

"I don't know. We got pretty close, then all hell broke out."

"When did you get hit?"

"In the morning. I don't know what time it was."

"They just gettin' you guys out?"

"Yeah. They tried to get in yesterday, but I hear some of the choppers were getting hit, then the fuckin' rain got heavy."

The corpsman kept asking questions, but I didn't want to think about the answers. I was cold, and I didn't want to be, and I was hungry. "Doc, is chow over? Is there anyplace to get a sandwich or somethin'?"

"Chow hall is closed, but there's a snack bar across the road. If you want, you can go over," the corpsman said, pointing out of the tent and into the night.

When he left, I just sat for a while. The cigarette was good, soothing. As I inhaled I felt lightheaded, but it felt good, eased the throbbing in my neck. I could still feel the wound dripping beneath the big loose bandage around it.

I had seen it.

I had looked in a mirror; I wanted to see it. Then I didn't want to anymore, I didn't want it to be there. Just below my mouth was a big hole where the bullet hit, then it had gone down into my neck, and when it had come out, it had torn the whole left side of my neck apart. My neck was just a big raggedy hole with shredded skin hanging from it. I could see all that stuff in there, veins and that stuff, and bubbles of blood over everything.

I wondered when Mom and the others would know. Then I wondered what they would think. I could see that bright day so long ago, in a different time, Mom standing on the porch. I could see her face now, feel her hug, her fears. I saw the streets of home, different-colored cars. Heard voices and laughter, saw Macky, Georgie, and them up by the tracks. I could see lights, streetlights, window lights, then I could see pretty lights, different colors, reds, greens, and Christmas lights. Then it was dark and Vernon was behind the gun, and he wanted to go home for Christmas. And I could hear that little girl screaming.

I stood. My legs were shaking, but I wanted to walk away. I went out of the tent and into the night. I looked around and was quietly stepping, stopping, looking, then stepping again. I was still there, still in the nights before, looking for shadows beneath the tents, looking, waiting. I stopped. I was shaking now, and my neck was throbbing. I thought about going back to the tent. I started talking to myself, whispering, "Come on, man, settle down."

I went out onto the road. I could hear my footsteps, then electric generators puttering, distant talk and laughter; I could even hear song. I saw lights, guys walking, but mostly it was the dark I saw and my own footsteps I heard.

Across the road was a half-open tent. Inside it were guys sitting around at little tables and a guy standing behind a counter. As I entered, the guy behind the counter looked and then stared at me. I felt spotted, out in the open. I wanted to duck, crouch behind something.

"Hey man, you all right?" the counter guy asked quickly.

"Yeah. Doc said I could come over."

The counter guy sighed and kept staring at me.

"You have any sandwiches, maybe a hot dog or somethin'? And you have any coffee, somethin' warm to drink?" I asked quickly.

"Got hot dogs," the guy said, still staring.

"I'll take one. You have any coffee?"

"Nope, but I can put some on."

I was still feeling cold, and now not a part of this counter-and-hot-dog world. I had never been behind the lines before, and I was feeling uneasy and alone. I saw this thing, and then it became a cash register. It hadn't dawned on me that I'd need money. I didn't have any.

I spoke quickly, almost yelling. My neck jolted with pain, but I had to say, "Never mind, I don't have any money with me."

The counter guy paused and turned from the grill, asking, "What outfit you with?"

"Echo two-seven. We were out of Chu Lai."

The counter guy turned back to the grill and yelled over his shoulder, "It's on the house, pal."

I sat at the end of the counter and ate the hot dog. It hurt when I chewed, but the food was warm. The coffee was good, it was hot. I sat sipping it quietly. The other guys were talking and laughing. It was good to hear talk, just the sound of it. After the coffee and hot dog were gone, I felt cold again and wanted to leave. I felt strange. I guess it was the lights.

Walking back to the hospital tent, I really got the chills. I hurried through the night and into the tent. I climbed under the covers and pulled them over my head. I remember just shaking and quivering. It was dark under the covers, and the little girl screamed again. Those guys were lying still in the rain and muddy water. Glickman's hair was blowing, and Vernon's eyes wouldn't close and go away.

Morning came out of the long, slow dark. The chill of the night had gone, but my neck seemed stiff and swollen with pain. I didn't want to move. Then I felt I couldn't, and just lay for a while. Maybe time and all the rest of this shit would take its ass someplace else for a while. Go make somebody be born, play marbles with some kids, ride a horse in a cowboy movie. Just leave me the fuck out of its shit.

"How you feeling?" the corpsman asked as he took my pulse.

"I feel all right. I had the chills last night, but I feel okay now," I answered, then asked, "What happens next? Am I going back to Chu Lai today?"

"The doctors want to look at you. Chow's going to be brought in. Just set tight, you'll probably be sent to a hospital today. Doctors will let us know," the corpsman said, then moved on.

I sat up on the side of the rack and just looked around. Everything seemed so neat and clean. The corpsmen had on clean uniforms; some had on clean white jackets. I could see other tents with neat little paths around them.

In the morning shadows I could see a face I knew, a guy from third platoon; I didn't know his name. His shoulder and chest were all bandaged up. I went over to him.

"Hey man, how ya doin'?" I asked quietly.

He looked up, saying, "Hey, you here too?"

"Yeah," I answered, and we were silent for a moment. Then he asked, "What, you get it in the neck?"

"Yeah," I answered, then said, "You get it in the chest, huh?"

"Yeah, fuckin' mortar. I got it all in the chest and up in my shoulder too. It hit right on the fuckin' dike. I got it good."

"How ya feelin'?"

"Shit, I can't move my fuckin' arm. I think a bone's broken—they got to take x-rays. They said they can't do it here. Shit. Did you get shrapnel?"

"No, fuckin' bullet," I said, seeing it in my mind again.

"Oh."

"How far did you get before you got it?"

"We were close, man, could see those sons of bitches. We went to move up and that fuckin' mortar got us. Felter was beside me, he got it."

"Huh, Felter?"

"Yeah, him and Ski."

"Is Felter dead?"

"Yeah."

"Oh man. Jesus fuckin' Christ, damn. We were together back in the States for two years. He was crazy but a good guy. Shit."

We talked for a while, and I heard other names. I could see Sergeant Ituarte, his Indian or Mexican look. I could remember how it had seemed that he didn't like me. Then that thought went away, but his face stayed with the other faces I tried to see again in my mind. There were too many to keep there; one would vanish before I could remember his last name or where he was from, but another would come.

Chow came. I just got some soft shit; a corpsman said I was on a soft food diet. Then the doctors came and looked in my neck again. That's when they told me how lucky I was, because the bullet had only scratched my jugular vein. One of the corpsmen brought in a bunch of C ration cigarettes. I sure was glad about that. A colonel came in all dressed up and passed out Purple Hearts, said some things, then left.

I remember I was sitting on the rack smoking a cigarette and just thinking. A corpsman came up and asked, "You were with two-seven, right?"

"Yeah, Doc."

He turned and said to a sergeant behind him, "Here he is—he was with two-seven."

I watched the sergeant approach, then I looked up as he said, "Corporal, what company were you with?"

"Echo two-seven, weapons platoon."

"We got some KIA in that may be from your outfit. We can't identify them. Can you go over and see if you know who they are?"

"Yeah, okay. Where is it?"

"Right up the road, next to the motor pool. You'll see a big gray fence. There's a gunnery sergeant up there—tell him you're with two-seven."

"Okay."

When the sergeant and the corpsman left, I just sat thinking until one of the other guys asked if I was with two-seven. I told him I was.

"Damn, man, you all got fucked. How many guys got lost up there? A couple hundred?"

I told him I didn't know. I didn't. I only knew the battle was still going on. It had started up the next day.

I had to go, I had to. I grabbed a cigarette and lit it, then walked out of the tent. I followed the neat little path up to the road, then turned and kept walking. A few jeeps and trucks were going by, but I kept walking. Each step seemed to mean something, seemed to count. I wondered if Vernon was there. Did they get him in, would he be one of the faces?

I passed the motor pool, jeeps and trucks all stuffed together. Past the motor pool was a big gray tin fence. I walked along the fence until I got to its gate. At the gate there was a wide path, big enough for trucks to go in. Looking down the path, I could see a couple tents, and across from the tents were two large refrigerator units. The putt-putt sound of electric generators was the only sound that could be heard, yet it seemed to be a silent sound.

I took a breath and started down the path. My eyes kept looking around but not wanting to see. Would it be Vernon they didn't know, or couldn't tell about? Would I know him without half his head? Was I alive and just walking through the death shit again, or was I dead, a ghost, and just hadn't laid down? Was I here too?

I could see a lot of folded-up ponchos lying on the ground. There were a few big green bathtub-looking containers with water hoses and brushes with long sticklike handles attached to them. Piles of ammo belts and bloody boots were off to the side.

I neared the tent. I could see a couple guys sitting inside, their white T-shirts popping out in the shade in the tent. I yelled, "I'm with Echo two-seven. They asked me to come down."

"Yeah, hold on, I'll be right out," a voice said from the tent. I turned, looking around and knowing what the green bathtubs were for and why the brushes had long handles on them, what they scrubbed. I knew what the folded-up ponchos had been taken off of.

I lit another cigarette and waited. Soon the gunny came out. He was an older man with a slight potbelly. He was chewing on a cigar and carrying a clipboard. He came out of the tent and quickly walked by, saying, "I got a couple KIA without ID." Then he slowed and looked back at me and said, "Damn, son, looks like someone tried to cut your head off."

I followed him. We were going to one of the big refrigerator units. When we reached the door, the gunny quickly pulled it open and stepped inside. I stood in the doorway looking in. I could smell the sour dampness seeping out. One light bulb hung from the ceiling, dimly lighting the pile of dark green, almost gray body bags. A layer of frost covered the bags. They weren't in order, in line; they were just piled up on top of one another. I could see shapes of heads and feet pressing from within the rubber bags. White tags could be seen hanging from the zippers.

"Let's see here," the gunny said as he stood chewing on his cigar and flipping through the papers on his clipboard. "I got two that need IDs."

I stood looking around, and then I just stared at the gunny as he stepped onto the pile of bodies. He climbed on them and over them as if they were logs, grabbing one of the bags from the top of the pile and pulling it down over the others.

"This one here came from up your way," he said, bending over and unzipping the bag. I stepped over the bodies in front of me, looking for spaces between them to step into. I reached the gunny and looked down at the face in the bag. It was all ugly yellow. The guy's mouth was still open; his blue eyes still begged.

I stared.

"Gunny, I don't think I know him. I can't tell." I was almost whispering.

"Got one more," the gunny said, then climbed again over the pile. "Here he is," he blurted out. He pulled the body over the others, then unzipped the next face.

I looked, then wanted to turn away. It wasn't a face, just twisted, bloody meat. The eyes had rolled back into its head, leaving an unreality that was real, would be real forever.

"Gunny, I can't recognize him."

"Damn," the gunny said and zipped the bag back up.

I stepped back over the bodies and stood looking around, trying to read the names on the white tags in the dim light.

"Gunny, I got a buddy that got it. Did you get a lance corporal Vernon Carter in? Is he here?"

"Carter, Carter," the gunny said as he flipped through the papers on his clipboard and chewed on his cigar. "Yeah, should be right over there. Came in this morning." The gunny pointed to the far side of the pile.

I climbed back over the bodies to Vernon's bag, bent over, and read his name tag. I was still, looking at the tag and I guess just thinking, maybe trying to say a goodbye or something like that.

For the first time the gunny spoke quietly. "You can unzip him if you want."

Without turning, I said, "I just wanted to make sure he was here." I put my hand on the bag where I thought Vernon's shoulder would be. The bag was cold, almost icy. I said some things again, just to him, then stood and turned away.

Walking back down to the hospital tent didn't take long, take time. It had nothing to do with time or steps, browns and greens, trucks going by. I kept thinking of Vernon. Thinking I should have opened the bag and looked at his face.

Maybe I should have looked at you, but Vernon, I didn't want to see your head all torn up and your mouth frozen open. I wanted to remember you talking, man. Your eyes alive and moving. I wanted to remember you the way you were when you were alive. You saying things and stuff like that.

I'm sorry I didn't look, couldn't look. Sorry you had to see me get all fucked up. I'm sorry I didn't keep going, keep moving. Maybe I might have said, *Let's go this way, keep down, spread out.* Maybe I would have seen something, seen it coming, got us out of the way. I don't know, man, but I think just maybe I was too scared to move on. Just wanted to lie behind the dike, not wanting to know who was dying, not wanting to die.

It was a long time ago, but not for you and me. Not for Felter and Glickman and the others. It was not long at all. Nothing passed, nothing passed that has the meaning. The feeling won't go away. Ain't it funny, time can't do a fuckin' thing with it.

I should have died with you, been there too. I shouldn't have let them leave you out there all night, dead and in the dark. We went too far, man. Into that shit you can't come back from. That shit that takes all of you out of you.

Sometimes I tell people about you, but they don't understand, can't understand. I don't even know if I understand. Everything is too close to separate. If you take it apart, look at it in pieces, it's not the same.

I don't even know where you're buried. What they said, what kind of day it was. I hope it didn't fuckin' rain that day too. I hope they said something that people could remember, not that put-you-in-the-ground shit. Ashes to ashes, dust to dust, forget about you, glad it ain't me. Run away from that grave with their nickel life stuck further up their ass. Get away from that death, go on doin' that Mr. Rogers shit. Ain't real shit. Ain't no dirt in it—can't grow, just be there.

Man, I never thought you'd be the one to get it. I thought—and I didn't tell you—I thought I'd be the one. Never thought you'd be dead. You know, sometimes I think it didn't happen, sometimes I think you never existed, never a Felter, Glickman, or the others. Never me there with you. Hey man, I didn't even know you. Then sometimes I think that when I wake up, I'll be back at the bunker. And all this life I've lived since you died is just some long fucked-up dream and you and me can go on. Maybe have a chance to say goodbye and you be able to live too. Maybe everybody will be able to live.

I don't know what we did, man.

Dear God, whatever we were, whatever we are, please forgive us, forgive us. Vernon believed in you; even Felter wore a cross. God, if it's like they say it is, if there's a heaven and all, please pick everybody up and hold them all together. And God, wipe the tears from that little girl's eyes. And those guys we killed, tell them I'm sorry. And those guys who killed Vernon and them, if they're still alive, bring peace to their lives.

Vern, I'm sorry you're dead every day I live.

I had been sitting on the sandbags behind the hospital tent. Chow had come and gone, cigarettes were running out, but I was just sitting. The corpsman came up saying, "Man, I've been looking all over for you. I need some information from you. What hospital do you want to go to?"

"I'm not staying here?"

"Nope."

I was trying to think where I wanted to go. I never thought I'd be leaving Da Nang. I was thinking maybe I could go to Saigon, or even back to Okinawa.

"Where you from, man?" the corpsman asked as he shuffled through some papers in his hands.

"Pittsburgh," I answered, still thinking of Okinawa and Japan.

"Well, can't get you to Pittsburgh. How 'bout Philly?"

"Huh, Doc? You mean . . . you mean I'm goin' home?"

"Yeah, man, you're going home. It's going to take about a year to get your neck together. You're going to need plastic surgery. You're going home, today."

After the corpsman left, I just sat there on the sandbags. I could not believe I was going home. I just could not believe it. I was happy, and I wasn't happy. My mind was spinning around. Fucking things were fucking up being happy. I saw home, but I could not see me there, I could not touch the things I was seeing in my mind. I wanted to, but I couldn't touch that far away. I still had on the same clothes I had been shot in, still had the bloodstains on my jacket.

Later I climbed onto the plane and sat looking out the window as it took off. The greens and browns seemed to melt into blurs of color as the plane climbed into the sky, but I kept watching and staring out the window. I was thinking of home, what it was going to be like. Then I just started thinking and seeing the rain, mud, dark nights, flashes of fire in the treeline. I could hear screams, could hear that little girl crying. Then I thought of Vernon, and I wondered if he was still in the refrigerator, and I was cold again.

14

The plane flew through a time.

Philippines was more doctors, nice base, clean Air Force chow hall, guys who didn't want us, me, in there. Didn't want the bloody clothes I had on fucking up their dessert. A night, a morning, then another plane. Japan, and it was cold, an airport and people looking. Then San Francisco and home, America and I didn't see anyone, just night and lights. The morning was sky again, then Kansas, then Alabama, and I just looked out the window. I didn't want to see any more of it.

I was going back through that space shit again. I could feel it going into what I was but wasn't anymore. I was trying to put my me face on. A mask, but I couldn't cover my eyes.

U.S. Naval Hospital, Philadelphia, Pennsylvania—big gray buildings, cold walls. People doing their paperwork, busy. Asking me, *Who are you, what's your name?* Then looking up at me and wanting to say, *Shit, what the fuck, you a nightmare-looking motherfucker.* They're going home at five and here I come at four with jungle shit on. I'm trying to tell them where I'm from: *I'm in Echo Company, two-seven, out of Chu Lai, I live in a bunker.* But I ain't fitting in with their stuff.

Fuck it.

A million doctors all want to look. Well, look at this, we can do this, hey, let's do that. And all I want to do is look out the window, check out

146

that girl I saw downstairs. I figured out I ain't dying and I ain't dead; fuck the rest. Enjoy this shit—they got beds, sheets, TV, and I've already seen swaying skirts with wiggling asses. This being alive shit isn't bad, except something is wrong.

I'm scared.

Don't want these people near me, touching me, looking in my neck. *Don't get near me, I don't know you.* Don't want to, either.

There were a few other guys, none from my outfit but some from two-four and three-three—close enough.

"Hey man, what outfit you from?"

"Echo two-seven. What outfit were you with?"

"Hotel two-four."

"How's things here?"

I found a phone and hurried up and called.

"Operator, I want to call Pittsburgh."

"What number, please?"

"Ah, Fremont one-three-six-four-six. Oh, operator, I want to call collect."

"Your name?"

"I'm callin my mom."

"Oh, okay."

I listened to the buzz, buzz. I was waiting. I wanted to hear me again. What I was. Someone saying, *That's me, I know you, you belong here.*

"Hello."

"This is the operator. I have a collect call from your son. Will you—"

"Yes, yes. My God. Thank God . . ."

"Mom."

I could hear the sound of tears.

"Mom, it's me, I'm in Philly."

"Are you all right?"

"Yeah, I'm fine. Don't worry, I'm fine."

"We got the telegram . . ."

I could hear a voice that was still me, an echo from a time.

Real hospital stuff became dumb shit. Pajamas and robes, stay down, don't get up. You sleep, they think you're there in the bed. You ain't nowhere near there. And they want to sneak up on you, give you some pills, touch you. Then they stand there stupid, don't know why you jumped, why you're scared. Don't know you're not scared of them, you're scared of yourself. Scared of what you might do to their silly asses.

I started talking, but just to us, guys from two-four and three-three. I climbed in their hole, felt covered, could get away from those hands poking at me.

We play cards, but not for money; we're not allowed to do that. That shit's like taking the black out of blackjack—just got silly jacks left, kid stuff. Fuck 'em. We tell the silly shits we're playing old maid or something. Stick the money under the covers or someplace.

Preacher man comes by, real nice dude, keeps telling us to come on down if we want to talk. I don't know what he wants to talk about—maybe that cross Felter wore around his neck. He wants to talk about shit he hasn't seen. Fuck that.

Meet Lewis, quiet guy, reminds me of Vernon. He was with two-four in a flame-thrower team. The hose on the flame-thrower broke; he's burned all over. He has brown skin, same color as Vernon, but he's half pink over his face. His hair is all burned away too. We talk about stuff.

Malone talks too. He's real crazy, like Felter. They have to stay on his ass, watch him. He sneaks out of the ward, wants out of this shit, says he needs a beer. Greco is real fucked up. He was with two-four, one of those guys they landed in the VC headquarters by accident—simple mistake. He got one of his balls shot off and had been married just before he went over. He doesn't talk too much, but when he does, it's just to us. They put some old dude by us, but he was okay. He was in Korea but had cancer. He'd moan a lot in the night, but you knew he didn't want to. You knew he wanted to keep his stuff straight and not bend. One morning he wasn't there—death shit again.

I saw a guy from first platoon. He's in another ward, he can't walk. He was in Sergeant Ituarte's squad. He said the lieutenant got shot in the arm. Wiggins got it too.

"What about third squad?" I wanted to know.

He didn't know about everybody, but he knew Bright got it in the leg. Lee got hit in the leg too. Grunwald went way past where he could go. The word was he took a rifle off a dead guy because his was broken, then went into the bushes, aimed that rifle at his foot, and pulled the trigger. I didn't ask about Glickman.

A couple days later I saw Franko in the mess hall with the crazy guys.

He smiled and we talked for a while. Said we'd check each other out later, but I never saw him again. Didn't worry about him, though. I knew something those head doctors hadn't figured out: Franko would be as crazy as they wanted him to be.

Christmas was approaching. I could see the lights, reds and greens, blinking and glowing out the window. The staff hung stuff up in the ward too, stockings, pictures of Santa Claus. They had a tiny little tree. If you just looked at it, got real close so you couldn't see anything else, it was pretty. But I wondered what Christmas was like in Florida.

Time was days that fell and just lay still. Stayed morning, stayed whatever was going on, not going on, wouldn't turn into the next thing, wouldn't turn into *Let's go, saddle up, move out*. But the waiting and watching still came with the nights. Seeing the little nurse's light on, waiting for it to swing and come toward me, watching anything that moved. Hearing things coming long before they got close, or maybe just waiting for them to move.

My neck was still dripping. They talked about fluids, kept changing bandages and looking inside. They were going to do this or that, then changed their minds and thought of something else to do. Let's sew it up. Oh no, let's let all that dangling, shredded, loose neck meat grow back together. We can take some skin from here and put it there, cover that shit up. I was saying, *Yeah, okay, do what the fuck ya want. Sew it up, pin it up, put Christmas stuff on it, light it up, just get me the fuck out of here.* But they weren't asking me anyway.

I wanted out, away from there. I could see out the window, but it wasn't what I wanted to see. It wasn't what I had seen in my mind, what I had sat and looked at while I was still in the bunker. It didn't have the spark; I wasn't in its glow.

TV was funny, all the time. Cowboys shooting Indians and not getting shot back. Motherfuckers getting killed and not dying; you'd see 'em again next week someplace else. Presidents telling Mother America, *You've got to stop that communism from spreading over there, send more guys, build more bunkers, save freedom's ass.* King moving out, spreading out in Mississippi, Alabama, looking for that freedom shit they were trying to save. King was telling folks, *Let's go, move out,* and was taking folks across the rice paddies, all out in the open, singing.

A sergeant came and told us he'd be back with some uniforms and some checks. I had forgotten all about paydays. Mom had sent some money just to have, for the snack bar, to sneak some real food and not that dumb crap they were still trying to feed me. I played some cards too.

I don't remember where I was when the word came down: *If the doctors say okay, you can go home for Christmas. Leave Christmas Eve and stay a week, then come back.* I hadn't thought about that, hadn't thought I'd be home for Christmas; I never did think that. And now, hearing it, thinking maybe, counting days frontward (four days, Christmas Eve), counting days backward (ten days ago, another place and time), I was scared. Scared of who was going home for Christmas.

My neck kept dripping, but just a little bit. Doctors said that was all right, I could go home. I got to looking for a ride and found a homeboy, Tyler, who was going home too. I knew Tyler from before, way back, projects and all. He was stationed over at the Navy Yard.

It was time.

The day was a uniform, dark green with red stripes on the shoulders. Somebody stripes, corporal stripes, what-I-was stripes. Had ribbons on my chest too. The ribbons said, *He saw some shit*, if you knew what they said at all. If you didn't, they were just pretty decoration stuff.

The car was looking out the window at Philly streets, people going, coming, bundled up against the cold. Sometimes I could see quick waves, smiles, and laughs and could almost hear a Merry Christmas. Then it was the road, speed, and more space shit again.

Tyler kept talking. Hey man, you remember that and that? Hey man, you ought to see Darlene now, she's lookin' good. Joan's lookin' good too, shit, she's lookin' better than her sister. You got to check that out.

I was saying things too. Yeah, man, I remember her, remember that too. I was saying I remembered things, but I was hurrying to see them in my mind, match them up to things, separate them from the other stuff which kept grabbing at things. But the road felt good.

Tyler kept talking and the night became the Pennsylvania Turnpike curving through the mountains and speeding through the tunnels. I knew the road well: exit 12, exit 11, exit 10. I waited for exit 6; I could feel it nearing.

Streets came, stop signs, lights in store windows. I could see people on sidewalks with packages. I knew they were going home too. I tried to see if I knew anybody, if I could wave and say, *Hey, it's me*, then waited to see if they looked back, knew me.

The streets became one street, my street—up the hill, around the curve, and I could see houses, porches, my home. I could see red Christmas lights. I could feel me just coming home from school, from a party, from down the way. Then it was dark and just lights in the night, still lights casting shadows that wiggled and squirmed, made creatures that stared at me. Made me look away, then quickly look back and slow my steps.

I touched the door.

Mom, Harry, Sherry, Stacy, home and hugs and hugs. So many words, just one sound. Quick looks around, looking at faces again. You were always way deep in my heart, where I kept you safe and dry. Kept you away from me when I went out too far, too far for you to see and touch, far enough to change the smiles in your eyes. I didn't think of you then, didn't want you in my mind with those demons in the dark, didn't want them touching you. No matter who we were, what we did, no matter, there's a me that's only you.

"Merry Christmas, Mom."

I could see the Christmas tree, its pretty lights, its softly glowing reds and greens. Brightly colored presents with ribbons and bows lay in wait. And stockings hung from the mantel. One from a time ago, with my name on it. A time when I would wait, try to peek at Santa Claus, think I saw him, know I had heard him come or leave.

Mom tried to look away, not stare at my neck. I could see her looking down when she wanted to look up. I'd turn away, point to something, ask something, say something to the kids. Looking at Sherry, just nine, I felt that she was cuddling beyond her understanding. But I was home and it was Christmas.

Stacy was just a baby, only three. Seeing her shy, then coming to me. I took her up into my lap, told her I'd be better soon, and her eyes just stared, and I could feel her cringe.

I asked, "Is Santa comin'?"

The time did not pass; it was still and gentle. Some laughs, but mostly soft lingering words that just settled into *All we have is together again.* The Christmas songs played; a choir was singing on TV. After the kids went to bed, Mom and I talked some, but just a little.

It was dark now. I was in my room. I remember thinking, and wanting too. Maybe trying to say some things in my mind, my heart. The moments stilled around me, but it was good. I wanted them to be still, to stop, so I could reach back and touch some things.

I don't know what happened or what time came again. I guess I was asleep and did not hear myself screaming, only my mother and Harry calling to me.

PART II

15

THE ROAD AND THE ROADS

I remember the drive downtown, the noon sun and all the light. I remember wanting to turn around, go back, or maybe just stop the car and get out, tell Mother America to go fuck herself again. Then walk, keep walking, maybe walk to the sea. When I reached town, got stuck in all the traffic, saw the red lights glaring in the sunlight, I still wanted to turn around, go back, get away from all the stop-and-go, the waiting, the flashing signs. Maybe I wanted to yell up to where the sun was, yell up there and see if Jesus was there and just ask him why. Maybe just keep yelling and asking him why, why? But I knew he wasn't going to yell back down and answer my question—he never answered the ones I had before.

It was 1987, the summer of the year. Mother America was doing well. Howdy Doody was President and other Presidents had come and gone. Cars weren't big and fast anymore, had safety belts in them. Buckle up; be safe so you won't die, splatter blood all over the road. Don't fuck up, bleed on America; keep it pretty. Mother America cares about everybody, Howdy Doody says so. I never did like Howdy Doody. I met Mr. Rogers one time, didn't like him and his little make-believe world either. Sometimes I'd try to make believe shit didn't happen. I was safe in America as long as I buckled up, did the right thing. Go into the service, get out, and get a job. Go work in the mills; coloreds could get jobs there. I was a good janitor, cleaned a hundred toilets real fast. Worked up on the furnace too. Got close to the fires and tried not to see the treelines burning in my mind. I was real good in the mill, went almost all the time until I said fuck it. I wanted to be something. I had been there a year. I didn't stay a day longer.

I remember the time and the year I left the mill. It was the winter of 1968. King was still alive and the war was still living too; body bags were filling up real quick, but I was safe in America. I grew a beard and tried to hide the scar on my neck. I didn't want people to see it. Sometimes I didn't want to know it was there either. I just wanted to live, be something. I went back to school, got into some community college. I didn't know what I wanted to be, but soon I knew I didn't want to be in school again, study about stuff I didn't care about, be a part of stuff I didn't care about. College didn't last as long as the mill. A Christmas passed again. I had taken my camera out, the one I had bought in Vietnam. I wanted to take some pictures of my little sisters. I liked taking pictures, so I didn't put the camera back. I started taking pictures of girls, then just people doing things. I wanted their faces to tell the stories of their lives. I wanted to be a photographer, work for a newspaper or magazine.

Bullets went through the air in the South, and King was caught out in the open. America caught on fire; colored people were burning her cities. Washington, D.C., was a glow when I went through, heading for Atlanta to take pictures of King's funeral. I wanted to learn how to be a newspaper photographer. I figured I could learn on my own, so I went my own way. But that was a long time ago, a different time, a time when I was young.

By 1987, twenty years had passed since I had picked up the camera. But I stopped at the door I was going through to look at the pictures in the store window. They were old black-and-white photos with young faces in them. I knew the fear I saw in some of the faces. I could see the fear on the face of a guy sitting behind a machine gun, the fear on the faces of some guys crossing a rice paddy. There were a lot of pictures in the window. I looked at every one of them before I went through the door of the Vietnam Veterans' Center. There was a woman sitting at the desk; I wondered if she was the one I had spoken to over the phone. She looked up, smiled, and said, "Hi, can I help you?"

I remember it was hard for me to answer quickly, but the woman kept smiling and looking up at me. "Hi," I finally said, and then I told her my name. Then I said, "I'm the guy who called a little while ago. I think I may have spoken with you first, then I spoke with Roger. He said I should come down at one o'clock."

"Oh yes, have a seat. Roger will be able to see you in just a few minutes. Do you want a cup of coffee?"

"No, thank you," I said as I took a seat. I remember I didn't want to be there, I wanted to get back up and leave and keep going. I could feel myself starting to feel empty inside, like there wasn't anything left of what I was. In my mind, I could see me sitting back at the office, getting mad and knocking stuff off my desk. The magazine was dying; seven years of my life were quivering, bleeding in my hands. I could see Teresa walking past my desk. She can't stop—she knows I am waiting to talk to her, I've been waiting. She knows the magazine is dying, she knows because she's killing it, letting it die; she wants it to bleed in my hands. I'm telling her we have to talk. She said she would meet with me. But she won't, she's just walking by, leaving. I'm up from my desk, telling her we have to talk, it's important. She's not stopping, turning around, nothing. "We have to talk," I'm telling her, but she's not stopping. She hasn't stopped in days, weeks. She's always busy with the TV show, busy doing stuff to fuck things up. I'm yelling now, "Teresa, we have to talk!" She's not stopping. It's happening before I know it's happening. It's not waiting on me to do it, it's doing it. It's showing me my hand going through the air, grabbing her shoulder, turning her around. Her sleeve is ripping, ripped. Stuff she was carrying in her arms is floating in the air, falling all over the place. I'm looking into her face, seeing her eyelids batting. Cold feelings are rushing up in my head, telling me, *You've gone too far, don't go no further. This shit ain't worth it, it ain't you and you don't want to be it again. You don't want to be jerkin' around in the night, firin' in the dark before you even know you're firin', killin' something that's tryin' to kill you.* I'm saying, "I'm sorry . . . I'm sorry, I didn't mean to." She's glaring at me, saying, almost hissing, "Now I've got you just where I want you."

The woman behind the desk is telling me, "Roger can see you now. You can just go on back. His office is the last one on the right."

"Oh. Okay, thanks."

There're pictures and posters on the walls of the hallway. I'm glancing at the pictures as I pass them, seeing guys sitting out in front of bunkers smiling because they're getting their pictures taken. I'm thinking of the bunkers, seeing all the sandbags again. I'm feeling like I'm going back to the bunker; maybe I never left. Maybe Vernon's still there, everybody's still there, still alive and none of this happy home shit ever happened.

Roger doesn't sound like he did over the phone; his voice seems softer when he introduces himself, but his handshake is firm. He is a tall guy, but slim. His hair is dark brown or black, but the dim light coming from the lamp on his desk shows some of the gray in it. When he closes the door to his office, the small room seems smaller, becomes darker. The lamp on his desk seems to have the glow of only a candle. He asks me to take a seat and I sit in a big soft chair next to his desk. There is another chair in front of his desk, and he takes that. Even though he has started talking a little, telling me about the Vet Center, the room seems as quiet as it is dark. But that is okay; I don't want to see the light from the outside world anyway.

"How are you feeling?" Roger's asking.

I'm sighing, looking down at the floor. It's real dark down there, and I stare into the dark for a while before telling Roger that I don't know how I feel.

"What's been going on in your life? Seems like there may be some problems," Roger's saying.

I'm thinking of days so long ago that don't seem that far away now. I'm thinking of Bright always wanting to go see the chaplain and me worrying about all that loose stuff inside his head just coming all apart real fast sometime. Then I'm hearing and seeing Rayburn sitting in the night. I can see the rain falling on his face and I can hear him naming the names of the dead all over again. It keeps raining, but I don't think Rayburn's mind knows it's raining. Now I am worrying about *my* mind and I start talking a little bit. I tell Roger how I left the newspaper after being a photographer there for thirteen years to start a magazine. I tell him about Teresa, my business partner, and how we started *Pittsburgh Premier*, a local women's magazine, together. I tell him about my conflicts with Teresa and the financial problems I'm facing as I try to keep the magazine afloat. I tell him about everything, my grabbing Teresa's arm and how I got scared, felt stuff I didn't want to feel again. I can hear myself whispering now, telling Roger, "I'm being pushed too far."

"What are you feeling?" Roger asks when I stop talking and just sit there staring down at the floor. I start talking again, but I'm not thinking about Teresa or the magazine. That stuff ain't on my mind anymore. I tell Roger about stuff that won't get out of my mind, is stuck up in my head and won't get out. I tell him about Rayburn talking about the dead, Glickman's dead face but the wind from the chopper blades making his hair blow, move, look alive. But his face didn't come alive, it's still dead. Vernon's still dead too; he gets killed again every night of my life. I hear myself saying, *I should have moved on too, I should have moved on with Vernon and them. I could have moved on, I just wasn't shot. I was scared too. I still get scared. I can't even walk in the park without lookin' in the treeline, lookin' for shit I know ain't there, is just in my mind.*

Roger's talking now. It was quiet for a moment; I didn't say anything and was still thinking about what I had said. Then Roger started talking. He's telling me that a lot of vets have the same feelings I do. I'm staring into the shadows along the wall of the little dark room. Sometimes I can hear every word Roger's saying. I can hear him saying, "There's help, there can be help." I'm still listening for his words and he's still talking, but it's just the sound of his voice I hear. It's only the words in my head I want to understand. They're my words, I keep hearing them. But I don't understand them. I look away from the shadows and look at Roger and ask him, "Do I really need help?"

"We all need help sometimes," Roger says. We talk for a while and I know why I have trusted him all along. He has seen the same fires in the treelines as I have. He came back too, had his problems but got his degree in psychology. He's telling me he'd like to see me twice a week for a while. He's saying that I'm dealing with a lot of loss and uncertainty in my life. I'm still thinking about this when he says, "If you can, I want you to come down tomorrow night too. We have a group of guys who meet once a week. They're all combat vets. We just sit around and talk things out. I think you need to talk about some things. If you don't want to talk, that's okay, you can just sit and listen. No one has to talk if they don't want to."

It was dark when I finally got home, it was dark. I had left the Vet Center and gone back to the magazine's office. One of the interns, Kate, was still there answering phones. She asked how my meeting had gone in town. I told her it was a good meeting and asked her if there were any phone messages. She was a young girl, had some freckles on her face. She was going to school and wanted to become a writer. I hated lying to her. I had told her I was going into town for a business meeting. When she left to go home, the office was empty. I stay for a while, trying to think of how I could get the next issue of the magazine out. It was already late. Advertisers were calling, wanting to know where it was. The printer and everybody else was calling, wanting to know where their money was, money I didn't have. The phone rang a few times, but I didn't answer it. I let the ring echo through the empty office. I didn't want to pick it up, tell somebody some lie, tell them the magazine would be out soon, tell somebody their money was on the way. I didn't want to say to somebody, *Oh, Teresa's not in now, do you want to leave a message?* I'd want to tell them, *She left, left the magazine in pieces on her art board. She's Miss TV Show now—she left the magazine. She ran out, used the pieces of the magazine for stepping stones to get to the TV show.*

I'm at home now, trying to sleep, but I can't sleep. It's dark, but I want it to be dark, darker than it is. I can see well in the dark, hear things coming too. But I can't sleep; I've got to listen, look.

I know hours have passed, but I'm thinking about the years that have passed. I can't sleep, won't sleep. I've got to watch Teresa, see her creepin' in her dark shit again. I got to hear the phone ringin', hear people askin' about the magazine and their money. I got to feel stuff I ain't thinkin' about, don't want to think about. I don't want to think about Roger, me tellin' him everything. Vernon, I don't want to think about you either. Your mother thinks you're still alive, might be comin' home, but I know you're not. Maybe I shouldn't have called her. You knew I would call her, didn't you? It took me twenty years to find her. I couldn't remember what part of Florida you were from. I know you told me a thousand times, but I just couldn't remember. Every year around Memorial Day, I'd try to find her, call different parts of Florida to see if she was in the phone book. When I did find her, I was afraid to call; I didn't know what to say. But I knew I had to call.

I remember when I first heard her voice. I can hear it now, her sayin', "Yes, this is Mrs. Carter speaking." I remember I was quiet for a moment, couldn't say anything. Then I told her my name and said, "Mrs. Carter . . . I was a friend of Vernon's . . . I was with him in Vietnam . . . I've been tryin' to find you." I could hear her gasp, say, "Oh my God—God have mercy." I could hear her grabbin' for words, savin' 'em, sayin', "Oh Jesus . . . Jesus have mercy. Tell me, son . . . Please tell me, son, is . . . is he really dead?"

All my thoughts broke into little feelings that I could not gather into words. I could see your face, Vern, when I got hit and you saw me. I could see the dark gray rice paddy and the burning fires. I could hear them again telling me that you got it. I could see the dark green frost-covered body bag you were in. I could see it lyin' in the cold refrigerator unit at graves registration. I was wishin' I had called sooner, wishin' I had never called too. I didn't know what to say, but I could hear myself sayin', "Yes, ma'am, Vernon's dead."

Quickly she asked, "Did you see it happen?"

"No, ma'am . . . when it happened, I didn't see it."

"Then he might be alive. I know he's alive. They wouldn't let me open up that coffin—could have been anybody in there. I know he's alive—I know it. He might be just missing in action."

I didn't want to say anything, but I had to tell her the truth I knew, saw, felt. I had to say, "Mrs. Carter, Vernon died a little ways up from where I was. The other guys saw him. They told me what happened. Mrs. Carter, Vernon was hit pretty bad—that's why they probably didn't want you to see him. I saw him later, but he was covered up. I saw his name tag, though. Mrs. Carter, Vernon's dead . . . I just called to say I think of him too . . . Ma'am, I'm sorry, I'm so sorry. I didn't know you weren't sure . . . I'm sorry."

Vernon, I told your mother how you were thinkin' about her, how you were thinkin' about Christmas comin' and wantin' to be home with her. I told her how brave you were. But I couldn't tell her I didn't want to look at you dead, see the left side of your head all gone. She still thinks you might be comin' home, thinks you'll get out of a cab one day and be home. I know you can't, but I hope you come home anyway.

Morning finally came. I think sleep had come too. I didn't want to get up, go into the office, and see it all empty, see the magazine still in pieces on the art board. I knew the phone would be ringing and I wouldn't want to answer it. I didn't want the day to go by, either, because I didn't want the night to come. I didn't want to go back down to the Vet Center, I wanted everything to go away, leave me the fuck alone. But nothing went away; the telephone rang and the evening came too—it wouldn't stay away.

It was hard to see the pictures in the window of the Vet Center when I looked at them again. The night was nearing and the guys in the pictures were seeping into the coming darkness. When I went into the little reception room, it was filled with other guys. They were standing around, sipping coffee and smoking cigarettes. Their faces seemed old, and I wondered if my face had aged like theirs.

Roger must have seen me come in, because he came up to me and said he was glad I could make it. Then he started introducing me to some of the guys. He would say what a guy's name was and the guy would shake hands with me and give the name of the outfit he had been with in Vietnam. I shook hands with a fellow named Billy, whose hand was already shaking before we shook. His face had stayed young-looking, still looked like the faces in the window pictures. His hair didn't have any gray in it; it was all brown and almost hanging down over his eyes. Maybe he still looked boyish because he was small and thin too. We got to talking and I found out it was his first night too. I asked him how things had been going for him. He sighed and looked away, then turned back but kept his eyes lowered when he said, "My wife is leaving me. She wants to take the kids. I love my kids. Everything I do to try to keep things together doesn't work. I don't know what to do, plus I got laid off last week. I don't know what to do, but I'm not letting her take the kids away from me."

Billy and I kept on talking, and I told him about all my stuff that was coming apart. We talked until it was time to go into the meeting room. Everybody seemed to go through the door slowly, the way you walk into a church or some funeral parlor. The room wasn't that big or real bright. The guys started sitting on the floor in a circle. I sat on the floor too and leaned back against the wall. Slowly I started looking around the room. I wasn't trying to look at the faces, because I didn't want anyone looking at mine. Roger came in and took a seat on the floor across from where I was sitting. I couldn't tell how many guys were in the room, but it looked like about twenty or so. Some of them were still sipping out of coffee cups and smoking cigarettes. I lit one and watched the smoke floating into the air. I kept watching the smoke, because I didn't want to look around anymore. It was getting real quiet; nobody was saying anything. It stayed that way for a long time, maybe longer than it really was. Maybe time was passing, but nobody was givin' a fuck about passin' time.

When Roger started to talk, his voice was as soft as the silence in the room. When I looked up at him, he had his head down, and I could see the other guys had their heads down too. I lowered my head and watched the smoke from my cigarette still floating in the air beneath my face. But I kept listening to Roger. He was saying things like he was glad everybody could make it. Then it got quiet again until Roger said, "Let's have a go-around and see how everybody is feeling. I think everybody has met the new guys. I just want to say before we get started . . . ahh, we're all here together. We're all here as brothers. Whoever wants to talk can, whoever doesn't want to or doesn't feel ready to doesn't have to say a word. So let's go around the circle and see how we're feeling."

It was real quiet again before this guy started talking. When I heard him I only looked toward him for a moment, then I lowered my head again. He was talking about how his week had been and what he was still having problems with. He kept talking about regular stuff until he started talking about the dark. Then he started saying how he still couldn't turn the lights off when he slept. He said, "My wife's pretty good about it, but I still can't talk to her. You know, I just can't do it. Man, I still see that shit all over again. Anytime the lights go off, I can see that shit all over again. That night we got hit, they were all over us before we knew it—man, I can still hear all that screaming. They shot this one kid, I didn't know his name, some new kid that just got in country. They hit him in the legs. It was dark, man, but I could still see this kid crawling and trying to get away from them. He's screaming and calling for his mother and those fuckin' bastards are runnin' alongside him and stickin' him and he kept on screaming for his mother. Man, they could have just shot him, finished him off. I guess they thought I was dead after they threw that grenade in on me."

While the guy was talking, in my mind I could see the night he was talking about. Then I was out of his night, I was in my night, he was still talking but I couldn't hear him for the screams I was hearing in my head. That little girl was screaming and screaming again out in the dark.

When the guy stopped talking, it got real quiet. Then the next guy started talking about this guy he knew. I could hear him sighing and sounding like he was getting ready to cry, then he got to saying, "Man, I'll never forget. Jake was a good guy, do anything for you. He always had this smile on his face. Man, he had just come up to talk, just stepped right in front of me to say something. Some gook got him right in the back of his head. I seen his face come off, man. That was my bullet, man, that was my fuckin' bullet he took."

Some other guy said that when he got back from his R and R, nobody was left in his platoon. The whole platoon walked into an ambush and all of them got wiped out. Another guy told him, "Hey, man, that's okay, man. You got to be okay with that. That's fate, man, you couldn't have changed that. That's fate, man, you got to let that go."

I'm seein' Vernon's eyes lookin' at me. Then I'm seein' him move on and me not going with him. Seein' me just lyin' there and not doin' nothin'. Every time some guy starts saying something, I start seein' and maybe start hearin' stuff up in my head. That guy named Billy ain't sayin' nothin' at all; it's his turn to talk. I'm watchin' him; he looks like he wants to say something, but when he tries to, his lips just move a little and no sound comes out. I can see him trembling. The next guy talks and Billy's still trembling. I'm still looking at him, but he can't see me because he has his head down.

The guy next to me is talking, and I know my time to say something too is nearing. He's done talking and it's quiet. It's time for me to say something and I don't want to. But I can hear me talking, saying how I always have stuff on my mind too. I'm telling how that little girl got shot and how she was screaming and crying out in the dark. I'm telling how Vernon and the others moved on and I didn't go. I'm seeing Glickman's face as I'm telling how the wind from the chopper blades blew his hair and made him look still alive. I'm saying other stuff, but I don't want to say some things. I'm quiet now; the guy on the other side of me is talking, but I'm still hearing and thinking about the things I said.

Roger begins telling everybody that he's hearing a lot of guilt and that it's okay. He says, "Look, it takes time to let some things come out. Most of you were in country one day and the next day you were back here in the States. You didn't have time to work out anything. World War Two and Korean vets came back by ship, they had some time to work things out some. And they came back to a welcome we didn't come back to."

He kept talking for a while, telling us some of the reasons that stuff stayed in our minds over the years. Some of the other guys talked afterward, but I didn't say anything more, and Billy didn't say anything at all. When I drove home, stopping at red lights, driving under streetlights, it seemed like I was driving in a world I had never seen before, some kind of place I didn't feel a part of anymore. I kept thinking about the meeting and what guys had said, and how they were just like me. We were talking about and feeling ugly stuff, and I knew it, but at least

I belonged there. There weren't any phony fuckin' streetlights tryin' to light up the darkness.

The next seven days passed slowly, and quickly too. When the days and nights were too long, passed too slowly, I'd try to hurry them up. And then sometimes I'd think about what day it was and how close the next meeting night was getting. I managed to get away from the office during the days I was to go see Roger. I'd talk about things with him, tell him how things were back at the magazine. I guess he could see how close to the edge the magazine was, and I knew he knew I was on the edge too. Sometimes I would try to tell him good things about the magazine. I think I wanted him to know that I had been successful some with my life. I told him how hard it had been to get the magazine started, but how Teresa and I had got it off the ground. Maybe I wanted to say, *Hey, look, I made things work in my life, started the magazine from nothing and made it something, got big department stores and banks to advertise in it. I can do things with my life, I'm a publisher, I don't belong here sitting in this big pile of shit I'm stuck in.* But I knew that when I got back to the office, the magazine would still be in pieces.

It's night; the faces in the window are hidden by the dark, but I know they're there. I see Billy in the reception room with the other guys. He sees me and comes over. "Hey man, how you doing?" I ask him. He takes a deep breath and looks down, but I can hear him saying, "Not good, not good at all. I've been looking for work, but I can't find anything. My unemployment checks haven't started to come yet . . . My wife's working, but I won't ask her for anything. We're not even talking."

I don't say anything back to Billy; there's nothing I can say. So I ask, "How's the kids?"

"Oh, they're great, I took them to the park today. We had a great time. After that we stopped by my mom's and stayed for a while. She's really great with them."

Billy's still talking, saying things about the kids, but he's keeping his head down. I put my head down too, maybe to look at the same spot on the floor. I don't know why—maybe I don't want to watch him looking down. Someone says it's time to go in. I glance up and see some of the guys slowly starting into the meeting room. I take a deep breath, but I try to do it quietly.

Everybody's in the room now. I sit in the same place I was sitting in before. It's getting quiet like it did before too. Roger comes in and sits across from me again. I put my head down and light a cigarette so I have something to do. Roger's talking now; I don't have to look up to see who's talking because I know the sound of his voice. He's saying stuff he said last time—anyone who doesn't want to talk doesn't have to. He finishes talking and it's not quiet, it's silent, as if something is wrong. I think, *Maybe it's just the silence in my head.* Roger says quietly, "Let's have a go-around and see how we're feeling tonight."

It's raining in my feelings, that cold rain that makes you as cold as it is, makes you shiver too. I'm wondering how long it's been raining. Rayburn and I are sitting together now. Maybe the rain doesn't make any difference. Some guy starts to talk, says how he went to see the movie *Platoon*, how stuff got back up in his head when he was watching it. He talks about how he heard people talking about the movie and saying how they think they understand Vietnam now. He says they don't understand shit—they think they do, but they don't. Some hour-and-forty-five-minute flick doesn't give them the fuckin' right to think they understand.

This real tall guy I saw in the hallway starts to talk about the movie too. He says how some of it wasn't real but some of it was too real and made him not want to believe things he did. He mentions some scene that shows the end of a big battle. Now he talks faster, saying how he was a medic and how it was his job to go around after the battles and put the dead into the body bags. He's quiet, but I can hear him sighing all the way across the room. Slowly he starts talking again, saying how during one battle he was on a chopper that got hit. He tells how the chopper's blade came off and flew across the rice paddy and how it happened real fast. This one guy didn't see the blade coming and it cut his head off. The speaker's voice is real low now and quivering. He says how he knew the guy and he was trying to find the guy's head so he could put it in the body bag. He didn't want to have the guy sent home without his head. He was really trying to find it, but the paddy water was knee-deep. The rest of the guy was lying on the muddy dike. He found the head when he was putting the body into the bag. It had fallen into the big gash in the guy's chest and was all covered up with blood and stuff. He says how he threw up all over himself and couldn't even help get the guy into the body bag.

This other guy's talking now, saying, "Man . . . This one time—

I'll never forget it—we were sent out to check on this platoon. HQ lost radio contact with them. Their last message said that they were pinned down . . . The shit was real hot . . . Man, when we found them, they had been over-fuckin'-run . . . All of them had got it. Man, all of them were fucked up, except this one kid. Man, we found this kid—he was sitting and leaning back on this tree. Man, this kid must have been so fuckin' scared . . . Man . . . He had killed himself—he had jammed his fist into his mouth. Man, there weren't any other marks on him."

I'm trying to look someplace else in my mind; I don't want to see this stuff I'm hearing. Another guy's been talking and now he's crying and Roger's telling him, "It's okay, man." The guy's still crying, but he's trying not to. He's trying to catch his breath, get himself together, but he's still crying some. He told about this night when it was raining hard. He was in his hole and heard some noise. He said he couldn't see anything because it was raining so hard, and he kept on hearing the noise, which was getting closer. He said he saw something and just started shooting. He was crying real hard when he said he found out it was his own guys he was firing on. They were coming back from a patrol, but he didn't know they were out there. He killed one of the guys and wounded two of them. And the one he killed, he knew really well. Roger and some of the other guys tell him to let it go. Roger talks about accidents, things that weren't anybody's fault. He says we have to let stuff like that go; time can only heal a clean wound.

It's quiet again and I want it to be quiet. I've got my head down; I want to close my eyes too, shut out everything from getting in my mind, but I'm just staring at the floor. I hear Billy's voice—he's going to talk. He talks about how things are going real bad for him and he can't find a job. I'm thinking about how things are so fucked up at the magazine, but I can still hear Billy talking about being laid off and about how he can't sleep. Then he just shuts up and gets real quiet and the next guy starts talking.

When I got home from the meeting, I did the little things I always did, had to do. I checked the mailbox for bills, trying not to look at the ones that were already piled up on the table. I didn't have to open them to know what they said. Gas man, electric man, mortgage man—they all wanted their money. And if they didn't get it, they were going to shut off stuff, take stuff back. I didn't open the bills, I left them in their nice clean little envelopes and tried to pretend that all that ugly shit wasn't inside each one. I hated pretend shit, hated myself for pretending. I turned off the lights, sat in the dark smoking cigarettes, and tried not to think about anything. Maybe I tried to pretend I didn't have anything to think about, be worried about.

I knew my mother was worried about me, had been worried. Sometimes I could still see her face when I told her I was leaving the newspaper to be with the magazine, give it all my time. The newspaper was going to fire me anyway; I was going to make them do it, had to. My mother said, *Think about it, think about what you've done to get there.* I had been there thirteen years and had done well. But I was making them fire me, making them do it while I looked in their eyes. I didn't want to leave the newspaper, but I couldn't stay any longer. I had seen the signs and I had seen them before.

Sometimes I could still feel, see in my mind, the last day at the paper. Somehow I knew it was going to be my last day. I had already started the magazine and was spending time after work and on weekends working on it. Other people at the newspaper did outside stuff too. One guy who wrote about dining out even had a TV show. A guy who reviewed plays had his own radio show. I wanted to grow too, maybe learn how to do art layouts, maybe even write stories. But I couldn't move up or move over. I had been allowed to come in the yard, but I damn well knew I'd never be allowed in the house to be a part of their white-faced family. When they hired me I was everything they were looking for: a black fist that wasn't balled up, an escapee from welfare. I would be their first colored photographer. They had only two other colored faces, but those belonged to clerks who didn't leave the office to show people the paper hired coloreds and had taken their signs down. But I knew the signs were still there; I could feel them even if I couldn't see them, and I knew what they said. I had seen the signs before, seen them in South Carolina, North Carolina, Virginia, seen them all saying the same thing: White only, no coloreds allowed here. I had lowered my head and followed the signs.

The manager of the paper was showing me the signs again. He didn't want to, he was an okay guy, but the editor told him what he had to do. He said I had to either give up the magazine or give up the newspaper. He talked real softly and it was real quiet in his little office. He asked if I had made up my mind about staying at the paper and letting the magazine go.

Now he's waiting on my answer. I can feel myself shaking inside. "Listen, I have to say something here before I give you my answer. Is that okay?"

"Sure," the manager says.

"First of all, I want you to know that I understand and I know you are not acting personally in this matter. You have always been a fair guy and I appreciate that. I know this is not your doing."

I pause for a moment, trying to find the words I want to say. Thirteen years and a lot of my life are coming to an end. I want these last moments to mean something; if not to anyone else, I want them to mean something to me.

"This whole thing is not right," I say, "and what I'm about to say is not going to change anything. But it is important for me to say it. The magazine is not just pages, pictures, and advertising to me, it's a chance to learn something and do something more. It's the chance I'm not getting here. But even that chance I could give up. It's important to me, but I could still give it up. But what I can't and won't give up is my right to be treated equally. When I was a kid in the Marines, I remember the first place I saw the WHITE ONLY, COLORED ONLY signs. They were on the wall in this train station in Rocky Mountain, North Carolina. You don't have the signs up here at the paper, but you have the same standards. I can't publish the magazine in my own time, but Pete can do his TV show, Curtis can do his radio show. That's not right. When I was a kid, I followed the signs; I couldn't do anything about them. I'll never forget seeing them, never. We all had our green Marine Corps uniforms on, but the colored kids had to go one way while the white kids could go the other way. All of us probably ended up in Vietnam. I know I did. I don't know whose freedom I was fighting for, but I know whose freedom I won, and that was mine. Now I can't stop you from doing what you're doing. But I'm going to make you do it. I'm not giving up the magazine. And I'm not resigning from the paper."

I didn't know what the road was going to be like up ahead. But I knew I had burned the bridge behind me, wanted to, had to. I knew I never wanted to go back and see the signs again, follow their ways. The magazine became everything, it had to; there was no bridge to run back across.

16

FIND HELP SOMEWHERE

I hated to see the mornings come; none of them were ever pretty anymore. When I got to the magazine's office, I'd hate to open up the door and go in. I could feel the hopelessness as soon as I stepped through the door. I'd try to push it away, take deep breaths and tell myself, *I've got to keep going, I can make it.* Sometimes Roger would call during the day to remind me of our appointments, but I knew he was really calling to see how I was doing. I hated to hear the phone ring, hated to see the little light flash every time it rang. I hated to pick it up, pretend that everything was fine. The magazine would be out soon, *Mother America and Jesus are my best friends.* I knew the printer would be calling. He knew Teresa had left and the magazine was hurting, knew I was hurting and half dead too.

It's him on the phone—I'm hearing "Hello, how are you doing?" I say, "It's been better" and try to get a cigarette lit. He's saying, "We've had a meeting here, and quite honestly, we are very concerned. You're into us for a lot of money. And we haven't had any payments from you in weeks. How are you coming along out there? We have to get some money in here. How are you going to get the magazine out? Do you have someone to do layout? How are your sales going?"

I don't want to hear what he's saying, asking, because it ain't nothin' but the truth of things. Red fuckin' blood with flies stuck in it, that's truth shit. Cold stuff fallin' on you in the night, you know it's rain. You ain't got to see it to know what the fuck it is. He's sayin' stuff I know is real. Five big empty rooms and a long silent hallway and I'm sittin' in the empty shit, stuck in it. It's real and I don't want it to be. It's that truth shit that I've got to lie to get out of or lie to stay in. Real soon I'm thinkin', *Fuck it.* The shit don't make no difference—the truth hurts, the lies hurt too. Just stay the fuck alive.

"Listen," I say, "I need some time to turn things around here. I can get things going again, but I need more time."

He says, "I understand that, but we need some money in here. What are your advertisers saying? You're late with the issue. They have to have their concerns. How much do you have out in receivables?"

I want to yell out, scream, but I can't. I want to say, Ain't no money here. I don't know when it's comin', if it's comin', 'cause ain't no place for it to come from. But I can yell out, make a quick move and let him know where I'm hidden. I say, "Receivables are a little slow, but I still have enough to cover the last run."

"How much money do you have out?"

"About ten thousand."

"That's hardly enough to cover what you owe me for the last issue. What about your other expenses—how are you going to cover them? What about the rent out there, how are you going to cover that? I'm very concerned about what your other creditors might do. I have to know, what is your situation out there?"

He's comin' after me, sees where I'm hidin'. I'm thinkin' fast, but I can't make no fast moves. Slowly I'm gettin' my head down, coverin' up. I tell him, "I'm not having any problems with them. Sure, they want their money too, but I explained the situation to them and told them I need a little time."

He moves off, says to give him a call next week. He said that about ten minutes ago, but I can still hear his voice in my head. I don't want to hear it because I've got to think, make the things I told him come true. He can stop printing the magazine, kill it the rest of the way. I'm up now, can't sit still in my chair. I have to walk some, walk up and down this silent hallway. I'm trying to think, say things in my head, like *I've got a week, maybe two. I have to come up with something.*

It's another meeting night and I don't want to go. I want to keep driving, find some road that just keeps going, but I'm passing the faces in the window. The little waiting room is all filled up with guys drinking coffee, waiting for the meeting to start. They all have that quiet look on their faces; even when they see someone they know, say something to him, their faces are still silent-looking. I see Billy and nod to him. He comes over to where I'm standing and asks how I'm doing. I just sigh some and shrug my shoulders.

I'm in the meeting room now; Roger's getting the meeting started. There're some new guys and he's introducing them and telling them they don't have to talk if they don't want to. One guy's all dirty—he looks like he's homeless or has been drunk for a long time. His eyes are sunken into his face and real dark. I'm wondering how he got that way. I'm not looking at him, I've got my head down and am staring at the floor, but I can still see his face in my mind while Roger's talking. He's asking how we're feeling tonight and whether we want to have a go-around. I wonder if the new guy's going to say anything.

Some other guy starts talking first. He tells how he had to go up to the VA Hospital during the week because he kept getting bad headaches. He says he's been getting them a lot—he has a steel plate in his head from when he got hit. They had to put the plate in because part of his skull was missing. He's pissed off because the VA Hospital said they couldn't do anything and told him to take aspirin.

Some other guy's talking now, saying how he has bad dreams all the time and he doesn't like to go to sleep. I'm trying to listen, but I keep thinking about the magazine. I don't want to think about the magazine, I don't want to think about anything. I don't want to hear this guy talking about dark stuff in the night. But maybe I'm in his night anyway and just looking out at stuff, seeing shit that I don't want to be a part of either. I hear Billy's voice; he's saying how he can't sleep either. He's talking but he sounds like he doesn't want to talk. His words are all choppy, I peek at him and I can see him sitting with his head down. He's just staring at the floor and trying to talk. I guess he's seeing what he doesn't want to say. He explains how when he first got to Vietnam they sent him to the infantry. He's talking about his platoon and how he didn't know any of the guys. He had been there only a week when he was picked to crawl down into this tunnel to see if there were any VC down there. He's shaking now, but he explains how they gave him a pistol and a flashlight and he had to crawl into the tunnel first—some other guy was going to follow him in. He says how dark and damp the tunnel was, and even with the flashlight he couldn't see well because the tunnel had a lot of curves in it. His face is turning red now and he's really shaking. He tells how all of a sudden the light from his flashlight was shining right in this VC face, and the VC stared back at him and pointed a gun right at his head. He tells how fast it happened. He couldn't move, and the VC shot at him and just missed his face by inches, and the guy behind him shot the VC. He was so scared he couldn't move, and the guy behind him had to drag him back out of the tunnel. He's saying how scared he was the whole time he was there and how he still can't sleep. He's real quiet now, but he's still trying to say something. His lips are moving, but no words are coming out. The group is quiet too because everybody knows he hasn't finished trying to talk. He says something about this time when they had to search a village. He's bringing his hands up to his face and putting his face into his hands so nobody can see him. He says, "After we searched the village, our CO . . . our CO said . . . he said we had to kill everybody in the village . . . He said it was a VC village and we had to kill everybody . . . He said we had to kill the . . . He said we had to kill the kids too. I swear to God I didn't want to, I swear I didn't. Some of the other guys started shooting right away . . . The villagers were screaming, and the kids were all crying too. I swear to God I didn't want to . . . I didn't . . . but I did it. I shot some of them kids too. They were screaming and crying and I still shot them . . . I did it."

Billy isn't saying anything now, he's just shaking, and he's still got both hands up in front of his face. Other guys are talking now, but they're saying things to Billy. They're telling him, "Hey man, you gotta let it go. You got to let it go. Let it go, man, that stuff happened. That's the way it went down sometimes."

I ain't sayin' nothin'. I can't. My head's back down and what my eyes are seein' on the floor my mind can't see at all. I'm hearin', "That stuff happened . . . Let it go, man," but it sounds real far away. I'm seein' the blue shirt again, that kid trying to sneak away. He's runnin', he's runnin' again, he won't stop. He's runnin' into them green bushes, but I'm still seein' that blue shirt. It's bouncin' up and down in front of my black rifle sights. I'm seein' things I ain't told myself, didn't want to say I saw. I'm seein' the blue shirt, seein' it wiggling in the green. I'm feelin' my finger pullin' back the trigger. I'm firin' at the back of the blue shirt, seein' it falling or something in the green. I don't want to see it again, see that other color I saw. That red color sprayin' real quick-like. I'm seein' that red anyway, know I saw it then. Didn't want to see it then, didn't want to say I saw it. Maybe I been wantin' to say, to believe up in my head, that the kid ain't dead, wasn't even hit. He ain't lyin' there on the other side of that creek. He's still livin', ain't even thinkin' about me here thinkin' about him. I'm thinkin' *Fuck it, one way or the other I'm still here. Fuck it, I should have crossed the creek and checked the shit out. Fuck it, he was a VC and had a gun. Fuck it if he wasn't, he shouldn't have run.* I wouldn't have fired at him, but I did and kept firin' until I didn't see him no more. *Fuck it,* I'm thinkin', but I ain't feelin' what I'm thinkin'.

Roger's talking now, telling Billy something. I'm trying to listen because I don't want to think about that kid in the blue shirt anymore. Now some other guy's talking, telling about shit he can't put out of his mind and throw away.

I'm talking now, but I'm not saying a lot—I just don't want to. Now I'm saying a little bit more about what I'm feeling, but I don't want to be shaking on the outside. Maybe I'm not shaking and just feel like I am, but I'm still talking and saying stuff about the kid.

Roger's still talking, saying something like "Time can only heal clean wounds." He isn't saying it that way, but that's the way I'm hearing it. I'm thinking, *Are we dirty?* but I know he doesn't mean it that way. He means sometimes we have to get those festering memories out of our minds before we can start to feel better.

Now he's telling us about what's going to happen next week. I look up now because I hadn't heard anything about a replica of the Vietnam memorial wall being brought to Pittsburgh. He's saying how it's going to be set up in some park over on the north side. In my mind I see the stuff I saw on TV when they put the real memorial wall up in D.C., and I wonder where Vernon's and the others' names are on it. I don't know whether or not I want to go see the wall. I know I want to one day, have to before I die. But now it's coming to see me and I have to be ready for it.

Sometimes I don't want to know what time it is, what day it is. Things that are coming, I don't want to come—don't want to know how close they're getting. Advertisers call, wanting to know when the magazine's going to be out. I tell them things I believe myself, keep believing until I hang the phone up. The landlord doesn't believe a thing I'm telling him. His office is right upstairs and he can see that the magazine isn't moving and his money isn't coming up the steps. I want to pray, but I can't. I can't be asking Jesus to come get me. He won't come and I know it; I've gone too far from his reach. I wanted to get away from it, didn't want to bend back and turn the other cheek. I knew he wasn't going to take a big ad out in the magazine, I already asked him a long time ago. But my mother's still telling me I've got to pray. *He's with you, you got a friend in Jesus.* She says, *Don't be thinking you're sitting out in that office all alone and no one cares about you.* I don't want to say anything back because I know she's so worried. I don't want to say, *I know I'm all alone.* I push away people who want to touch me. I don't want them to touch me, because it might hurt. I don't want them to get too close, because I don't know when things are going to blow up in my face. And I don't want them to get hurt too.

I've got to keep moving, find ads for the magazine, find somebody to lay it out, find things I can't see in the dark. I make phone calls, trying to find the things I need. Sometimes I can see time, see it standing in the corner of my office. It has an ugly gray face that doesn't smile. I can't see its eyes—it doesn't have any eyes—but I can feel it looking at me anyway. It's dark gray, but I can see it in the dark too, see it there in my bedroom when I'm trying to get to sleep. It's there in the morning too, and it won't smile even when the birds sing.

Roger calls me to see how things are going, I tell him, "Ain't too many things going right." He says, "Hang tight, man, you've been through worse. Are you going to be able to get your magazine out in time?"

"No," I say, "I've got to skip an issue. Maybe I can combine it with the next issue, make it some special issue or something."

He keeps talking to me, telling me to stay calm and asking me if I'm coming with the group to see the memorial wall. I tell him I'll be there because I know I have to go. It's as if Vernon and the others are coming to town and I have to be there. But I don't want to go, see their faces when I see their names. I'm tired of death and being a part of it. I had to take pictures of it too. I had to be a photographer in a hospital, go down and take pictures of autopsies. I had to see some pretty teenage girl lying there dead and still looking alive with her high school ring on her finger. I had to watch them cut her open, bring her heart over to me so I could take pictures of it. I had to hear the blood dripping on that cold cement floor and pretend it didn't bother me. Then I had to whisper to her heart that I didn't want to see it this way.

It was time to go over to the wall. The little reception room was full. Some of the guys there I hadn't seen before; they had come to see the wall too. Some vans were parked outside; we were all going over together in them. Their parking lights were flashing, little quick lights lighting up the dark street. The ride over to the north side didn't take long—didn't take as long as I wanted it to take. The outer part of the park was dark, and the trees had become creatures in the night. They stood like silent ushers along the dark path that led to the park's center. Beyond the path I could see a glow coming from lights, and then I could see the lights. They were lighting up the memorial wall. It was still far away, but I could see it, see its dark V-shaped form within the light. I could see people in front of the wall, some moving slowly, others standing still in the stillness in front of the wall.

When I was closer, I could see a soft white glow coming from the darkness of the wall. I knew it must be the names being lit up by the lights. I kept walking, but I tell you, Jesus or whoever else can care, give a damn, hear me when I ain't sayin' a word, I didn't want to be there, I wanted to turn around and crawl away, then get up and run into the night. But I had to keep going and I knew it. *I'm going to find your name, Vern—I don't know where it is, but I'm going to find it. I'm going to find yours too, Glickman. I'm going to find all of you guys. I know you're all close together—I'm coming.*

When I found the names, I just stood and stared at them. I had to reach up and touch them and say I was sorry. Say some things I guess I just had to say. Sometimes I had to look down, look away from the names. When I did, I could see other people standing around me and staring at the wall. Some of them had tears in their eyes, and I could hear soft whispers all around me. I started staring at a woman standing near me. Maybe it was because of the way the light fell so gently on her face, making it a tender glow in the dark. She was an older woman, maybe my mother's age. Her face was brown and weary but looking up toward the wall. Her face wasn't moving; she didn't turn it away, kept looking at whatever she saw. Only the tears rolling down her cheeks gave movement to the moment.

Maybe I wanted to cry too, put my head down in front of this wall and cry for a long time. I couldn't do that, though. I felt like I wanted to, but I couldn't. I was looking at the wall, and I knew I was smiling a little. *I found your name, Felter—didn't see it before. I should have known you wouldn't be where you were supposed to be anyway. I'm lookin' at your name but seein' that face of yours always lookin' like you ain't shaved in three days. I'm hearin' you talkin', man, makin' fun of stuff that would make most people sick. I'm hearin' you in them dark nights. Everybody else be down in them holes, half scared, half asleep, half the time all wet from the goddamn rain. Everybody be tryin' to be all quiet, but not you, man. You'd start makin' them Donald Duck sounds, get somebody else to start makin' them cartoon sounds too. You made us laugh in the dark, didn't you? You didn't live too long, but you laughed at the shit, made us laugh and smile too.*

I stayed at the wall until it was time to leave, when I said goodbye to Vern and the others. It was like being at a funeral, feeling stuff like that. Feeling sad but feeling good about being there and showing you cared. I guess I never really thought about it, but I never had a chance to say goodbye to everybody like I did when I left the wall. When I got home, I felt different from the way I had felt before. I wasn't all happy and stuff like that, but it was a real good feeling. When I lay down on the bed to get some sleep, I could feel my body rising, floating like some kind of cloud. I guess it was peace I was feeling.

In the morning I could still feel the peace, and I tried to keep it all day. But I had to move on, keep moving.

Some good things started to happen. A kid named Hank called; he was an art student looking for layout work. He came in and we talked. He didn't have much experience, but he said he would try to help out. I started getting the office cleaned up, and I got the intern to come in more often and try to get the stories ready to go to the typesetter. When I was alone in the office, I tried not to feel alone, to keep things going. I found a salesperson, Kerry, to work part-time. A week went by, and then that time that I didn't want to watch passing came and went too. I needed money, twelve thousand at least, and it had to come in prepaid ads. I knew the printer wouldn't take any more promises. He didn't know it, but I had learned a lot from him over the years. He was always businesslike, but even when I had to meet with him to talk about how much money the magazine owed him, he'd show me ways that I might be able to make things work. In a way, I didn't want to let him down. I knew he could have pulled the plug on the magazine a long time before this.

I had to keep going, selling ads, putting little pieces of the magazine together. I told the advertisers, *Yes, the magazine's still alive. Teresa left and we have to reorganize, but we'll be coming out with the fall/holiday issue soon.* I called the printer to let him know what was happening, where I was with things. But I wasn't where I wanted to be, had to be. The days were getting shorter and the nights had a chill in them. September had come and it wouldn't stay forever. Kerry was trying, but I needed more salespeople and I couldn't get them. And if I did, they didn't stay. One lasted two days, never came back. Every advertiser she went to told her they had heard the magazine was going out of business.

Roger still calls to see how I'm doing. He wants me to keep coming down to see him for my daytime sessions. I can't—September is passing and October is only days away. Some money from new ads is coming in and I'm sending it out real quick to the printer, the landlord, and anybody else who can kill the magazine. Sometimes I forget the peace I found—have to, because I can't be peaceful and fight to stay alive at the same time. I hate Sundays, because I can't sell ads, keep going. I have to think on Sundays, but I try not to. I just want to be alone, away from everybody and everything. But I'm too alone and I know it. Ain't no love in my life, warm arms I can come home to, fall into and just say, *Hold me.* Me and love could never hold hands too long. Maybe I wanted too much, wanted something to last more than the time it did. More than the couple of years or months, overnights in a strange bed whispering to a stranger and smelling her perfume, wanting to keep her scent beyond the next sunrise. Warm breast against my chest ain't close to me. It's Sunday and I'm alone.

Mondays and I have to move out again, up the fuckin' hill in the mud. One advertiser says yes, a hundred million seem to say no. But I have to keep going, find another to say yes; noes don't count, can't count. October didn't last long, it's gone and November's cold. I still need six, seven thousand dollars, and I don't have six or seven days left to get it. That ugly face of time is everywhere I look, gettin' up in my face. Sometimes I want to see its eyes, stare back at it, but it's too ugly. The magazine is going to die, but I can't fool myself anymore: I'm the magazine, always was. I'm dying. I'm going to be dead and still alive to look at myself, smell myself stinkin', see me going back to Homewood and no one knowin' my name.

The printer is on the phone, wanting to know when the rest of his money's coming. He knows my hours are few. I tell him soon; I'll pull through. I'm running out in the open, too scared to stop—I have to get where I'm going.

I'm on the phone talking to one of the big advertisers, one who's been with the magazine since it started. I'm saying, "Listen, Ed, I have some situations here, they're serious. I'm going to get to the point. I need six thousand dollars. If I don't get it, the printer won't print. I don't have any time left. This is what I want to do. Our back cover is fifteen hundred in color. I'll give it to you for a thousand an issue for the next six issues. But I need you to pay up front. You understand? I have to do this, I have to ask you."

I can hear, feel the silence between us. Now I hear him saying, "I know you have been struggling out there. And you know what we think of the magazine here—we've always been behind you. Let me check my budget and have a quick talk with my advertising agency. I'll call you back within the hour."

"Ed, if you can't do it, I'll understand. If you can do it, please do so."

"I hear you."

I wait, looking at the clock and hearing my breath fill up my little office. Cigarette smoke is floating through the air; sometimes I watch it instead of the clock. I have fifty more minutes to wait. The phone's ringing and I don't want to answer it, answer some question I don't know the the answer to, try to sound all normal.

I pick the phone up, say that good-afternoon stuff, can I help you. It's Ed calling back already, and he's saying, "We'll do it, it's a go. Get me a letter stating the terms. I'll see to it that we cut you a check by tomorrow."

"Oh my . . . Thanks!"

"I'm just glad we can do it. We don't want to see the magazine go under."

I'm everything I wasn't a moment ago. I'm alive and I can feel it, I can feel that feeling I had the night I left the wall. I'm still talking to Ed, going over the details about artwork for his ad. Now I'm talking to the printer, telling him his money will be there. Now I'm looking at the calendar, counting days I have and need to get the magazine ready to go. I've got to keep moving. I'm calling the art school kid, telling him to get in as soon as possible, we are going to print. I'm calling the new salesperson, telling her to keep selling until the end of the week, then we're closing and going to print.

Everything is moving now and I have to keep it moving. I'm doing work I've never done before and don't know how to do, but I'm doing it anyway. I'm speccing type, editing stories. If a story is a few inches too long, I find a few short paragraphs that are an inch long and cut them out with the scissors. If a story is too short, I make the picture bigger to fill up the space. If the art school kid doesn't know how to do something, I tell him to pretend he does and do it anyway. I have to keep moving, and I ain't stoppin' for nothin'.

Everything kept moving fast. The magazine was at the printer's. Then the first copies came to the office. I took one from a box and sat quietly at my desk and just stared at it. The battle was over, and I was still alive and alone with the memories.

The year was coming to an end. December tenth had come and passed with peace. When it came, in my mind I could still see the fires burning in the treeline, but I could see the dark wall beneath the lights and feel its peace. Christmas was coming and I was in town looking for presents. It was cold, and I walked fast through the crowded streets. I had neared the end of a block and stopped to wait for the traffic light to change. I knew it was him, felt it was him when I saw him. I just caught a glimpse of him through the window, driving a passing bus, but I knew it was him. I knew it was Nooty, I felt it, felt that time of Macky, Georgie, and Nooty. I felt the trains going by again and could see me and Georgie up on the railroad tracks. I could hear Macky yelling, *Daddy's comin', Daddy's comin',* and see them running to meet the car driving up. I could see their daddy getting out of the car, giving them dimes and nickels. I could see me standing there watching and knowing I had to remember the moment, remember him looking at me and asking how I was doing.

It's night now, the day's gone, but I can still see the bus passing and Nooty through the window. I started thinking of Richie, years had passed, maybe even ten since that day I saw him at the park. Me knowing he was my younger brother and him knowing I was the kid who lived up the street. He is a man now, but I still recognize him. I call to him, "Hey, Richie. You're Richie, aren't you?" He sees me, knows it's me, and comes over, saying, "Hey, how you doin'?"

"Okay, man. Damn, it's good to see you. I thought it was you. How's Macky and them?"

"Mack's fine, he's in D.C. Nooty's doin' great, he's been with the Port Authority, drivin' them buses. He's making good money down there. I was just up his house yesterday. George—well, you know George, he ain't changed."

"Oh, what's he up to?"

"He's doin' better, he's outta the joint. He's been outta there for about five years now. He was working for a while, had some job at some factory. But you know George, that wasn't going to last but so long."

"How's your mom, she doing okay?"

"She's fine, she's doing good. She lives right over there by Food Land. You know, that new one they built over behind the school."

I have to ask and I know it. And when I do, I can feel the sounds of my words coming up from inside me. "How is your father, Richie, is he okay?"

"Ahh . . . he passed away, just last month."

I sigh and hear myself saying, "Oh, that's too bad, I'm sorry to hear that . . ." But I'm feeling stuff inside starting to shake. It's starting to hurt, too. Richie's still talking, he's saying, "Yeah, he got real sick and died" on this date or that date. I keep saying things back, like what hospital, was he sick long, what happened to him. But inside I keep seeing him coming, Macky and the others running to him. He's passing by me and I'm looking up at him. But now I'm reaching for him, trying to turn him around and say things to him. Say, *What about me? What about me? Touch me too.*

He was dead now; a touch would never come. *I didn't even know you were dead. I wanted to see you just one time, then maybe again. I wanted to look into your face. I don't hate you, I just don't understand. I wanted to say some things, tell you I'm okay. I got shot, but I didn't cry. I did okay, never got in trouble. I took pictures for the paper. I started a magazine. I made it, I'm not mad at you. I'm your son too.*

I said goodbye to Richie and went home. I wanted to get away and be alone. I wanted to say, *Fuck it, it never was anyway, he didn't care anyway.* But feelings inside wouldn't go away. They didn't have words to say what they were; they didn't need any. I knew what hurting stuff was anyway.

Christmas passed and the new year came. I was waiting for it, wanted it to come. Christmas decorations were still up on some of the houses, pretty colored bulbs still hanging around windows. People were still wishing each other a happy new year. Everybody was still happy. The printer was still happy; he got some of his money. Advertisers were happy; some even called to say how nice the issue was. I wanted to be happy, but I wasn't, I just felt good and alive. The office was still empty, but I was going to fill it up, get new people in whom I could depend on. I needed a new editor, new salespeople, new everything. I had time, lots of time, not that last-breath time before I had to get the next issue out. It was a good issue to get out; it was the bridal issue and always easy to get ads for. But I was still afraid that the magazine's reputation was damaged beyond what I knew.

The days started going by again and I was trying to go faster, get ahead of the bills. I was finding salespeople and getting them started. I found two in the first week and was still looking for more. I found and hired a young woman from Massachusetts to be the editor. Her name was Christy, and she had just moved to Pittsburgh and really loved becoming editor of the magazine. She was in her early thirties and carried herself well. I got hold of Hank, the art student, and told him to learn how to pretend he was an art director, because that's what his title was going to be for the next issue.

The magazine was coming alive again, I could see it and feel it. Ads and money started coming in every day. There were always people in the office doing things to get the issue ready. The printer didn't have to call to see when his money was coming, I was already sending him payments. Sometimes I couldn't believe what the new year was bringing. January had not passed yet and the ad board was just about filled up. I'm telling the salespeople to keep selling. I'm telling Hank to stand by, get ready to make the magazine bigger. Lots of full-page ads are coming in. I'm calling the printer to see how many pages of color I can get if I add two more spreads. He's still happy; he's been getting checks in just about each day. I'm telling him how well things are going, and he wants to know when I'll be ready to print.

Spring came quick and I was moving fast, making things happen. I didn't know the death of the magazine was waiting, I thought I had gotten past it. When it came, it came slow. It couldn't die fast, say *Oh my God* and go in peace. It had to look in my eyes, beg me for help I couldn't give it because I was dying too.

I thought help had come, some attorney named Ross wanted to invest, help out, but it was only another ambush in the night. He wasn't anything he said he was. I was caught out in the open of a corporate ambush, he stole the magazine. He knew I would probably die without it, he didn't know it couldn't live without me. It died too.

17

THE LIGHT BULB

I had not been to the magazine's office in days, long days that had passed slowly. I watched them pass, felt them go by. Sometimes I'd stand by the window and just look out, see people walking up and down the sidewalk, kids playing. I'd see the same people pass at the same time each day on their way to work. Same kids would play across the street, same sun would set in the same place in the sky, but I didn't feel a part of anything I saw. I didn't want to be a part of the fucking world.

When the phone rang I didn't want to answer it, hear more hell and shit trying to squeeze into my ear at the same time. The sound of its ringing filled the room each time it rang. I stared at the phone, then held my breath as I reached for it.

"Yes," I answer, trying to hold on to some hope that it just might be somebody calling a wrong number. Maybe it's Jesus calling to tell me everything's going to be all right. But it ain't him callin'. I can hear the landlord's voice. I'm holding my breath while he's talking, telling me I have to get the magazine's stuff out of the office. He's telling me what he'll let me take and what he's going to keep. He's keeping the desk, the other furniture; he's going to sell it and try to get some of his money back. I'm not saying anything—I can't. He's right and I know it, but it just doesn't feel right. He's asking when I can come get the stuff he doesn't want. Now he's saying that if I don't get there today he's going to have to throw stuff out. I say I understand, I'll be down later to get the stuff.

I look back out the window: same kids playing, same world still out there. But I'm not thinking about what I'm seeing—I can't. It's over for me, everything's over. The magazine's dead, I'm dead. Motherfuckers is pickin', gettin' ready to gnaw on my bones. I'm dead, but I'm still feelin' shit. I would have been dead, but that bullet didn't kill me. It just made me think I was dying. Maybe it did kill me and I just think I'm livin'. Maybe I'm dead, someplace where fucked-up souls go, and I'm sittin' there wishin' so hard I was here that I see myself here. I can see myself, feel myself here, feel all this shit around me. But I ain't really here, never was. I was lyin' there with Glickman, I just didn't look at me.

I don't want to look out the window anymore, don't want to see anybody. I'm not in that bright sun-shining world anyway. It's August, somewhere in the middle of it. It's 1988. I don't want to think the way I'm thinking. I want to walk away from myself, say, *This shit is crazy, it ain't real.* I can hear myself sighing, see something dark I'm staring at. I don't know how long I've been staring into the corner of the room. I want to yell, scream. Maybe go to the window and scream out of it, scream *Help me. Somebody come and help me, go tell Jesus to come. Tell him I'm in trouble.* But I can't, I've got to keep still, keep down. I don't want anybody around me, nobody. *Mother, I don't want you around me. I wish you didn't even have me, know me. I don't want you around this ugly shit, don't want you around if I have to go out in the night again. I'm going, too, sooner or later.*

I'm still looking out the window, seeing the same shit. But it ain't August no more and I ain't me. I ain't nobody, I ain't doin nothin', can't do nothin' except wait. But I can't wait, I'll never come back alive if I wait. But I got to wait. Maybe I can get the magazine goin' again, get even with that lawyer and the rest of them. I know it's them callin', makin' funny sounds in the phone, then hangin' up. I'm goin' to kill them. I'm scared, scared of me, scared of what I might do. I don't want to see them. I know time's goin' by, I know it's September, but I'm stuck in one moment of shit, right in the center of it. I can't move, got to keep still. I don't go out of the house unless I need cigarettes, food. Then I come right back and get down again, keep still, wait until night comes. I can get in the dark then, breathe easier. I don't have to be anybody in the dark. The gas man doesn't come at night and pound on the door like he does during the day. I don't open the door; I know it's him. If it's not him, it's the electric man wanting to tell me the same thing the gas man wants to say. I know they'll go away, just leave their tacked-up notices stuck on the door. I don't read the notices, don't have to. I just look to see what date they're going to cut the shit off. See how much time I have to come up with money I know I can't get. I don't want to think about money, can't think about it. It's too far away to think about, and it ain't comin'. I got to stay down, keep still, wait.

My life is over, I just don't want to say it. September is over and I don't want it to be October, November. It ain't, it's just time, faceless time, nameless time. Just time you feel, don't want to feel. But it comes anyway, crawls over you like a snake in the night. You don't want to move, can't move. But it's night, you can keep your eyes closed, keep dreaming. You can dream stuff away, go where you want, run back into a different time. I hear noises, little scratchy sounds. It's cold now, fuckin' mice are comin' into the house. I watch for them, stare out from my bedroom door, see the quick little blur they make runnin' into the kitchen. There's a lot of them. I should get some traps, kill them. Fuck it. I can't do anything, I just wait. I can't kill the mice, that would be doin' something. I can't, I have to wait. I don't want to make decisions anymore, I don't want to do anything anymore. I can't anyway, can't even flush the toilet. I stand there, stare at the shit, piss. I got to flush it, got to. But I don't have to look in the mirror, I don't want to do that. I don't want to shave, shower. I don't want to get out of the bed, take a shower. Fuck the goddamn mice. I see you motherfuckers. I can see you sneakin', can even see you in the dark. I know you're comin' before I see you, I can hear you, feel you comin'. You're comin', mouse mother-fucker, wigglin' your ass up through that hole. Then you peep at me, see if I'm asleep. Phone ringin', I know it's you, CitiBank, World Bank, Universe Motherfuckin' Bank. All you-all callin', tryin' to call at the same time. I told you, I don't have any money, business went down, I'm havin' a real bad time, I'll send somethin' if I can. They don't want to hear that "if" shit. But they don't know I ain't nothin' but an "if." My whole world is "if." "If" shit all around me.

December comes, gets in my mind. It's December tenth all over again. I ain't no better off now than what the fuck I was then. Twenty fuckin'-some years and I'm in the middle of the rice paddy again.

Motherfuckers shootin' at me, tryin' to kill me again. I'm hidin' all over again, listenin' for the gas man to pound on the door. Duckin' from the electric man. Christmas is comin', can't be far off with its red, green, all kinds of colored lights I don't want to see, be a part of.

Christmas came and I hated myself, hated hearing myself say Merry Christmas and trying to be happy around my family. I hated myself because I was lying to them too. Trying to make them believe I wasn't fucked up, I was just waiting—that's all, just waiting. I could go out any day, go find a job, start life all over again. Yeah, I could do it, I did it before. Ain't nothin' wrong with me, I'm just waitin', waitin' to kill motherfuckers. I want them more dead than I want to be alive. My mother can't say nothin' to me, I won't let her. I won't let nobody talk to me. I ain't gettin' a job, draggin' my ass out and bowing. I ain't beggin', tellin' anybody, *Oh yeah, I used to be a big-time magazine publisher, but I just have a high school education. Make me something important so I won't feel like shit for the rest of my life.* Fuck it, I ain't nobody anyway, never was. Just some bastard child, fucked-up accident that keeps fuckin' up. Yeah, I'm a nigger too. Let that white-ass Jones fuck me up. I ain't nothin', mice don't even give a fuck about me. They come out whenever they want, don't give a damn if I'm lookin' at them or not. One motherfucker's real bold, climbs up the toaster wire and gets on the kitchen table. I'm tryin' to figure out what the hell they're findin' to eat. Spiders are havin' fun too, got webs all over the fuckin' place. I look at them, see if I can see the spiders. I can't see them all the time, just them other little bugs caught in the web. I'm caught in a web too, 'cept I can't see, just feel it. Sometimes if a little bug ain't dead, I pick it out, let it go. Sometimes I don't, I let them stay in there. That's their fuckin' problem. I got my own web and they ain't helpin' me.

Months and months, weeks, days, going by. I know it, I see the time passin' the window. Sometimes it's snowin', looks real cold, wind's blowin' a broken branch all over the place. It gets warm again, kids outside playin' again, but I'm still waitin'. Ain't a fuckin' moment went by in my head, 'cept if I'm sleepin' and have a happy-ass dream. I don't want to wake up, have real shit slappin' me in the face. Windows opened or closed, I can still hear the mailman comin'. I can hear the sounds of his footsteps comin' across the lawn, comin' up the steps. I don't breathe, keep still, listen for the sound of his footsteps to go away. I wait until I know he's gone, then I open the door real quick. I keep holdin' my breath while I look at it, hope it ain't what it always is. Some of the bills I don't open, I know what they say. I hide them from myself, put them in different little places so I won't have to see them. I got them hid all over the place. Sometimes I'll forget I stuck some bill somewhere, be lookin' for something else and find a bill.

Sometimes I try to be me again, feel like I'm still alive and can do stuff. I'm alive again, yeah, I'm goin' to make it. I'm going out there, I'm going outside and be around people, start the magazine again. People are going to know I'm still alive, I didn't quit, run and hide. Yeah, I know I can do it again.

I can't, I can't do nothin' except find shit I'm hidin' from myself. Sometimes I can't even do that, can't even see, fuckin' light bulbs keep burnin' out. Sometimes I got one left, got to unscrew the motherfucker and carry it with me. I want to see to piss, got to take the light bulb to the bathroom, screw it in there. I'm done pissin', fuck it, I could have pissed in the dark, what difference would it make. Ain't nobody givin' a fuck where I'm pissin', fuckin' friends ain't friends anymore. Nobody wants to talk to me, hear me sayin' the same thing over again. Fuck them, I can't talk about nothin' else. They get tired of hearin' how my life is destroyed. They get tired of hearin' how I'm goin' to get even, get the magazine up again. Fuck them, that's why I ain't tellin' them I got one light bulb, burn my fingers on it when I'm tryin' to unscrew it and take it someplace else. It's hot when I'm carryin' it in my hands. But I can't drop it, it would be all dark then.

I can't cry, I wish I could. Maybe I won't wake up tomorrow, all this shit would be over. I got to do something, but I ain't goin' outside. Ain't goin' to do that, can't anyway. I don't like it out there all in the open. I got to go and get cigarettes, coffee or somethin'. Ain't a long walk but I don't want to go, have people lookin' at me. I don't want them askin' me how I'm doin'. I ain't nothin' worth askin' how I'm doin'. Just give me the cigarettes, leave me alone. I hear myself sayin' things, talkin' back to people. I'm smilin', sayin' some nice shit about the weather. I can hear me sayin', *Yeah, you have a nice day too.* It's hot, cold, don't make any difference, I walk real fast. I want to get back home, get back in the house, get away from all that outside shit. But I don't want to go in the house either. I don't want to be in there, stuck in its fuckin' spiderwebs. I'm going to kill them damn mice. Phone's ringin', I ain't answerin' it. It's done ringin', I'm still shakin', wonderin' who it was. I ain't got no money for nobody. If I did, I'd pay all you-all. Take the motherfuckin' money and shove it up your fuckin' ass. It ain't about money, never was. It was about livin', and I don't have no life no more. I'm a ghost, fucked up my chance at livin'. I'm hurtin' and I can't make it go away. I don't want to kill nobody, but I don't want to be dead like this. Dead stuff just stinks, turns ugly colors. Gets ugly yellow, green, purple, black-lookin'. I ain't cried, ain't goin' to cry. I ain't dyin' without takin' some motherfuckers with me. I can't die now and I can't live. I don't want to go outside, either.

It's some night, late in some night. I know it's late because it's quiet, been quiet for a while. I'm thinkin', seein' stuff in my mind. I keep seein' you guys, seein' me in our time, seein' us in the night. I can feel the rain comin' down on me, feel the cold wet ground I'm lyin' on. I can see the raindrops drippin' on them leaves, branches. But I keep lookin' at the path, keep tryin' to keep my eyes open, keep rubbin' my finger over the trigger. I can feel everything I'm seein' in my mind. I want to do something now. Maybe I'll try it. Yeah, why not. I ain't got nothin' else to do.

I'm up, lookin' around the house for a pen that writes. I find one, find a notebook that has lots of empty pages in it. I'm still seein' stuff in my mind, but I'm lookin' at the empty page. I want to put the stuff I see in my mind on the page. I want to draw it with words, draw the feelings of it, draw the feelings into little words. I want to see Vernon's face in the night, make it into a portrait with words. I want to bring that time back, but I know I can't change it. Vernon still has to die; the wind is going to blow Glickman's hair again, I'm going to be afraid again. I'm writing now, I'm sitting in a chair and using the end table for a desk. Words are coming, feelings won't go away. I see what I'm writing about, see fear on faces all over again. I can hear things too, the cracking sound of a branch breaking in the night. I keep writing, trying to squeeze feelings until little words come out. I'm on the next page already. I can't stop writing; I don't want to, either. Light is coming through the window; it's nearly morning. I can hear the birds singing; the sun will be coming up soon. I don't want it to come up and bring its bright new day. I want it to stay dark, I want to stay in the dark, I want to keep writing. I don't want the sun coming and bringing its mailman, its gas man. I'm on page ten, I want to keep going. I don't know what time it is, don't care either, but I'm tired. I don't want to go to sleep, I want to stay up with Vernon and the others. I want to keep moving out, be something again, feel something again, feel alive.

It must be near noon now. I lay down for a while, but I'm up again and writing. I'm done with one chapter; it's twenty-three pages long. I'm going to do another one, write about something else that happened. The phone is ringing, but I'm not answering it. I keep writing; fuck the mailman, the fuckin' mice, and everything else too. I'm not counting the days and weeks going by. I'm just counting pages. I write stuff in my notebook first, then when I'm done with a chapter I do it over again on the typewriter. I can't type, but I can push the *A* key if I want to make an *A*. I can find the little letters that make the words. I can't spell, but I don't know I can't spell so it's not a problem. I was just going to do one short story, but now I have a lot of them. Each little story has its own title and chapter number. I'm not writing a book, but maybe it will be. Sometimes when I write, it hurts when I see stuff happen all over again. Sometimes I stop writing and light a cigarette, sit and try to wait until the blood goes away. I don't know what I'm going to call the book, if it is a book. I don't want it to be some kind of Rambo book. I'm not writing it that way. We were scared. We were just average guys. I know that now; I want to write about how we were. That's what I'm doing. Felter wasn't brave, he was just out of his fuckin' mind. Franko was way out of his fuckin' mind; if he's still alive, he's probably still crazy. I'm crazy now, I know I'm fucked up. I can think it, but I can't say it out loud and hear myself saying it.

A fuckin' spider just crawled over the paper. I didn't kill it, just watched it. Let it live.

Outside it's summer again; kids are playing across the street, the sun is shining every day. I don't want to look out the window and see it. I have to go to the store, get coffee, cigarettes, and stuff. It's hot, but I'm still walking fast. I'm thinking fast too; stuff keeps bouncing back and forth in my mind. I know I'm not anybody anymore, just some man walking to the store with a couple dollars, quarters, dimes, pennies, all in one pocket. People at the store are used to me buying stuff with quarters and dimes, giving them a lot of pennies too. But I'm not thinking or giving a damn about the people in the store. I want to get back home, write stuff. In my mind I can see things, feel things I want to write down when I get back home. I don't want to think about the other stuff, mailman stuff, phone-ringing, bill-collector stuff. But it won't go away; when it's not the phone ringing, it's still a feeling. That kind of fucking feeling that can wiggle and crawl, sneak into your head when you don't want it there at all. Sometimes I want to be alive again, but that feeling keeps on killing me.

I've got lots more pages done; maybe one, two, or more chapters to go and it will be a whole book. I'm going to finish it, but I don't know what to do for the next chapter. I don't want to do it because I know what's going to happen and I can't stop it. When I start the chapter, Vernon and the others are going to be alive. I know when I finish it, they're going to be dead. I'm going to be all fucked up, bullet-through-the-throat shit. Big ugly face of death, smiling, killing guys all day, all night. I know I'm going to feel that death finger poking at me all over again. Fuck it, I'm writing anyway.

It's nighttime, real late. Vernon and the others have only a few more pages to live. But I ain't writin' slowly, I'm writin' real fast. I'm tryin' to keep movin'. I'm scared because I'm runnin' across that rice paddy again. This time I know what's goin' to happen, I know where and when. I'm livin' in fucked-up time shit, all at the same time. I'm livin' in twenty-some-year-ago time, I'm writin' in now time. Sometimes I can't tell the difference, there ain't no difference. Motherfuckers are out there sneakin' around in the night, fuckin' mice makin' the same kind of little sneakin' sounds in the kitchen. I got to keep writin', keep movin'. I can see everything again, feel it. I'm writing about how I feel, how I felt when the bullet hit me. I'm hit, but I keep writin', tryin' to tell how it felt, I felt. I'm tryin' to tell how Vernon's face looked when he saw me, how big his eyes got. I can still see his eyes, but I got to keep writin'.

It's still dark outside, morning ain't come yet. I know it got to be near. I'm tired, I want to go to bed. I want to get far away from this night. But I can't, or won't. I'm still writin', but not as fast. The words want to come, but I won't let them come all the time. If I ain't writin', I'm starin' down at the paper, seein' the stuff that's in my mind. I can hear words I want to say, I can hear the sounds around the words. I can hear the sounds of artillery shells, the whistling sound they make going through the air before they hit the ground and burst. I can hear machine-gun fire, sometimes screams and calls for the corpsmen. I can see myself lying behind the rice paddy dike, see the fog floating through the darkness like some big gray ghost. I can feel the hours passing again, feel my fears again. I'm writing slowly, trying to tell about when

I heard my platoon coming back and how they saw me lying in the water. I'm trying to tell how I got to my feet and looked back across the dark battlefield, looking for Vernon. I'm writing that all I could see was the patches of fire burning through the gray fog. I'm seeing it again and hearing somebody tell me, *He's dead, they got it back there.*

Birds are singing, I know it's morning, time to sleep and hide from the fuckin' world again. Days go by with the normal stuff lingering behind them, but I wait for the night and write. One night, I don't know what time it is, but I know, feel, it's done. I did a book, I did something, I finished it. I will call it *Patches of Fire.*

18

JESSICA AND JESUS

I didn't know how many days, weeks, had passed since I finished the book. Sometimes I would pick it up, just to hold all the pages in my hand and feel how heavy it was. Sometimes I'd look at one of the chapters and read a page or two. Then I would set it back down, maybe go to the window, sigh as I looked out. I could not see out as far as I wanted to. I could only see the uncertainty of the moment and hate myself for being where I was. I hated standing by some window and just looking out, afraid to go out. I still didn't want to be seen, have somebody come up to me and ask me what happened to the magazine. Maybe someone would ask how it feels to be Mr. Failure of the World. Maybe I would accidentally run into Attorney Ross. Maybe I would kill him, then kill myself and end all this shit. Sometimes I could hear a voice inside me saying, *Go out there and be something again.* Then I'd hear that other voice screaming inside my head, telling me, *You ain't got a damn thing to fight with. You ain't nothin', and nothin' can't do nothin'. It don't make no difference what you were, it's what you are. And you ain't nothin' no more.* Sometimes I could hear a little voice inside me whispering, *At least I wrote a book.*

When the phone rang I didn't answer it. I let it ring for a long time, then I figured it might be my mother calling. I didn't want to talk to her, answer her questions with that same old lie. I hated lying, especially to my mother. But I had to if it was her, I had to say, *Yeah, I'm all right. Yeah, I got something to eat. Yeah, I'm thinking about becoming alive again. Should be any day now, maybe tomorrow.*

Holding my breath, I pick up the phone and hear myself saying, "Yes." Then I hear my cousin John's voice asking me if I was asleep and saying if I was, wake the hell up.

I pretend like I'm laughing some, and say, "Hey man, what's up? Are you in town?"

"Yeah, we just got in about an hour ago. I'm up at my mother's."

"How long you going to be in town?"

"About a week."

"I've been meaning to give you a call."

"Well, why didn't you?"

"Telephone company got a little upset with me and cut off the long distance. If I don't pay the bill soon, they'll be cuttin' off the short distances too."

"How are you doing?"

"It's been a little rough."

"Yeah, I hear."

"But I've been meaning to call. I got somethin' to show you. You'll never guess. I wrote a book. I want to talk to you about it. It's about Vietnam, it's no Rambo shit. It's titled *Patches of Fire.* I was going to call and tell you about it."

My cousin was very close to me, even though he had gone his way when we were young and I had gone my way. His way was the other side of the mountain. He had gone to school, college, universities, was an All-American basketball player, Rhodes scholar, author of a whole bunch of books. Two of them won big national awards. I'd see him in national magazines and on TV sometimes, big TV shows like *60 Minutes* and *Good Morning, America.* I'd brag about him, tell people he was my cousin; our mothers are sisters. I was glad he was on the phone, but I was lying again. I hadn't been going to call him, couldn't. I was ashamed of what I was, and I knew he knew. I didn't want to be seen that way.

He asked me a little about the book, then I could feel myself cringe when I heard him saying, "Why don't you come on up?"

Quickly I tried to think of something to say, some excuse so I wouldn't have to leave the house. I said, "Man, that's a long walk up there."

"What happened to your car?"

"It died—been dead for a while."

"Okay, I'll be down in about an hour to pick you up."

"Okay, see you then."

I was sorry I had answered the phone. When it rang again, I didn't answer it. Enough of answering the damn phone for one day. Now I got to shave, take a fuckin' shower, try to look like I give a fuck about how I look. I know the hour ain't going to take too long to pass. I'm getting ready, shaving and seeing myself in the mirror. I know I have to have that normal look on my face, that look I show my family. It's different from the one I'm seeing now. The one I'm seeing now doesn't even want to look at itself, hates itself.

I don't know whether or not an hour passed; I didn't look at the clock when my cousin called. Maybe an hour passed, maybe it didn't. But I was looking out the window for him and waiting anyway. I was trying to remember the last time he was in town, the last time I saw him. It was sunny outside; it must still be summer. It was cold when he was in town before. Damn, it had been a while since I'd seen him. I tried to remember what-all had happened since we had last seen each other. I didn't want to feel what I was thinking, so I wasn't thinking about it anymore. I could push stuff away, put it with those bills I hid from myself. I just wished I could hide me from myself and not accidentally find me when I was looking for something else.

My cousin came, and the ride up to his mother's house was only a short distance, too short for a long talk. We only had time to say the quick little things to each other, the "Hey, what's up? What have you been up to? What's your mother fixin' for dinner?" We kept talking small talk, and I kept trying to keep my pretend I'm-okay face on. I had *Patches of Fire* with me in an envelope I had found. John had asked if that was the manuscript. I said yeah and asked if we could talk about it later; maybe we could find some time to talk after dinner.

I wasn't hungry, but I ate anyway. Everybody in the family was stopping by to see my cousin and his family. Kids were running all over the place, and everybody was talking at the same time. I was hearing voices, seeing faces I'd known forever. Faces looking like other faces—my aunt's face looking like my grandmother's face. Memories of my life, long gone, kept coming into my mind, making me feel as if no time had ever passed in my life. I'm home, it's Homewood, I can just be me and

Jesus ain't never goin' to let nothin' bad happen. Trains passin' my grandparents' house ain't comin' from nowhere and ain't goin' nowhere, just passin'. Ain't no crosses burnin' in the night, ain't no Vietnam nowhere. And I ain't all fucked up in my head, tryin' to hide stuff from myself. Me and Jesus are still friends. I ain't never wanted to kill nobody. Ain't nobody tried to kill me either. I'm tryin' to keep the memories in my head, see my grandmother's face, see my grandfather comin' up the alley with his jug of wine and his big smile on his face. He's singin' one of them songs he was always singin'. My grandmother's goin' to be mad at him when he comes in the house all drunk. But he's goin' to keep on singin' when he gets in the house. He's goin' to have a pocketful of candy for me and my cousins, but my grandmother's still goin' to be mad at him for bein' drunk. But that ain't goin' to stop him from singin'. Candy's gone, I want to keep the memories, but now they're gone too. And I'm sitting around people I love being afraid they might touch me, see inside of me, see that I ain't nothin' but a memory of myself.

Talking is still going on. I'm not talking too much, just listening, until my cousin's wife, Judy, starts asking me about the book I wrote. She's sitting next to me at the table and quietly asks me some questions about it. We can hardly hear each other at the big dinner table. We're in the kitchen now, sitting at the little table. I tell her about the book, things I wrote about. Judy keeps asking questions. I feel like she really wants to know. I say, "You want to see it? You can be the first person to read something in it." Judy tells me she would love to take a look at it. I'm up and going to get the book; it's on the mantelpiece in the other room. I get it quickly and hurry back to the kitchen so no one will ask me what I have in the envelope. When I give the envelope to Judy and she takes the book out, her eyes get big. She says that she is surprised that I have so many pages. I say, "You don't have to read the whole thing. You can just read a little bit. Just read the first chapter or first ten pages. Can you do that and let me know what you really think of it? I'll go back in the other room so you can read it without me sittin' here watchin' you. Okay?"

Judy stays in the kitchen reading the book. I'm back at the dinner table. It's a little quieter now; some of the family has left, and the kids are outside, playing. It's just me, John, and his mother sitting at the table. We're talking quietly about some things that are always spoken quietly about. We're talking about the ones in the family who couldn't come to dinner. Sometimes my aunt stops talking and just puts her head down, shakes, while her face is a portrait of despair. Robbie, John's youngest brother, is still in prison. One of John's books told his brother's story, but that was years ago. Maybe the despair on my aunt's face and this quiet moment at the table can only find comfort in silence. It's still quiet; I'm waiting on John or his mother to say something. Some of the kids come in, hollering at each other. It isn't quiet anymore. My aunt gets to hushing them up and telling them it's their bedtime.

Judy's still in the kitchen reading the book. John and his mother are talking about something again, but I can't keep my mind on the conversation. I'm thinking about what Judy's going to say about it. Seems like she's been in there reading for a long time. I don't know what to think. Maybe she isn't going to like it and will just try to say something real nice, try not to hurt my feelings. I don't want my feelings to be hurt anymore, I don't need any more pain. I can't deal with the fuckin' pain I've got. And I'm tired of feeling sorry for myself and being sorry for feeling sorry.

John's asking me something and I have to say, "Huh?" because I'm not listening. I want to go home, but I don't want to say I do. I want to know what time it is, but I don't want to raise my wrist to look at my watch. I want to be family, feel stuff like that again, but I want to go home too and be alone. I look up quickly; Judy is coming back into the room. I look at her face, trying to see what it's saying, what it's going to say. Her eyes are big again; she's not smiling, but she has a different look on her face. I don't know what she's thinking. I'm trying to think of something not too serious to say. I can't, so I laugh a little and say, "Well, what did you think? It wasn't that bad, was it?"

Judy still isn't saying anything, she's just looking at me. I have to say something again, I have to know what she's thinking. I laugh again and say, "Well, was it that bad?"

Judy is still looking at me, but she says, "It's incredible! I mean it, it is really incredible writing. I don't believe you wrote this. It's great."

"Huh?" I say, because I'm not certain she said what she said. I want her to say it again so I can be certain. I have to be certain.

"I've read a lot of books about Vietnam. I've never read anything like this before."

"How far did you read?"

"I didn't want to put it down. I read about the first four chapters. It's very moving."

"You're not just saying that, are you?"

"Of course not. I can't believe you wrote this."

Judy sits back down at the table and tells John more about the book. I'm not saying anything, but I feel all warm inside. I don't want to feel happy, because I know I can't trust that happy shit. But I can't and don't want to stop that warm feeling inside of me. John asks me if I have a copy for him to take back so he can read it. I say no, that's the only copy I have. Now I have to tell him I don't have enough money to get it copied. Quickly but quietly, he says not to worry, he'll get copies made in the morning.

"Thanks."

The ride back home didn't take long. John and I talked a little about how I was doing and feeling. We set aside some time to talk more. I knew he was worried but didn't want to ask too much. I think he knew I was trying to hold on to what dignity I had left. I was.

When I got home, in a way, I didn't want to go in the house. I knew it was going to be all dark and dirty in there. Fuckin' mice runnin' all over the place as soon as I turned the light on. When John dropped me off, I sat on the porch steps a while, smoked cigarettes, and looked up at the stars. I hadn't looked at the stars for a while. I remembered how I used to look at them in Vietnam. How they seemed to be so pretty and peaceful all the time. They have a way of saying from up there, *All this ugly stuff down here just ain't worth it.* When I did get up and go into the house, I went right to bed, but I didn't go to sleep right away. I couldn't; I was still thinking of what Judy had said about the book. I still had that warm feeling inside. Maybe my life was coming alive again, maybe not, but I still wanted to keep the warm feeling.

A week or so later, John and his family left Pittsburgh to go back to their home in Massachusetts. I hid the little warm feeling I had; I didn't want it too close to me. I didn't want it to hurt me, or some fuckin' bill collector trying to take it away. I wanted hope, but I didn't want it too close to me, I didn't and couldn't trust it. I started writing again, I needed to. It was like a diary. Every time something happened, I'd rush to my notebook and write about it. Sometimes I'd write down things minute by minute. I'd write stuff like "10:53am—I'm up, drinking coffee. The phone ain't rung yet—Maybe everyone thinks I'm dead to-day—Good. Got to go to the store, just three fuckin' cigarettes left—Need coffee too. I wonder if the mailman came yet—Wonder what shit he's bringing today. I need money—I need more than that. The tail end of waiting is slippery with despair—I don't know how much longer I can hold on."

It was late in an evening when my cousin called. When I answered the phone and heard his voice, I braced myself. He spoke slowly, and I listened closely. I wanted to hear every word he was going to say; I had to know. I'm listening and feeling that little warm feeling I try to hide from myself. My cousin's telling me that he read the manuscript and he thinks it is a very exceptional, strong piece of work. He's saying he's glad that he can say this, because he wouldn't know how to tell me otherwise. Now he's saying how he has already sent the book to his agent in New York and how highly he thinks of his agent. He's saying how he already talked to his agent about the book and how his agent will read it. He's telling me it may take a while before his agent can read it and just to be patient. The book needs some editing, he's saying, and the spelling is so bad it's colorful.

I had to ask my cousin some questions about how stuff works in New York, what agencies do and what happens if they like a book too. He told me what a long shot it is to get a book published. But it's one step at a time and be patient, he said.

It's around midnight. I'm still up and just sitting on the side of the bed, thinking about what my cousin said. I know I can't let myself feel different, but I want to. Everything is a long shot—me bein' alive is a fuckin' long shot too. Long shots—damn, I'm tired of long shots. Maybe I might be good at making long shots; I'm a fuckin' long shot anyway. I ain't nothin' but a long shot, always have been.

Another winter was on the way; leaves had already turned their pretty colors and were falling off the trees. I hated to see the winter come again. Snow, cold, was one thing, but winter has a way of throwing time up in your face and making it stay there. Frozen, icy time stuck all over you. I hated to see it come again. I didn't need the leaves reminding me that time was passing and I wasn't doing a damn thing about it except waiting.

I'm going to kill the fuckin' mice—fuck them, I'm gettin' tired of their sneaky shit. I got some traps, going to put some peanut butter on them. I hate peanut butter, but my mother says my Aunt Gerl says that's the best stuff to put out for mice. I got a little jar of peanut butter. I hate the smell of it. Fuck it, it ain't for me anyway. I'm at war with the mice, I'm ambushin' their sneaky asses. I'm puttin' the traps right near their holes, behind places they like to hide. I know where they go, I watch them. There's one big-ass son of a bitch, his daddy must have been a rat. I'm gettin' his ass—he don't know it, but he's dead. I'm hearin' them *smack* sounds in the night. I'm gettin' up to see if I got the big-ass mouse. I don't know whether it's him or not, but it's dead. Eyes all poppin' out of its smashed-up head. I'm pickin' up the trap, lookin' at the mouse's face. It's dead all right; death always looks the same on faces. I don't want to look at it anymore, its blood is the same color Glickman's blood was. I'm in this death shit again. That's why I didn't want to kill you, mouse, that's the only fuckin' reason why I put up with your ass. I didn't want to kill you.

It ain't winter yet, it's still some fall day. I don't want to get up, ain't no reason to get up. Phone's been ringin', but I ain't been answerin' it. It's those nine-o'clock-in-the-mornin' calls. I know what time Mr. and Miss Bill Collector call. Banks don't call no more, must have said I wasn't worth their dime, let the vultures have his ass, he's dead anyway. I must be first on their list and last on it too, 'cause they call the same time at night. I guess they call just before they leave to go home. I don't think they like me, they're never nice. Fuck 'em, I don't like them either. It might not be them callin'. The phone keeps ringin'. If it rings again, I might answer it.

I can stare at things sometimes and forget I'm starin' at them. I'm starin' at something that's all dark, fuzzy-lookin'. It is just the dark bottom of the dresser I can see when I'm lyin' under the covers and just peekin' out through some small opening I need to breathe. I know it's just the dresser, but I'm still lookin' at it. I can't get up, and I don't want to look at the clock to see what time it is. Shit, the phone's ringin' again. I reach for the clock to turn it around so I can see what time it is. It's late afternoon. Maybe it ain't the assholes callin'. Fuck it, I'm pickin' up the phone.

It's Judy, who talks real fast, saying, "Where have you been? I've been calling all morning. The agency called, they read your book. They think it's great and they have sent it out already to a few publishers."

"Huh? You mean they really liked it?"

"Yes."

"They sent it out to publishers too?"

"Yes, they said they sent out copies to about five publishing houses. The ones they named are all big houses."

"I can't believe this is happening. I mean, they really liked it and sent it out to book publishers—I can't believe it. Does John know?"

"He's teaching today, he's not home yet. But I'm sure he's going to be delighted. He'll call you, I'm sure."

"Are those people from the agency going to be calling here? Do they have to talk to me? Judy, I don't know anything about writing. What about the spelling in the book? Will someone fix that? I mean, what do I say if someone calls here? Are they going to call?"

"They were going to call you, but they didn't have your number. They were calling John to get it. They'll call you soon, I'm sure."

I'm still talking to Judy and she's telling me the names of some of the publishing houses the book was sent to. They're all big-sounding names; they sound real important, but I've only heard of one of them. I think that one used to publish John's books. They're all in New York except for one; it's up in Boston. Now she's asking me if I'm excited and I'm telling her yeah. But I don't want to be excited and start trusting that hope stuff. I know I have to keep down, can't get out in the open. But I know I'm already in the open. I've got to start answering the fuckin' phone now.

I don't want to call my mother and tell her about the book. That's just passing that hope stuff along; I can't trust it, and I don't want her to grab on to it if it's going to break. I'm dropping anyway, I don't want everyone else dropping with me. But I have to call and tell her; it's not a lie or anything, it's happening. At least it's real hope, maybe something real to wait on. I don't want to think about what the publishing people might think. I know I have enough problems dealing with little pieces of hope; I can't deal with that big-hope shit.

It's nighttime, I think it's nearing midnight. I'm sitting on the side of the bed. I know my mother's worried about me, and that bothers me. When I told her what Judy said, I could hear her deep sigh. I could hear her thanking Jesus; I can still hear her saying, "You got a friend in Jesus." I'm thinking about Jesus now, church, and all those songs of hope. Sometimes there wasn't anything but hope on all those different colored faces. Maybe there was hope on mine; maybe I was their hope.

Maybe I was one of the children they were talking about when they asked God to save the children. But I ain't no kid anymore and I've seen too many dead young faces. I ain't worth savin', and I ain't askin' to be saved. I didn't know a day was comin' within the comin' years. And in a not far-off year, I would be able to call Mom and say, "I made the center of *Time* magazine, Mom. It came out today."

It's morning now, I'm up and hoping the phone will ring and it'll be the agent calling from New York. I got up early and had some coffee so my head would be clear. I didn't want to sound completely stupid if they asked me some questions. I keep looking at the clock to see what time it is. It's not even nine o'clock yet. When I'm not thinking about waiting, I'm staring at stuff and still feeling that waiting feeling. Shit, the fucking bill collectors aren't even calling. Maybe they cut the phone off and I don't know it. I pick up the phone real fast and listen to see if there's a dial tone. It's there, so I put the phone back down as fast as I can. I don't want the agent to call and get a busy signal.

It's past the noon hour and the phone hasn't rung all morning. It's lunchtime now; normal people are probably out eating lunch. I'm at the window watching the lunchtime hour pass. It's taking a long time, but I can wait. It's sort of funny—the first phone call I'm waiting for and the phone hasn't rung all day. Maybe it isn't going to ring again.

Lunch hour has gone on by. The phone rang and I got real excited. Of all days to call, some salesperson was calling to see if I wanted to buy a funeral plot, a fucking grave. I tried to be polite and just say I wasn't interested. He kept on talking about how nice the cemetery was. I wanted to yell into the phone, ask him why in the hell everybody is trying to bury me, I ain't fuckin' dead yet. When I got off the phone, I kept thinking about the grave, some cold hole you can't get out of, don't even know you're in.

The phone is ringing again. I rush to it, but I don't want to answer it again. Fuck it, I've got to. I try to sound calm, say a nice "Yes?" A young woman's voice asks for me. I know it isn't a bill collector, her voice is different. She has some kind of an accent. She says, "This is Jessica Clarksdale calling from Herbert, Hunt and Scott Agency in New York."

"Hi, thanks for calling," I say, thinking about the sound of her voice. It's different; it has to be English. Every word she says is clear, can stand on its own. It's bringing me into it, taking me away from somebody trying to sell me a grave.

She tells me how everybody at the agency likes my writing. She tells me the same things Judy told me, but it's making me feel even better. Her voice is coming from the outside world; Judy's and John's voices are inside-world voices, they will always be caring voices. This voice has a choice; it doesn't have to care, but it does, and I feel it already. I have to ask her a question, I'm telling her I have to ask if she's from England. She says yes, she's from some small town outside London. I tell her that I have been to England, long ago. I was in Plymouth for a few days when I was in the service. I say how much I liked England; it was the only place I ever went where I could understand what people were saying. We keep talking for a while about what will happen next, when she thinks she might hear from the publishers they sent the book to. I feel myself feeling like somebody again; even if I don't want to, I am. Maybe I have something to fight back with now, to crawl out of this hole I didn't dig.

Stuff outside the window is still the same passing time; mailman comes every day except for Sundays and some damn holidays. I don't want to think about the trouble I'm in. I may be fucked up and crazy, but I'm not stupid. I know that shit isn't going to go away. The mailman isn't going to knock on the door and say, *Hey, give me all those bills and legal notices back. You're special—everybody has forgiven you for being a fuck-up.* I know I've got to hold out, keep down until I can get back up on my feet, fight back. Sometimes I feel I'm going to win, just sometimes.

Days without names, time-filled weeks, pass without that day I'm waiting for in them. I keep waiting anyway. I know the call has to come one day; fuck the other fuckin' calls coming, I got to hold out. I got to keep thinking of things to help me hold out, hold on. I keep remembering a speech Martin Luther King made, him saying something like "Only when it's dark enough can you see the stars." I'm trying to remember stuff like that. I don't want to think about those dark raining nights in Vietnam. Those nights when there weren't any stars, you couldn't even see your own hand in front of your face and death waitin' for you in the dark . . .

Jessica's got to call. She calls. She tells me they have had some unusual responses from publishers who have read the book. She says that one or two publishers just sent those "not interested" letters, but the others sent real good rejection letters; some of the editors were very impressed, and she tells me what they said. One editor almost made an offer on the book, but he said it needs too much editing. She tells me how he even called her to talk about the book. He may want to call me and talk to me too. I don't know what to say back. I'm not hearing what I wanted to hear, but I'm hearing that everything isn't dead. She's going to send me copies of the letters and call me back when she hears more.

It's nighttime, deep in the night, and I'm still up thinking about things. Days have gone by since Jessica called. The letters came. I couldn't believe what they said, how good the editors thought the writing was. I'm thinking maybe I'll write another book, maybe I'll write a novel and show that to them too. I'm thinking about what I can write about, I'm writing some ideas down on my notebook paper, trying to think of what I can write about. I've got four or five ideas; two of them I'm thinking about real hard. I've circled these two, and I'm trying to make up my mind which one to do. One could be about this program I saw on TV a long time ago, about how young kids were executed in the South—Mississippi and South Carolina, places like that. I think real hard about that idea. I never forgot that program; I tried to imagine how it would be to be just a kid and put to death. I tried to imagine how a mother would feel, knowing her child was going to be put to death in some electric chair. Sometimes I'm thinking that all this shit's a joke. I ain't really no fuckin' writer, I just wrote down what the fuck I lived, just saw the shit all over again and wrote it down.

It's a night, another night. I don't know what time it is and I don't care. I'm starin' at a blank piece of paper tryin' to see Mississippi. I've never been to Mississippi, but I'm still tryin' to see it in my mind. I got to see it, feel it the way it was in the thirties. It couldn't have been much different from North Carolina. Probably had the same set of tracks runnin' through it. Them kind of tracks that say, *Niggers better stay on one side.*

I'm still starin' at the paper. I can hear and feel myself sigh, I can hear me whisperin', *Let's do it.* I'm writin' words I never wrote about places I ain't never seen. I'm just naming people as I see their faces. I'm writin' down words the way they're sayin' them. "Let's see . . . Mister Pete, he be dead just before a spring ago . . ." I'm seein' an Indian-lookin' colored woman and callin' her Cinder, seein' her only child and callin' him Billy. I'm there the night he's born and hearin' Cinder screamin' out with pain into the dark of a Mississippi night. I can see the sweat on her face, the dark face of her Aunt Katey callin' on her

God to have mercy in the night. I know Cinder's child, Billy, is goin' to grow up and kill somebody, be put in the electric chair. But I can't tell her that; she can't hear me. I can see in, but she can't see out. She don't even know I'm there.

Days ain't days again, they're just pages. Weeks ain't nothin' but chapters. Jessica calls, lets me know what's happening. She's sending out *Patches of Fire* to more publishers. The editor who really likes it still wants to talk to me, but he's on vacation. I keep writing anyway; I can't leave Mississippi now for anything. I got to keep going. Billy has killed a young white girl named Lori. She's dead and I watched her die. Cinder got Billy and is tryin' to hide out in the dark swamps from Sheriff Tom. Sheriff Tom's lookin' for them in the night.

Bill collectors are still callin', gas man still ain't happy. Snow hasn't fallen yet, but it's comin'. But I haven't stopped writing, I'm past a hundred pages. I want to get to a hundred and five before I sleep. I ain't going to sleep long, I got to get back up. I got to finish, I got to finish soon. If *Patches of Fire* comes back in the mail, I want *Billy* done, ready to go to New York the same day. I'm not giving up hope, can't, not anymore.

Jessica calls. I wait for the sound of her voice, always hope it's her when the phone rings. She tells me this publisher says this, this one says that. It's still good stuff, they like my writing. But no checks are coming. That's okay, I can hold out. That editor who was to call is still on vacation, busy or something, but he'll call. I try to see her face as I listen to her voice. She's so important to me, and I don't even know what she looks like. I've told her about the new book, I keep telling her how far I'm getting with it. Each time she calls, I'm a whole lot further. I keep writing, I've got to. Gas man knocks, I keep writing. Mailman brings real bad stuff, I keep writing. When I get to thinking, *I ain't no real writer, I don't know what the fuck I'm doin'*, I keep writing. It's night and I see Billy, hear him cryin' in his cell. He only has moments to live. I want to cry too, turn off the typewriter, but I can't. Billy's dead, Cinder is cryin' in the night. I don't know, just feel it, there's nothing else to write. I did it; the book is finished. I don't feel happy; I can still hear Cinder crying in the night.

Daybreak came. I watched it get light outside. I was tired, but I was still thinking about Billy and Cinder. I didn't realize it, hadn't been thinking about the outside time that had passed—I didn't realize that I had written *Billy* in six weeks of that passing time. I wanted to be happy, I thought I would feel good when I finished it, but I didn't. Maybe I was too tired of everything to be happy. But I knew that wasn't why. Being happy was too far away for me to see; I could barely see hope. But at least I *could* see it.

I had to wait for Jessica to call so I could tell her *Billy* was done. I hadn't told her that I didn't have long-distance phone service. I didn't want her to know how poor I was, that I didn't like giving the people at the store all those nickels, dimes, and pennies and trying to keep my dignity. I had told her that I used to have an English Jaguar, had been a photographer, a magazine publisher, stuff like that. I told her things weren't going so well now, but I didn't tell her about the fuckin' mice and all the other fucked-up things running around in my head.

Jessica calls to tell me that the editor is going to be calling me in the evening. I tell her that *Billy*'s done and ask if I can send it to her. She says, "Gosh, you completed it already?"

"Yeah, I finished it a couple nights ago."

"That was awfully fast. How many pages is it?"

"It's just a little over two hundred. I don't know whether you'll like it, but it's done."

"Please send it. I would like very much to have a look at it."

In the evening, the editor calls. I'm excited, nervous, and feeling stupid all at the same time. He says how much he likes *Patches of Fire* and asks me questions. I want to answer all of them, but sometimes I don't know what to say. He asks about Vietnam and what made me start to write about it. I don't want to say, *I'm all fucked up, hidin' from everything that reminds me of myself now. That was me then, I was alive, I counted. I don't want to be a writer, but maybe I can count again.* I say stuff like *Oh I'm in between things now, I have a little time to myself, so I decided to write some.* We keep talking, and I try to figure out what he's thinking. I want him to say, *Okay, you're great. I'll buy the book. You'll have enough money to pay the gas man.* But he doesn't, he just says he'll be talking to Jessica soon. I don't know how to feel, except just to hope a good thing might happen.

I kept copies of both *Patches of Fire* and *Billy* on the corner of the end table where they were written. Sometimes I'd put one on top of the other, pick them up, and just hold them. I wanted to feel the weight of all the pages, how much I had done. I kept trying to remind myself that

I had done something, even after Jessica called and said the editor had called her. She said he would really like to take *Patches of Fire*, but he couldn't get his associates to go along with him. It needed too much editing and stuff. She said maybe I should rewrite it, get some help on the editing. She would read *Billy*, but it might be a while before she got a chance to read it. But she would read it and call me.

I kept waiting for the phone to ring, to pick it up and hear Jessica's voice, but she didn't call. Sometimes I would stare at the phone while it was ringing, trying to will it to be her calling. It wouldn't be, and I would feel it getting all dark again. I could hear that hope stuff laughing at me and telling me it was just a joke. Fairy-tale shit all over again— wasn't nothin' real, never was. I could feel myself getting ready to go back into the night, and then the phone would ring. I'd rush to it, hope, then hear myself sigh when it wasn't Jessica.

Maybe a couple of weeks went by after I sent *Billy*, maybe even a month passed. I kept writing in my notebook journal. I'd tell myself things I didn't even want to know. I wrote about time a lot, how precious it was and how you could never get it back once it passed. I knew it was passing and Jessica hadn't called. Maybe she had read *Billy* and didn't want to call and tell me how bad it was. Maybe she hadn't read it yet. Maybe she was reading it now. Maybe I'd do it again, maybe I'd write another book. Fuck it, why not.

I'm staring at another empty page again, trying to see stuff in my mind. I know what the book is going to be about. It's going to be something like a love story, except it's going to take place in the South. The girl is going to be white and she's going to fall in love with a colored guy. It's going to take place in the 1940s, during the Second World War. It's going to be set in a small town in North Carolina named Supply. At least I've been to North Carolina and I know there's a town called Supply. I've never been there, but I met a girl one night who said she lived there. She said it wasn't too far from Wilmington. I can't remember the girl's name, but she was pretty and we fucked in the car. I remember the name of the town she was from. I had never met anyone from there before, and it had such a military-sounding name.

I'm writing now. I can see Supply. It's sittin' off from some two-lane blacktop highway. I can barely see it from the road. I'm tellin' how folks drivin' down the highway might see the little roadside sign that says, WELCOME TO SUPPLY. They might look over from the car, get a glimpse of them far-off little buildings, see that one big building that looks like a courthouse or something, then keep on going to wherever they were headed. I can feel Supply now; I've passed a thousand little towns that look like it. I've driven into them a lot too, seen those faces that time ain't touched since the Civil War. White faces that smile at one another. Dark faces that know those smiles on them white faces can vanish real quick if they say or do the wrong thing. I know Supply got to have a railroad track, creek, or somethin' that keeps coloreds separated from whites.

I've got a page done, but I'm not writing now, I'm just starin' at the paper. I'm thinkin', *All this shit's stupid, why am I sittin' here doin' this writin' stuff? I'm out of my mind with this shit—fuck this damn writin' shit. Fuck you motherfuckers out there. Death before dishonor. If you're goin' to get killed, get killed good. Yeah, take some motherfuckers with you, kill 'em all. Get a machine gun, kill all day long.*

I'm still starin' at the page, thinkin' about stuff that I don't want to think about. I'm seein' magazine shit runnin' around in my head. I'm the stupid nigger again, I'm waitin' on something that ain't comin'. I know it ain't comin'—magazine's dead and ain't comin' back. But it didn't have a chance to die with dignity. I could die with dignity, but I ain't dyin' without it. One way or the other, I got to get those motherfuckers back. I got to get myself back. I can't do that, I ain't nothin'.

I'm writing again, just because I ain't got nothin' else to do. It's late in the night, but I ain't tired. I'm tryin' to see a young white girl in my mind. She's got to be real pretty, and bold too. I can see she has blond hair, blue eyes. She's got to be about nineteen and have that southern way of sayin' things. I want to see her face, see how she moves when she talks real fast. I can see her now, she's flingin' her hands while she's talkin'. She's remindin' me of the young girl who used to come and see the kid next door. She was from the South too, had that southern accent. She wanted to be an actress and was going to school here. I took some pictures of her for her portfolio. I liked talkin' to her, she had so much life in her. I'm thinkin' of her and seein' the girl in the book. I'm callin' the girl on the page, in my mind, Holly Hill. I'm smiling and thinking of the young girl who came next door and of how she really wanted to be an actress. I remember how the first time I saw her in a movie, I didn't know who she was; years had passed since I had taken her pictures. Then I smiled when I saw her name, Holly Hunter, in the credits.

I got to keep going, got to. Holly's just wakin' up, she's cranky and mad at her little brother for wakin' her up. She's mutterin', "Can't sleep past the chickens. Same thing every time Ah turn around. That little brat, wait till Ah git him. Can't wait ta git out of here. Do this, do that, do this, do that . . ."

I keep writing; even when I don't want to, I write. I hide in the pages, hide in Supply. I come out to sleep, go to the store for cigarettes, hide stuff the mailman brings. Phone rings, I stop and look at it, hope it's Jessica calling. It ain't her, has never been her, she ain't called yet. I don't know what's happening, if she read *Billy*. Holly's fiancé got killed in the South Pacific. She had just got a Christmas card to send and her mama is tellin' her his ship got bombed and he's dead. Her mother's holdin' her and she's cryin', shakin' in her mother's arms. She's tryin' to ask her mother something, but she can barely talk. She's using the breath of her cries and askin', "Will God let him know . . . Mama, will God let him know Ah got him a Christmas card?"

Jessica ain't called. Some man bought the big house down the street and opened up a fuckin' funeral parlor. Seems like every time I look out the window, some funeral is goin' by, death shit paradin', every day. I keep writin' 'cause I don't want to be dead too.

Everything keeps going by: weeks, pages, fuckin' funerals. I've done more pages than I ever did before, but I have more to do. Holly's met the colored guy. He ain't got but one arm and he's an artist. She's been sneakin' down by the creek to see him. Now she's runnin' through the night with him. Her daddy found out she's been with a nigger and he's after her and that one-armed nigger too. I keep writin', followin' Holly through the night. I can hear them distant dogs barkin', see Holly's breath in the cool night air. I can hear her heart beatin', hear her whisperin', "They didn't see us, Elias. They won't come this far."

It's done again, I feel it. I did it again, this time more pages than before. Three hundred and some, but it's done. I'm tired, it's late in the night, but I can't sleep. I'm done, but I don't know what I'm done with. I don't know that years from now, a book club in England is going to reprint *To Kill a Mockingbird* and I'm going to be asked to write the foreword to it. Harper Lee will read the foreword, like it, and approve it. The daughter of Richard Wright, the author of *Native Son*, will have my work read at a book fair in Paris. But I can't see that far out of the night. I'm not even lookin' out the window.

I was scared, too old and having seen too much to say to myself that I was. I hated the feeling, but sometimes I couldn't feel anything else. Jessica hadn't called. I wanted to call her, get a whole bunch of quarters and go to a pay phone. But I was afraid of what she might say, what she might have to say about *Billy*. In a way, as long as she didn't call, there was still hope that she might not have read it yet. *Maybe she'll like it when she reads it. Maybe if she doesn't like* Billy, *she'll like* Holly. *It's different, more like a love story, it may have more appeal than some child being put in an electric chair. Fuck it, fuck everything forever. Maybe she'll call. Maybe Mom's right, maybe I've got a friend in Jesus. Maybe Jesus will call.*

It's morning; I'm still under the covers, because I don't want to get up. I'm not thinkin' about anything, just that dark with me under the covers. If I don't look out from beneath the covers, it ain't got to be morning, I don't have to do anything, and I don't have to feel bad about doin' nothin'. When the phone rings, I'm not thinkin' about Jessica, I don't want to let myself know I care about writing. When I hear Jessica's voice, all that hope stuff rushes back into my head.

She says who she is, but I already know. Quickly, I say, "Hi, it's good to hear from you. How are you?"

"I'm well, thank you."

It's silent. I'm waiting on Jessica to say something else. I know she's going to say something, and I'm afraid in the silence. Now she's talking, sounding as if she's looking for the right words to say. She says, "I'm . . . I'm calling to tell you that I have just read *Billy*. It is amazing . . . simply amazing. I . . . I could not put it down. It is so beautifully written, simply beautiful."

"Huh? My God, did you really like it?"

"A great deal."

We kept talking and I was alive, feeling stuff inside me tickling me and making me smile. I hurried up and told her about *Holly*, said it was done too, I'd send it. She was surprised that I had done another book in such a short time. I didn't tell her how long that time had been for me.

Looking out the window became different. I wanted to be out there. If a funeral went by, I was happy it wasn't mine. I could deal with the mailman/gas man stuff. Jessica had sent *Billy* out to a whole bunch of

big publishers. Some very big ones got interested; some wanted a rewrite, some wanted to talk to me. One was about to make an offer but
didn't. I had to hold on, stay alive, keep down just a little bit longer. But
I was afraid, still shaking inside. I knew it was just hope I was holding
on to. And it was that shaky kind of hope; it could break any time.

19

AND A BAG OF WELFARE COFFEE

I remember it was a warm day, sun shining. I felt like walking some, going a different way, getting further away from the house and everything in it. I needed cigarettes, coffee, lunch meat, but I didn't feel like seeing the same people at the same store around the corner. I was tired of them seeing me with all my dimes, nickels, and whatever other little pieces of money I had in my pocket. Maybe when they saw me coming, they would say, *Here comes Mr. Poor Man again.* I didn't want that, didn't feel like walking that way.

Homewood wasn't that far, never was that far. Even if I pushed it away, refused to think about it, it was always there in my mind. If I went there, I was only passing through. Sometimes I'd go over to my grandfather's house, where Aunt Gerl still lives in the house across from the railroad tracks. Homewood was always on the other side of the railroad tracks; there was always something big and wide separating it from America. My grandfather's house was on Fiance Street, but Fiance Street used to be called First Street. I didn't have to go that far into Homewood to be home, to be around the ghost of a better time.

I was walking the other way. I could see the railroad bridge, the dirty, crooked sign hanging from its rail that read, WELCOME TO HOME-WOOD. In a way, it could have read, WELCOME TO A FORGOTTEN LAND. A land that Mother America and Aunt Pittsburgh stopped caring about when the last white family moved out. Old jobs moved out too, and new jobs wouldn't move in. But Homewood was still there, wouldn't go away, was waiting on Jesus to come and save it. Jesus is going to come, got to come and save the children, get the guns out of their hands.

It was dark under the bridge; no matter how bright the day, it was always dark under the old gray concrete bridge. When the darkness wasn't shade, it was the shadow of a time that had long passed for me. As I walked under the bridge, I could feel, see that time of long ago in my mind. It was still there, me, Pee Wee, and Brother playing underneath the bridge. Hollering real loud to make echoes bounce around in the dark spooky shade. We could always go as far as the bridge and feel the same as we had going to the bridge. But on the other side, we felt different, maybe afraid because we knew we had gone too far. Now I was coming from that far side of the bridge, that big-house-wide-street side of the bridge, that used-to-be-all-white-and-no-niggers-allowed side of the bridge. And I was greeting that same little kid, feeling that I had gone too far on the other side of the tracks.

When I got to Fiance Street, I kept walking down Homewood Avenue. Maybe I'd walk over to that little store on Hamilton Avenue, see if they had lunch meat, coffee; they'd have to have cigarettes. I felt myself veering from the sidewalk and cutting across that old empty lot as I had done a million years ago. It seemed like the same little path still cut through the lot, same broken wine bottles and rusty cans were lying in the bushes. When I got to the alley on the other side of the lot, I had to go down it. In a way that only comes sometimes, I could feel it calling me back into a time. I could feel it calling me back into my grandfather's time, my mother's time, that old Homewood time. I was passing places I hadn't seen in years, seeing old houses and remembering them from a time ago. I wonder if Mr. Benson still lives there, still has that big old brown dog that would come running and doing all that barking at the fence. But that fence isn't there, and I know the dog and Mr. Benson have to be long gone too. I wonder who's living in the house now. I wonder if they knew my grandfather, knew my grandmother, grew up with my mother. But I don't see anything in the alley, just old thrown-out refrigerators and other piles of junk that have been lying for a long time.

I'm out on Tioga Street now, walking past that church where Jimmy Pitman's mother used to go. That church where they used to do all that shouting and singing. But that singing sounded good, would have the whole street waiting on Jesus to come dancing down out of the skies. On hot summer nights, folks living anywhere near the church would be sitting out, patting their feet and giving a little praise to Jesus in case he did come. Pee Wee went in that church one time with Jimmy Pitman. Jimmy Pitman got mad at Pee Wee, said Pee Wee got to laughing at his mother. Pee Wee said it wasn't his fault that Jimmy's mama got to shakin' herself so much her wig fell off and showed all them naps she had hidin'.

I pass some old storefront and remember it used to be where the shoemaker's shop was. Some guy's sitting out in front, and he's looking at me and I'm looking back at him. His face is looking real familiar, and I know he's trying to figure out who I am too.

"Hey man, don't I know you?" he's asking.

I stop and say that I used to live over on Fiance Street, went to Homewood school and all that. It's dawning on me who he is. I say, "You're Claire's brother. You're Punkin. Damn, man, I ain't seen you since when."

He's remembering me and getting up to give me a handshake. I'm still looking at his face and seeing it in my mind when it was young. He was older than me, bigger than me, and used to pitch on Homewood's pony league team. He was real good; everybody knew him. We talk, saying how things have changed. He says, "Man, shit out here is a motherfucker. Niggas around here are outs they minds, put a bullet in your head just for a dime or lookin' at them wrong. They were shootin' the other night over there at Tina's Lounge. Some young dude offed this old dude. Get this, they were arguin' about the motherfuckin' pay phone in there. The old dude wouldn't get off the phone, must have said somethin' to the young dude. They said the young dude just offed him, pulled his piece out and just blew the man away while he was still talkin' into the phone."

We're still talking about stuff, old days. Now he's asking something that makes me feel stuff inside me, stuff I don't want to think about or talk about. He says, "Man, when I saw you comin' down the street, I thought you were George comin'. Man, you look just like him."

I hear myself asking, "George who?" But I can feel who he's talking about.

"You know George? You remember George, got a brother named Macky, one named Nooty too. They used to live over there on Fiance

Street too. You remember George, don't ya? He come by here all the time. Do you remember Macky? He used to play ball with me."

I'm thinking, feeling stuff I don't want to think about or feel. I can see Macky, Georgie, and Nooty in my mind. See my father coming by to see them and just looking at me. I can hear them hollering, *Daddy's comin'*. I can see me watching the big shiny car pull up. I can see him getting out, looking at me a little bit but not touching me like he did them, not giving me a dime or a nickel too.

I say, "Oh yeah, I know George and them. They used to live a couple houses down. Damn, last I heard, George was still in prison. When did he get out?"

"Oh, he's been out, he livin' right over there across from the field. You know, in one of them houses by the parkin' lot."

"Damn, I ain't seen him since I was in ninth grade or somethin'. Is he doin' all right now?"

"Oh yeah, he fine. You know he be drinkin' some, but he ain't into nothin' and ain't never bother folks. It's a wonder he ain't comin' down the street now. He come by each day, you know, goin' over to the store. If I got somethin' or he got somethin', we always give each other a little taste. George is my man, he's all right."

I'm walking again, looking at things I haven't seen in a long time. But I'm seeing George's, Macky's, Nooty's faces. I can see Richie too, see him up in the park that day. I can see him, hear him telling me his father died. He didn't know he was telling me my father had died too. I was the brother who didn't know Daddy was coming. I'm the brother with the empty space in his soul. I'm the brother who doesn't want to think about all that empty space. But I'm still thinking about it, walking back home, back through that dark shade under the bridge, thinking about that dark empty space in my soul . . . Fuck it.

I was trying not to think about what was going on in New York. Jessica hadn't called in a while. The last time I had heard from her, it was not good news. She had sent *Billy* to some other big publishers and they had only said what the others had said. I'd try to separate everything in my mind, I'd try to say, *At least they liked the writing*. And I'd sigh and say, *This shit's a joke, ain't nothin' never going to happen*. I think Jessica was realizing what bad financial shape I was in. I told her I didn't have long-distance phone service. I told her about a few other little problems. I didn't want to go into everything, I didn't want her to think she was dealing with some fucked-up, depressed, frightened man. Sometimes I was still feeling better, thinking some good might happen. Then I'd shake inside when I'd think, knowing that if something good was going to happen, it would have to be soon. I could still feel that raging battle going on in my head, me fighting me. No matter which me would win, I'd still lose. I'd just be half of something, dragging the stinking other half around.

When it was time to go to the store again, I stood for a moment, thinking about which way to go. In a way, I knew which way I was going, had to go. It seemed like the dark shade under the bridge was waiting on me, knew I was coming back. I was telling myself I felt like walking, needed the exercise or something. *Maybe I'll walk over by the old ballfield, I ain't been over that way in years.* I'm passing the old elementary school, looking at the schoolyard, the door, and then up at the windows. I'm stopping, leaning up against the schoolyard fence and seeing the kids playing. I'm thinking of me playing there one time, getting in that fight with Harry Francis and that old Mr. Bonner paddling us real hard.

I'm close to the field now. I know I should turn around, go back. I know I should leave things alone; got enough troubles, don't need no more. I want to turn around. *Don't go where I don't belong, never did belong. It's a nice day, I can walk wherever I want. I'm not botherin' anybody 'cept myself and can't nobody see that.* But I can see it, feel it. It hurts a little, been hurting forever a little. I can see the parking lot and the nearby houses. I'm feeling a weakness coming in my legs; seems like they don't want to take these steps with me. I'm in front of some of the houses now, looking at them and not wanting to look too hard. I want to look like I'm just accidentally glancing at them as I'm passing.

I hear a car nearing, coming up behind me real slow. It's pulling over to the curb to park. Some woman's getting out, then reaching back in to get some shopping bags out. I'm smiling, giving her a nod as she catches my eye looking her way. I'm a couple steps past her now, but I can still hear her rustling her shopping bags. I can feel myself slow and turn around. I can hear myself saying something to her. I'm pretending, lying to her. I'm not telling myself the truth either. I'm being real polite and saying, "Excuse me . . . I'm—I'm looking for an old friend of mine I haven't seen in years. Another friend of mine says he lives around here in one of these houses. Do you know anyone by the name of George that lives around here? He's about my age, looks like me a little."

The woman's looking at me. Now she's asking, "You a friend of George's?"

"Yeah, we go way back. We were kids together over on Fiance Street. Way, way back."

The woman's smiling a little and pointing to a house a couple doors up the street. I'm looking where she's pointing and I'm hearing her say, "He lives up there, that house with the green porch."

"Thanks a lot."

"You're welcome."

I still want to turn around, go home, leave this stuff alone. I haven't seen George in thirty-five years or so, and he hasn't tried to see me either. None of them have—Mack, Nooty, Richie, and the other two, whom I've never seen at all. I want to leave it alone, but I can't. I'm going up the steps, looking at the door. I'm knocking, waiting, looking back over my shoulder at the houses across the street, looking beyond them to the sky. I knock again, little nice taps, and I listen, waiting and looking at the sky again. It's all soft blue, with white clouds floating around. It's peaceful-looking; I want to keep looking at it.

Someone's opening the door, I turn away from the sky, waiting till the door opens. There's a woman looking at me, asking if she can help me. I wonder who she is. Her skin is dark brown, same color as her eyes. Her hair is pulled back from her face, letting her eyes and the dark features of her face fill the moment. I tell her my nickname and say I'm a real old friend of George's. I ask if he's at home. She says yes and tells me to come on in, she'll get him.

I'm in the house, standing in the living room. I can hear the woman calling George, telling him some friend is here to see him. A deeper voice says, "All right, I'm comin'."

I look around the living room and try to see the photographs sitting on the mantel. The pictures are too far away for me to tell whose faces are in them. But I keep looking and wondering. I hear the sound of footsteps coming down the steps. I sigh as quietly as I can and look toward the sound of the nearing footsteps. It's George, after all these years. It's George—same eyes, same look on his face, same funny little smile he gets when he likes something, gets something he wants.

He stops in the doorway and just stares at me. I say, "It's been a long time, a real long time. It's good to see you. How you doing?"

The little smile is still on George's face. He says, "I knew it was you. I just had a feelin' you were coming by."

"Huh? How did you know that? I just found out you lived up here yesterday. How did you know I was coming by?"

"So what, how I know."

We're shaking hands now and just looking at each other. He looks like me when I look in the mirror, except his face is thinner and his eyes are red. I feel they're too red, and I don't want them all that red-looking. I look away from his eyes, look down at his hand in mine. I ain't sayin' what I'm feelin' when I look back up into his eyes. I ain't sayin', *You're my brother, I had to come.* I'm sayin' stuff like *You got a nice place. What are you doing now? If you ain't doin' nothin' now, come on and walk over to the store with me. I need some cigarettes.*

We're walking, passing the school and talking about when we went there, how things have changed. He's still got that little bounce in his walk, that quick step that could get him in the middle of trouble in no time. In my mind, I can see him reaching up to that wall in the junkman's office to steal a big knife, then turning and running real quick. I had to run too before that man came back and caught us taking his big knife from the wall. We ran up behind the junkyard and then down beside the railroad tracks. Then we hid in the bushes beside the tracks, stayed there for a long time.

"How's your mom?" George is asking.

"Everyone's fine. You know my mom got married after Fiance Street. I got two sisters. Everyone's doin' fine. How's Mack and them?"

"Mack's still in D.C. He was here when my mother died. I haven't seen him since the funeral. That's been some time. I see Richie all the time, he's always stoppin' by. Nooty comes by sometimes, he's still drivin' the bus. Darly lives up on Frankstown. Ain't nobody seen Kevin in years, he got out of the service and stayed out west."

"I saw Richie up at the park . . . But that was years ago. Did he tell you?"

"Yeah, he said somethin'. What are you doin' now, you workin'? You were doin' that photography for the paper."

"Yeah, how did you know that?"

"So what, how I know."

"I left that a long time ago."

"What you now? You working?"

"It's a long story. I'll tell you about it later."

It's like we're hiding in the bushes again, just me and Georgie. And we ain't payin' the world going by no mind. We're sitting on the wall behind what's left of that old garage, the one Mr. Gibson used to have back in the alley. It's nothing but a little piece of wall still standing. We've got some beer and we're still talking. I know I've got to ask some things, I just don't know when to, or how. We haven't talked about it yet, but George knows I'm his brother. He hasn't said it; he doesn't have to, I feel it. Maybe he knew before me and just hasn't ever said. He's older than me, but just a year. We're talking about my being in Vietnam and almost getting killed when I got shot. He says he heard about it, but he doesn't remember who told him. I'm wondering if my father knew and I'm wondering if he cared. I'm listening to Georgie talking about something, but I'm staring down at the little pieces of broken glass lying in the alley. There's an old fence across the way that has some kind of green vine growing up on it. The fence doesn't have any color, it's just that old pale gray.

"George, I want to know some things about my father. I don't know anything about him at all, 'cept he was from Texas. It bothers me a little bit, not knowin' about him. What happened to him? How did he die?"

"He fell or somethin'. He was livin' down on the hill—he had fallen or somethin'. He couldn't get his health back from that fall. I can't tell you too much, 'cause I don't know. Don't anybody ever talk about it. I know he was in the hospital when he died, down there in one of them hospitals by Pitt."

"Where's he buried?"

"That cemetery on the other side of the river, that one out past Aspinwall. Green somethin'—Greenland, Greenlawn."

"I know the one you're talking about. What was he like?"

"He was all right, you know. I mean, he was always straight with me. I'd see him down on the hill sometimes. He used to hang out in them joints, he hustled with them cards. He liked to gamble, was good with them cards. After he and my mom split, I didn't see him too much. He'd stop by, see how we were doin'. I didn't see him that much. You know, I was behind the wall a lot."

"Yeah, I'd hear. What was he like to talk to?"

"Nooty could tell you more. Nooty would always go down and see him—you know, spend a little time with him. You know, I was always out there gettin' into shit all the time. I remember I ran into him a few times when I was in them joints down on the hill. You know, we'd off some from out this way, used to off them stores they got out in the mall, then take it on down the hill and sell it there. We used to off them jewelry stores, get them rings and watches. I remember runnin' into him a couple times in them joints. He knew what I was doin', he knew what I was about. I'll say one thing, he didn't try to judge me. I remember this one time, he just like pulled me aside, said something like 'You know what you're doin' now? You better be careful.' He'd help me out if he could. He got me out of jail sometimes, posted bail if he had it. He would have to have been Rockefeller or Perry Mason to keep me out."

"Did he ever mention me?"

"Not to me. You got to ask Nooty about stuff like that. He's the one that knows all that family business. My mom used to try and keep things together, but after she died . . . We don't see each other that much anymore. You know she died?"

"Oh yeah, I heard that a long time ago. My Aunt Gerl told me."

"I can't tell you a lot. I don't know myself."

"How did you know I was coming to see you? How did you know?"

"So what if I knew. I knew, that's all. Something said you were coming. I saw your Aunt Gerl, she said you live up there in one of them big Thomas Boulevard homes. I was going to check you out, but I didn't know which one. She said it's right up from Harris Funeral Home. I would have found it next time I was up that way."

I'm staring at the pieces of broken glass again. Georgie's quiet too; maybe he's thinking about the same thing I am. Maybe both of us ain't nothin' but two little pieces of broken glass from the same bottle. In a way, we ain't much different. He fucked up one way, I fucked up the other. But I'm thinking other stuff too. I'm thinking that fairy-tale stuff and trying to figure out how George knew I was on the way. I'm thinking maybe all this is happening for a reason, maybe it is our father's will, his wish. Maybe he asked Jesus to bring all his sons together. I don't know it, but a day is nearing when all but one of us will be together for the first time. The day will come soon.

Next thing I know, big trouble in the mail: water man wants his money and I owe him a lot. He's put a lien on the house; next he's coming to turn off the water. He didn't say when, but I know it won't be long. I'm not mad at the water man, the gas man, any of them. I'm the fuckin' asshole, not them. But I didn't jump in this hole, I was pushed. I want to get out, but maybe I don't. I'd have to look at myself, face all of me, not just that little hopeful part of my face.

I was retyping *Holly*, getting her in better shape for her journey. She had to be in shape to go as soon as *Billy* came back. I felt foolish doing it, sitting there and pretending that something was going to work right for once. I just retyped the whole book because I didn't have anything else to do. Sometimes when Jessica would call, I'd think I'd hear a loss of hope in her voice. She wasn't saying that things weren't looking as good as she thought they might. She didn't have to. I knew when hope sounded as if it were moaning, nearing its last breath.

George started coming by, and we'd sit for hours and talk. Sometimes I'd find out more about my father's life, just little things. George would only talk about little things. Life to George was whatever it was that day; if it was rain, life was raindrops and puddles on the sidewalk. He didn't work, hadn't worked since that big factory he was at went out of business. The woman he was living with was the mother of his son. She had always loved him, wanted him with her. George didn't say it that way; maybe he couldn't. He'd just say how she waited for him the whole time he was in prison. George would get to talking about prison sometimes, get to talking about all the guys he met in there and what they did. He said it was real bad in the federal prison he was in until Jimmy Hoffa was put in there too. He said Jimmy Hoffa got some changes made. He liked Hoffa, talked with him a few times. Sometimes Georgie would tell funny stories about prison; he'd laugh while he was telling them. I'd be laughing too, until Georgie's story would come to its end and he'd get real quiet. His face would get this silent look, and his eyes would get real droopy. He'd just stare at something for a while, anything. I knew the look; it was like guys laughing about something that happened during a battle. Then they'd think of some other part of the battle while they were still laughing. They'd stop laughing and get to staring off somewhere.

George was becoming part of the passing time. He kept stopping by. Sometimes I wanted to see him, feel that brother stuff. I wanted to feel that belief, feel like my father was sending George by to make sure I was okay. I wanted to see my father's face in George's face, see my face in George's, and feel a part of that missing feeling. Sometimes I didn't want to see him. I didn't want to see my face in his. I didn't want to see my eyes and face all red, that dry-blood-color red. I didn't want to watch George's face, see that sad hound-dog look get on it when he was getting ready to ask me for money again. Sometimes I'd give him a dollar or fifty cents he needed to go get a bottle. He'd always say he would give it back. Sometimes he'd go get his bottle of vodka, stop back by the house, and drink it. The whole fuckin' bottle would be gone in no time. He'd ask me if I wanted some, I'd say no, and then he would just pour that shit right down his throat. I'd be sitting there trying to talk to him, trying to be some brother, feel the empty-feeling stuff, and the only thing I was talking to was a bottle of vodka. Sometimes in the middle of the night I'd hear knocking at the door. I'd lie there in the dark, hope the knocking would go away. I knew it wasn't the gas man knocking, but the sound wouldn't go away. I'd get up, sneak to the door, and peep out. I'd see George, know he was drunk. I'd sneak back away from the door, hate myself, and leave my brother in the dark.

It's still summertime, late summer but it's still hot. Nothing is working right. Jessica's on the phone, telling me that some big publisher changed its mind at the last minute again. I ask why and feel my hands slipping off everything I was holding on to. She's telling me the reasons why, this reason, that reason. I'm hating reasons, every fuckin' reason in the world. The reason I'm here, the reason I'm not there, the reason I'm not dead, and the reason I'm still alive. I know I've got to hold on, but I don't have any reason to hold on. Jessica's still talking about what the publisher said about writing, editing, and all that. I'm thinking fast, saying, *I'll get some help. My friend Barry's a writer—I'll get him to help with the editing.* I hang up, call Barry. He'll help. I get him the manuscript. Months and all that time shit goes by. Barry and his wife, Myrna, are putting *Billy* on a computer, fixing this and that. I'm waiting, sighing out loud when I know I'm waiting and not sure what I'm waiting for. I'm not sure anything is ever going to work right, ever.

It's not summer anymore; leaves are getting their pretty colors before they die. Busted buckeyes lying on the ground; I see them on the way to the store. Sometimes I pick one up, break it the rest of the way open, stand a moment, look at the shiny brown color of it, get those kid memories back again. Maybe feel myself smiling, just thinking about the shiny buckeye and funny kid stuff before I get to thinking about other stuff that wasn't shining in my face. Sometimes I want to pray, still want to pray. Maybe pray and cry all at the same fucking time. But I can't cry and I can't ask Jesus to come running to me when I never went running to him. He might ask me about that stuff in the night, in the dark of my mind. He might ask me why I tried to blow the back off the kid in the blue shirt. He'll know I knew that kid just might have been just a kid and not no fuckin' VC. He'll know I'm still mad at him for lettin' Vernon and them get killed, for lettin' me see all that ugly shit and not be able to make sense out of it. He'll know I got a big problem with that "God works in mysterious ways." Maybe he does; maybe I'm part of the mysterious stuff. I just want to be part of the regular stuff.

Barry and Myrna are done with *Billy;* they think it's real good. It looks good, all typed neatly on that computer paper. I tell Jessica I'm sending the manuscript back to her. It's waiting time again. I hear the same stuff I heard before, that "almost" stuff. Fuck it, I'll rewrite *Billy* myself. I'm writing it again, typing it all over and taking Barry's stuff out, putting my stuff back in and trying to make it better. I ain't doin' nothin' but writin'; day, night don't make no difference again. This got to work; I ain't goin' to be nothin' forever. I'm done again, did it again in weeks. I talk to Jessica, tell her it's done again.

It's waiting time again and Georgie keeps coming by. Sometimes I can talk to him, want to. I want to tell him about the book and what it means to me. But if I do, he just says, "So what."

I say, "Hey man, it's important."

Georgie's half drunk, looking at me, waiting until I'm done saying what's important. I'm trying to explain things, but I hear him saying, "So what . . . So what . . ."

I don't want to hear his so whats. But I can feel them, feel them in different ways all at the same time. I can feel that so what saying, *All that outside world ain't important. It doesn't think about you, don't think about it.* I can hear it saying, *Ain't no hope out there, niggers are niggers out there.* I can hear it saying, *Be glad it's a nice day and you're breathing.* But I don't want to hear it at all. I keep waiting to hear from Jessica.

I'm coming from the store, the Homewood store. I'm about to go back under the bridge, back through its dark shade to my side of the tracks. I hear my name being called. I don't have to turn around to know it's George coming up behind me. I don't want it to be him. It's a bad day. Money ain't nowhere and money problems are waitin' for me everywhere. I don't feel like hearin' the so whats. But I can hear Georgie saying, "I was just on the way to see you. Here, I got this for you."

I look at the bag in his hand and ask, "What's this?"

Georgie's saying, "Just take it, you need it. It's a bag of coffee. Ain't you never seen welfare coffee before? Go on and take it, it's better than that Taster's Choice shit you have up there. Oh here, here's this couple bucks I owe you. Here, take this five, I don't have any change."

Georgie's lookin' at me, lookin' into my eyes, and I'm lookin' back into his. We're brothers, I can feel it. Whatever anything is, in this moment beneath the bridge, he's my brother. I walk on home with the bag of welfare coffee and the five dollars I didn't have before. I'm thinkin', *It's the only thing my father ever gave me, but at least it's something I need.*

I didn't know, so help me; I wish I did. But I didn't know I would never talk to George again. In time, and not a long time, just weeks, I'd see him lying in his coffin, see him dead and looking like me. I'd touch his hand, tell him, *I love you, brother.* Macky, Nooty, Richie, and a brother I had never met were all around. For the first time I was my father's son too.

When the call came, I wasn't thinking about good things. I knew Jessica would be calling, and when I heard her voice I knew it was going to be something bad. When she started talking, I didn't understand what she was telling me. She was saying, "We've had an offer for *Billy*."

"Huh?"

"We've had an offer from an editor at Viking. She has fallen in love with *Billy*. The offer is low, but there is money on the table for *Billy*."

"Oh, my God!"

I couldn't talk. I asked Jessica if she could call me back in five minutes. I think she knew I had to be alone, I had to. I hung up the phone, just sat, stared, saw the patches of fire in the treeline fading. I heard Jesus whispering, *You always had a friend.* I heard some voice way down deep inside of me saying, *It's over, the battle's over, put your head up. You can be proud, you were always something. You were always an eagle, you just had a broken wing.*

I didn't know in that moment what I had done. I didn't know that *Billy* would become one of the *New York Times*'s notable books of the year. I didn't know that *Billy* would be published in England, make the

London *Times* bestseller list. I didn't know that *Billy* would be translated into different languages and be published in France, Germany, Holland, and Italy. A day was coming when *Holly* would be ready to go too, to follow *Billy* wherever he went. In months, I would want to meet Jessica and the publishing people in New York. It would be just before Christmas. I would take a Greyhound bus at midnight, sit by the window and look out at the passing night. I would see the fog along the highway, see the ghostly figures of the treeline through the thick gray mist. I would think of the fires, but they weren't there. In the morning I would see Jessica, see the big New York publishing building. I'd see all the people in New York, the ones walking on the sidewalks, driving the cabs, singing in Grand Central Station. I would remember the Christmas songs they were singing. I remember how their songs seemed to fill the air with life, how I felt so alive. I would know then what all the waiting had been for.

YELLOW FLOWERS IN LONDON

A year passed with a face on time I hadn't seen before. Time had a smile on its face, and good things were happening, kept happening. *Billy* was getting good reviews all over the place, and some movie producer bought the film rights. I was out in the open again, way out in the open. I was going on book tours, reading from *Billy* in big lecture halls and bookstores. People were asking me a lot of questions: why had I decided to write *Billy*, what made me want to be a writer. I was being interviewed by newspaper and magazine reporters. I was on big national radio shows answering questions about *Billy*, about myself. I was on airplanes again, flying to different cities. Some cities I had been to before, seen in a different way. I remembered Philadelphia, the Naval Hospital there. It was still there; its walls were still bright-looking in the sun. I tried to look up, see if I could remember what floor I had been on, see if I could see the window I used to look out. I couldn't remember, but in my mind I could see the faces of the guys I was with. I could see us playing cards, see us all fucked up one way or the other. I could see the little Christmas tree they put up in the ward, see its pretty little lights. I could see me back in Vietnam, sitting on the sandbags. I could hear the corpsman telling me I was going home, I was being sent to the Philadelphia Naval Hospital. Thirty-year-old moments followed me even after I passed the hospital and couldn't see it anymore.

In a way, it was still dark in my world. I still wouldn't let all of the light come in. I didn't want people to be able to see me; I didn't, couldn't, trust things and didn't want people getting too close to me. I had an outside me that I'd show people and let them talk to. I let them touch that outside me, let them think they were really touching me. But they weren't; I couldn't let them get that close. I was happy about being somebody, feeling alive again, but I was still scared about its not being real. Maybe it was just some fucked-up dream and I would wake up, be poor and hidden in the dark again. Maybe I still liked the dark, had got too used to being in it. I knew I could hide in it and no one could see me, touch me. I knew if I really let them touch me, they could hurt me. Maybe they would pull my happy mask off and see the fear that was still stuck on my face.

The gas man wasn't knocking anymore, and the water man went away too. The bill collectors didn't have to call anymore. I didn't have to count dimes and nickels, look for enough change just to buy a pack of cigarettes. But I could not forget the times when I did. If the phone rang, I still braced myself, like I did when I heard firecrackers on the Fourth of July. I had to hurry up and think, say to myself, *Cool down, man, that's just fuckin' firecrackers. Ain't nobody tryin' to kill you again.* The phone rang a lot. The publishing people from New York would call and tell me what was going on: *Billy* just got another good review. Jessica would call, see how I was doing. I think she knew I needed her to guide me through all that open space. The publishing people from England were calling too. I was going to London for a book tour. I was thinking about going to England a lot, because I wanted to cross the sea again, see another part of the world again. Maybe have that feeling of being in the wind again, a part of its freedom.

Another Christmas passed, a good Christmas. I could buy presents for my family. Another year was passing and I didn't want it to go; it had been a good year. I didn't want good things ever to go away. The new year came quietly; I wanted it to be that way. I wanted time to think about England. I wanted *Billy* to do well there too. Sometimes when I talked to the people there, I wanted to say, *Hey, I'm just some guy that wrote a book. I'm no real author, don't expect me to know a lot about writin' stuff.* But I didn't say that when they called, and I didn't want to sound all stupid on the phone. Jessica said I would do just fine. They'd like me, and *Billy* was already being talked about a lot there. The early reviews were very good, but I didn't know what the rest would be like. I only knew *Billy* was already there and I was going too. I guess I was getting a little excited about going—I started marking the days off on the calendar. When it was time to go, I remember looking at the corner of the end table where I had written *Billy*. I remember standing and looking around the room and remembering all the ugly stuff before I left the house.

It was mid-January, and the skies darkened as I drove to the airport. The plane would take off from Pittsburgh at six P.M. and fly directly to England. I knew when the sun came up again, I'd be on the other side of the ocean. The airplane was real big inside, much bigger than the ones I had flown on before. My seat was in the back and next to the window; the seats next to me were empty, and I was glad. I didn't want anyone close to me; I remember I wanted to be alone so I could think, be able to remember the moments better. I was looking out the window when the plane began to move toward the runway. I kept looking out the window as it began to take off. I watched the lights of Pittsburgh become dimmer as the plane climbed through the clouds, then I couldn't see them anymore. I looked out through the clouds and I could see the little distant stars glowing. The airplane had TV screens and headsets so you could listen or watch a movie. But I didn't want to see a movie, I wanted to look out the window and see if I could see the sea again. Maybe be able to see its whitecaps through the breaks in the clouds. I knew it would be a while before we reached the sea, but I kept watching anyway. Sometimes I could see my own reflection in the window, see the age that had come to my face since the last time I had flown across an ocean. Thirty years had passed, but I could still feel the feeling of the time. In my mind I could see myself on the hospital plane that brought me back from Vietnam. I could see me trying to look down and see if I could see the ocean but mostly still seeing where I was coming from. I didn't want to see the age on my face, so I looked away from the window for a while.

The airplane people served dinner and then the hours seemed slow. In a while the lights in the plane were dimmed. I could see my watch, and I knew we were flying through the midnight hours. I didn't want to sleep but sometimes I closed my eyes. When I did, I would only think of my life, think of the time I was leaving behind. Sometimes it seemed like I could think of everything all at the same time, feel everything in the same moment. I'd look back out the window, see the stars and look at them for a while. I knew we were over the ocean, but I couldn't see it. In a way, I could feel it, feel its emptiness. I could feel how it can show you nothing but its endless waves but in the same moment make you feel everything within yourself. Maybe feel a moment that was yet to come. I needed to feel the ocean again, pass through its open space. I couldn't see it, but I knew it was there.

I was getting tired, but I didn't want to sleep. I knew I couldn't sleep even if I wanted to. I couldn't sleep on planes, couldn't keep my eyes closed for too long with people around me. Sometimes I could lose the thought of where I was coming from and where I was going. I could find myself just staring at something, some star way out in the dark, the little light flashing out on the end of the airplane's wing. Then I would remember who I was, what I was, where I was coming from, where I was going.

The hands on my watch were moving very slowly. When I thought an hour had passed, sometimes only moments had. Except for the hum of the plane's engines, everything seemed so quiet. From time to time I'd look out the window, then down at my watch. I remember it was almost 2 A.M. and I was wondering if I'd be able to stay awake. I was tired of looking at the little stars and the flashing light, but I looked out the window anyway. I saw something beautiful and I kept looking at it. Way off in the far dark sky, I could see bright reddish, yellowish colors. The sun was coming up; I didn't think it would be coming up so soon. I kept watching it, seeing the rays of its beautiful colors shining into the darkness. In a while all the sky was brightly colored by the sun's light. I knew I could stay awake and be ready for the coming time.

The next few hours went by quickly. I could see other people stirring in the seats; some were getting up and going to the toilet. Soon after breakfast was served, the pilot announced that we were close to London. I was beginning to feel how far away I was from Homewood again. Maybe how far away from what I was, where I could hide. Sometimes I could feel both sides of myself at the same time. I could feel that side that was happy and wanting to do things, never hide again. And at the same time, I didn't want to go out in the open, get ambushed. But the plane was getting ready to land anyway; I could feel its engines slowing as it began descending through the clouds. I was looking out the window, waiting to see my first sight of the land, another part of the world again. The window had tiny bubbles of dew or raindrops on it. And when I could see the browns and greens of the land below, it seemed all misty. I kept looking down to see if I could see any people, cars moving. I could see little gray paths winding through the greens and browns, which I knew would be roads and highways. Then I could see the lights of the airport and feel the plane begin to bank into a curve. I kept looking out the window, watching the buildings of the airport come closer, get bigger, be different colors. Big gray buildings, some light blue with red trim around the windows. I could see people standing around some yellow trucks. Then I could feel the plane's wheels touch the ground, could feel the force of the plane braking its speed, slowing. I was in England again.

The plane was still slowing, coming to a stop. But I could feel myself rushing inside, wanting to see England. I hurried off the plane and up the ramp, then into the big customs room. I stood in line, waiting to show my passport. The English customs agent looked at my passport, looked at me, and asked, "What brings you to England?" I answered quickly, saying, "I'm here on book tour. I'm an American writer."

I knew there would be a car waiting; a driver would meet me at the international arrivals gate. I could see the man standing behind a rail holding up a sign with my name on it. I was feeling like some real important person, but I didn't want to look like I was feeling that way. The driver was very polite, saying stuff like "Good morning, sir, how was your flight? Is this your first time over?" I know I was smiling when I answered, "It's been a while since I've been here." In my mind I was still smiling, thinking, *Last time I was here, wasn't anybody with a car waitin' on me.*

The car was a long gray Mercedes limo. I really wanted to ask the driver if he was sure he had picked up the right person, but I didn't. He opened the back door and I got in. He said it would be about a forty-five-minute drive into London. I hadn't changed my watch to the new time; I still had Pittsburgh time, my time. It wasn't even 4 A.M. yet, but here it was already close to nine. But it was still a pretty morning. I sat looking out the window at the countryside, seeing sheep and cattle grazing on the green hills. Sometimes I could see kids standing at a bus stop with their bookbags over their shoulders. When we neared London, the traffic began to thicken, the streets became narrow. In a while I knew we were in the city: big buildings, lots of people on the side-walks, and funny old-time-looking cabs all over the place. I even saw some of those double-decker buses and something that looked like a castle with big statues of lions sitting out in front of it. The driver said we were getting close to Soho, where the hotel was. I kept looking out the window. There were so many people walking the streets. I saw colored people too—I knew there were colored people in London, but not as many as I saw.

We turned up a narrow street with lots of cafés on it and stopped in front of a light-colored building with a black fence in front of it. I asked, "Is this the hotel?" The driver quickly answered. "Yes, this is Hazlitt's." I didn't know how important to my life this place would come to be.

I told the man at the hotel desk my name. He rose to his feet, saying, "Oh yes, we've been expecting you. Welcome to Hazlitt's. You have a few messages already."

When I got to my room and looked around, I felt like I was back in the first century. Everything in the room was real old. There was a big bed with one of those canopies over it. The bathtub was huge and long with legs holding it up. I liked the toilet; the tank part was way up on the wall and had a chain to pull. I tried it and it made a big gushing sound when it flushed. I was in Sir Gregory's Room; the rooms were named after people who had lived in them hundreds of years ago. I was trying to see him in my mind, looking like those pictures of George Washington. I sat down on the side of the bed and read the messages. They were from the English publishing people. There was an envelope too; inside it was a schedule for all the interviews for the next week. It looked like there was a big bunch of them. I had a few hours before Rebecca, the publicist, was coming to get me for the first one. I knew I had to sleep; I couldn't keep my eyes open any longer.

When Rebecca came I was up and ready, but I had stayed in the room looking out the window. I couldn't see much, but I did see all the pigeons out in a little courtyard. Some of the pigeons were so big they looked more like ducks. When I wasn't looking at the pigeons I was thinking about important stuff, like how the interviews were going to go. One of the first ones was a radio show, and I hated talking on the radio. The phone rang and it was Rebecca telling me she was at the hotel. I had talked to her a few times when she had called me in Pittsburgh. She was nice, and I was looking forward to meeting her.

She is waiting for me in the hotel lobby. She has short dark hair and a face that is a smile itself. She's introducing herself all formally, but she is still smiling at the same time. She says how nice it is to meet me and asks how the flight over was. I'm saying, "It wasn't bad," but I'm looking at her smile and feeling good about being in England. She tells me how much she liked the book and about some of the reviews that just came out today. She says how good they are and that there's a car waiting to take us to the radio station. Outside there's a guy in a nice suit opening up the back door to a Jaguar sedan. I'm thinking, *This stuff ain't real.* The car goes up the little narrow streets; I look out the window at all the cafés, some right next to each other. Sometimes people are sitting out at the sidewalk tables. It's still January, but it's not that cold, more like a warm fall day. I thought it would be real cold, but it's warm. Everyone I see has just a light coat or a sweater on. Rebecca's telling me about the radio program I'm going to be on. She says it's a very popular show. I'm still looking out the window at all the cafés and little shops. They're all neatly painted different colors, some pretty light colors that make the whole street look bright. But I'm listening to Rebecca and feeling like I don't belong here. I like it, like the feeling of being here, but I'm starting to feel like Cinderella and hoping that I don't turn into some fucked-up pumpkin on the radio show.

All the people at the radio station know I'm coming. Some of them already have copies of *Billy* and want me to autograph them. It's time to go into the studio, and I can feel myself taking big breaths, but I'm trying to take them quietly. I hate talking on the radio, but I don't want to show it. The woman who is going to interview me is telling me how much she enjoyed reading *Billy* and explaining that we will go on the air after the commercials are over. I look at the microphone, stare at it and wait. The commercials are over, she's introducing me now. She's talking, rolling her words in her mouth until she can make them come out with almost an echo trailing each one. She's saying what she thought when she first read *Billy*. She says, "I must say that when I discovered that this book was written in heavy American Deep South dialect, I was a little disappointed. I was looking forward to reading it, but I don't enjoy reading books in dialect. But I had heard so many good things about this book, I decided I would give it five pages, just five pages. Two o'clock that same night, I turned the last page, and I was weeping. I was overwhelmed by the impact of this book. I was literally weeping, I found this book to be so devastatingly moving. How did you come to write *Billy*? This is your first novel, isn't it?"

I look up real fast while she is talking to see if she is really saying what I am hearing. I look back at the microphone. I have to answer her questions. I don't know what to say, so I just start talking and saying how I got the idea to write *Billy* and how I felt about writing the book. She asks some of those writing questions—why I did this and why I did that. I don't know what to say again, but I know I have to answer fast. I say, "I don't really plan things when I write, I just do it. I just try and see the people I'm writing about. They didn't plan too much, they just lived, and I just wrote about their lives, their time. *Billy*'s fiction, but I think the feelings are real. And I just tried to write them down, that's all . . ."

The radio show seemed to last forever, but it's over now and I'm back in the car, asking Rebecca how I did. She tells me I did great, but I don't feel great, I'm just glad it's over.

Dinner was next, a nice café and lots of talk between Rebecca and me. I had a lot of questions about England and she wanted to know about Pittsburgh and the States. She had never been to the States. The car waited and took us to another radio show, then back to the hotel. Rebecca told me what time she'd be back in the morning to get me; there were going to be a lot of interviews the next day.

Evening had come, and London was starting to look all gray, with pretty lights coming on. I was tired, went up to my room and lay across the bed for a while. But I couldn't sleep. I kept thinking about everything, about my life and what it was, what it had come to be. People asking me for my autograph way on the other side of the ocean, me in a different part of the world again, me being all fucked up and afraid to come out of the house. I lay on the bed for a while, then I decided to get up and go for a walk. I wanted to see London, just be a part of it. No one would know me. I washed up, grabbed my coat, and went down the steps. There was a little sitting room that you had to go through before you reached the lobby. Earlier I had noticed the little fireplace in it, the bookshelf and soft-looking couches. But I had passed through it quickly. This time I slowed as I entered it and looked at the flames in the fireplace, then toward the young woman sitting on the couch. She looked up as I passed and I could see her face, feel her eyes. I think I nodded my head, said hello. But I know as I passed her, I could see her in my mind, see her eyes, her face. An oval face with high cheekbones, blue eyes that kept their color in the dim light. Blue eyes, one gently covered a little by the strands of her light-colored hair.

I stopped in the lobby and said hello to the woman at the desk, then went out into the night. The streets were still filled with people walking about. I walked and watched the other people walking too, watched them go into cafés and clubs. It was cooler; a chill had come with the night. But I only felt it, I didn't care about it. I kept looking at all the people, but I wasn't thinking about them. Something had just happened; I didn't know what it was, I just felt it. I walked a little further, then turned and went back to the hotel.

She was still sitting in the room, her eyes still blue in the dim light, her hair still hanging softly over one side of her face. And I could still see her face and feel her eyes when she looked up to see who was passing. I nodded my head again, maybe said hi. Then I could feel myself slowing, stopping, and turning to her. It was almost as if she were in a painting, was a painting. The glow from the fire and the soft dim light from the lamp gently lit up her face, added red to her lips, let her gleam. Where the light did not fall, her dark sweater fell in the shadows, her dark leggings curled her legs into the dark. I spoke through the space between us, asking her, "Are you a guest here too?"

She looked at me as if just to glance, but her look lingered, and I asked again, "Are you a guest too?"

I saw her lips part, heard her voice. She just said two words: "Say . . . again."

"Are you a guest here at the hotel too?"

"Oh. I'm not a guest . . . I'm employed here."

There was something different about the way she spoke. She spoke slowly, softly. Each word she said seemed to stop the moment in which it was spoken.

I wanted to hear her speak again. I asked her, "Where you from?" Are you from here in London?"

"Please . . . please say again."

"Where are you from? Are you English?"

"No, I'm not English. I'm Polish."

"You're from Poland? That's a good ways from here. How far is it?"

"Sorry . . . say again."

"How far away is Poland? Ah . . . how long did it take you to get here from Poland?"

"Three days by . . . on the train."

I told her I was from America, the States, Pittsburgh. And I had come to London for a book tour, I was a writer.

"You . . . you from Pitsberg?"

"Yeah, Pittsburgh, in the state of Pennsylvania. I just got here this morning."

I moved closer to her while I spoke. There was a chair I was nearing, and I asked if I could sit for a while. I remember when I sat, I stared into the fire for a moment, then glanced around the room. It was a comfortable room; it looked like a place to rest, read, sip coffee. The bookshelves were along one wall and enclosed by glass. I could see the reflections of the fire's glow on the glass as I glanced at all the books that were in them. I didn't know what time it was; I didn't want to look at my watch. Maybe I didn't want to label the moments. I was tired, but not sleepy. When I looked back into the red, yellow, pretty flickering flames in the fireplace, they told me I was weary. I was weary from the roads, the paths in the nights, the open spaces of my life. I kept staring at the fire, listening to it telling me to rest a while. It was telling me, *I'm not the same fire that burned in the treeline, I'm a different fire.*

I was still looking at the fire and might have said something about how pretty it was. When I looked back at her, I could only see her eyes, feel them. I looked at her for a moment, then asked, "What's your name?"

"Katarzyna."

I smiled a little before I asked her to say her name again. I wanted to hear it again and be able to say it right. She told me again. Slowly she seemed to part the four sounds of her name, make them sound like three pretty notes of a harmony. I repeated, "Ka-tar-zy-na."

A moment passed and I told her my name and she asked, "You . . . Are you a writer? Ah . . . what kind of books do you write?"

I told her about *Billy*, how it took place in Mississippi, in America. As I told her about *Billy*, my writing, sometimes I looked into the fire and sometimes I looked at her. I wanted to ask her who she was and what this feeling I was feeling was. I didn't; I just looked back into the fire. But I could still see her eyes, feel the moments time was allowing to linger in peace.

"How long have you been here in England?" I asked.

"I come here, came here, a year ago. I came to learn English—how to speak it."

"What part of Poland are you from?"

"Say . . . please say again."

"What city, what part of Poland did you live in?"

"Oh. Warsawa."

In a while, the woman who was at the lobby's front desk came into the sitting room. She was off-duty and came to sit for a while. Her name was Anna and she was from Sweden. She asked if I wanted to share some wine with her and Katarzyna. I said yes, I would like that. I could see that Katarzyna and the woman from Sweden were friends. When I wasn't answering questions about being a writer, about America, I was watching Katarzyna talk with Anna. Sometimes her face, her eyes, her hands would make a picture of the words she was saying. I could see that she could not say all the words in English she wanted to say. When she couldn't, a quick silence would come to her face. Her eyes could still the moment, keep it still until she could find a word she wanted to say. Sometimes I'd see her smile, a quick smile that would go away but would stay in my mind. The wine came into my mind too, but it was a gentle wine. It eased, then pushed away, kept away the feelings I didn't want to feel. Her eyes were bringing a feeling I would never let go away.

In the morning, London was the sounds of pigeons outside the window, breakfast brought to the door of my room. Then it was a soothing bath in the big bathtub and a little time to relax, think about what the day was going to bring. Rebecca had said that some of the interviewers were coming to the hotel with photographers, then there were more radio shows to do, an early evening trip by train to someplace called Cambridge. A big bookstore there wanted me to read from *Billy* and sign books. It was *Billy*'s official release date; a lot more book reviews would start to come out.

London became a phone call telling me that Rebecca was waiting in the lobby. A reporter and a photographer from one of the big newspapers were waiting too. I liked the reporter; she had read *Billy* and really liked it. She asked me a lot of questions about myself, who I was and where I came from; she really wanted to know. I was being interviewed in the little sitting room where the fireplace was. As I answered the questions about myself, my writing, in my mind I could see and feel the night before. I could see Katarzyna's eyes all over again.

Another Jaguar came; we wound through the small streets again. A light rain was falling, made things look all foggy. But the colored umbrellas women were carrying made things beautiful anyway, put pretty colors in the mist. I had a bunch of radio shows to do. All the interviewers had read *Billy* and wanted to know so much about the book, about the American South. I was nervous before all the shows, but Rebecca kept telling me how well I was doing. I liked her, and when we talked, sometimes I'd try to say things with an English accent. She'd smile and tell me if I was getting closer to sounding like I was English. The train ride to Cambridge took us into the night and the people waiting in the bookstore for me to read. They had come through the rain to see me, had their books for me to sign. Sometimes I could see that they saw more in me than I felt in myself.

At night, London became Katarzyna again. We went for a walk, stopped at a little café, and had wine. I gave her a copy of *Billy*, watched her as she read what I had written to her. I can still see her as she closed the book and brought it to her breast and held it there. I had only written "I'll never let the feeling go away."

I watch her hold the book, looking into her eyes and wondering what this feeling is. There's a vase on the table; it has yellow flowers in it. The flowers are between us, blurry in my sight. But I love them being there, seeing her just beyond the flowers. I take one of the flowers out of the vase and give it to her, watching the smile come to her face and feeling it light up the moment. One of Louis Armstrong's songs is being played in the café. I've heard it before, but I've never liked it so much as in this moment. He's singing about what a wonderful world we live in.

I say, "There's something different about you, I have that feeling. I'm not certain what it is, I just have the feeling."

She's looking at me; I can see her eyes beyond the flowers. She's not saying anything, just looking. Her eyes are lowering, looking down at the table.

"Do you like it here in London?" I ask.

She looks up, and speaking softly, she says, "It's . . . it's all right. When I come here, I didn't know nobody—anybody, and I couldn't speak the language. I come to learn English . . . You see, it's very difficult to get a good job in Poland if you don't speak English. You see, when you . . . How you say . . . ah, ah, make an apply for a good job, they ask if you can speak English. I'm a journalist, and it's important to be able to speak the English."

"When I talk to you, can you understand me?"

"Sometimes."

"Just sometimes?"

She's getting a smile on her face, and says, "Your English is horrible. You have a funny accent—and you mumble."

"You're tellin' me I can't talk my own language, and I mumble too?"

"Yep, I'm telling you that."

I'm silent, but I'm smiling, looking at her. "You know," I say, "you have a smart mouth. Did anybody ever tell you that you have a smart mouth?"

"A smart mouth . . . What's that mean, a smart mouth?"

"It means your mouth is smart. You're pickin' on me."

"Oh. Um, pickin' on you . . . What's that mean, pickin' on?"

She's leaning toward me; the smile on her face looks like it's trying to hold a laugh back. "You . . . you . . . ," she's saying, "you should come to my English classes with me."

"You have a real smart mouth," I tell her again, smiling and looking down at the table. "When I go back to America, if I write to you, will you write me back?"

"Yes."

I look up. I can see a silence in her eyes, the blue is so still. The look on her face is changing, the little smile is going away. I can see now how her face can look so different from one moment to the next. I can feel the moment changing, and I am trying to see beyond this time in London. I don't know what it is I'm looking for, but I know I don't have it. I'm looking into her eyes, hearing myself saying, "When I leave here, when I go back to America, I'm going to miss you. I don't know why, but I'm going to miss you."

In the morning London was more radio shows and going to bookstores and signing lots of books. In a big bookstore on one of the big streets, *Billy* was already the number-eight best-selling book. I just wanted to stand there for a while and look up at the big printed list that it was on. I was thinking that of all the thousands of books in the bookstore, *Billy* was number eight. I was thinking, just feeling, that when I left, *Billy* was going to be okay in England.

It was a happy day; when I got back to the hotel, a message was there. The New York publishing people had called to tell me that *Billy* had reached number eighteen on a major wholesaler's bestseller list. The hotel manager wanted to meet me and have me sign a copy of the book so he could put it in the bookcase—the one in the little sitting room with the fireplace, where I first saw Katarzyna. *Billy* would stay there in that room after I left. I didn't know it, but in a time to come, *Holly* would be placed next to *Billy;* they would be together in that bookcase.

In the evening, I waited for Katarzyna in the lobby. I had asked her if she would go to dinner with me and maybe for a walk afterward. I smiled when I saw her looking so nice. A light rain had fallen and a little wind was still blowing. The pretty, pretty lights coming from the café windows brightened up the sidewalks and then fell in the little puddles of water, making them look like rainbows in the night. We went to the café with the yellow flowers and sat at the same little table. I told her about all the good things that had happened during the day. Dinner came, and I kept knocking the french fries off the plate. I could see the little smile that kept coming to her face. Then she said something I didn't understand. But she still had that little smile on her face.

I said, "I didn't hear you. What did you say?"

The little smile went away from her face but stayed in her eyes as she said, "You're a . . . mess."

"I'm a mess?"

"Yes. You're a mess . . . You're a mess of a mess."

I was trying to act insulted, but I couldn't. I could only look down at the french fries lying beside my plate, then look at her and laugh. Then I said, "You know, when you want to, you don't have any problems at all finding the words in English you want to say. You don't have any problems at all, do you?"

"Say again."

"You understood what I said," I told her, smiling and watching her little smile come again before she said, "You were mumbling."

After dinner the waiter brought the wine to the table. I had a few sips of wine, then I became silent. I stared at the yellow flowers, seeing her beyond them. I must have been too quiet. I heard her asking, "What's wrong? What are you thinking about?"

I looked beyond the flowers, into her eyes, and told her, "I'm thinking about my life, what it's been, what it is. I'm thinking about this moment. I'm thinking about you and the feeling I feel when I think of you."

She was quiet for a moment. Then she said, "It's . . . it's a special

time, isn't it? Life has so much meaning . . . so hard to understand. I
. . . I feel things too that I don't understand."

"I will remember this moment, you, the little flowers here, this time
in my life."

Slowly I reached across the table and gently touched her cheek. I
looked into her eyes; they did not turn from mine. We walked in a light
rain then, through the little streets. Sometimes I could feel her lean to
my touch on her arm. I knew I didn't understand this feeling I had, but
I could feel it trying to tell me what it was. I could feel it saying, *You're
falling in love with this young woman. Stop looking for words in your mind.
Go on—take her arm and walk through this time that you have.*

The days were more interviews, meeting people who wanted to meet
me. I met my English editor and thanked him for making it possible for
Billy to come to England. I was stilled when he told me how much *Billy*
meant to him. We went to have lunch, and he brought a friend he
wanted me to meet. I knew his friend—not by name, but I knew the
look in his eyes. I could see past his jokes, laughs, as we sat and drank
after the meal. I knew his feelings. He had been a combat photographer
in Vietnam. He had been wounded five times and had almost died too.
But I didn't know until we talked that he had been in some of the
battles I had been in. He had seen the same fires burning in the night.

I waited for the evenings to come, waited to take Katarzyna's arm,
walk with her and tell her about the days. I waited to stop as we walked,
waited for her to turn and look at me before I said, "You're important
to me. I'm going to miss you." A moment passed slowly before she said,
"I'll miss you . . . I'll miss you too."

When I touched her hand, held her, and kissed her cheek, there was
no open space between us for me to be afraid of. Sometimes when we
talked, she would tell me her fears, her loves, her secrets. I told her
mine, and sometimes when we talked, I could feel tears coming to my
eyes. I knew I was too old to cry, but I still felt the tears coming to my
eyes.

And I asked her to make one promise. I could hear myself saying, "In
a way, I've been very fortunate to live this long and see this time. I've
had the chance to do what I always wanted to do, just be somebody and
make a contribution to life. It was always important for me to do that—
even when I didn't think it was, it was. You're important to me—I will
never forget you. Some time from now, I want you to do something

that will also be important to me. When I die, that time will come. In the life that you have, if you ever come to America, I want you to come to my grave. Just come one time and leave one yellow flower on my grave, then go and live your life. Will you do this?"

"Yes. Yes, I will come—I promise."

When it came time to leave England, to go back to America, when it came time for one last walk in the night, when it came time to hold her and say, "I must go in the morning. I will miss you," I knew I would be back. And when I told her, she said, "I will be waiting for you."

Morning came and the car came to take me to the airport. As I left the hotel, I didn't want to look back, but I did. It was a quiet ride through all the little streets. At the airport, I saw *Billy* in one of the bookstore windows, and I knew he'd be all right. As the plane took off, I kept looking out the window until I couldn't see England anymore. But I could still see Katarzyna in my mind, and I knew the plane was taking me away from her. And I didn't like the ocean anymore, didn't like the big wide space it was putting between us.

But I had told her I was coming back. And I came back, didn't I? And we found the same little café with the yellow flowers and sat at the same table. And you picked on me again, told me I was still a mess of a mess, but you loved me. You already knew I loved you. But you didn't know that *Holly* would be placed next to *Billy* in the bookcase, the one in the sitting room of the little hotel in London. You didn't know that *Holly* was going to be dedicated to you and our names would be together in the little room where we met.

Years have passed in my life, and are passing. A day will near, then come, and I will go away with it. And it will be okay. And I have no doubt that wherever I lay, one yellow flower will be placed on my grave.